ROY BAINTON, author of *Honoured by Strangers* and *The Long Patrol*, served in the Merchant Navy and has travelled around the world three times. He has written extensively for newspapers and magazines and has been a regular contributor to Radio 4.

Praise for *The Long Patrol:*

'*A marvellous book, uncovering an important chapter of British social history abroad, engrossing and fascinating.*'
Ian Docherty, BBC Scotland

Praise for *Honoured By Strangers:*

'*A fascinating story, well-written.*' BBC Wales

'*A first class work – incredible research.*' Michael Wilson, author of *Baltic Assignment* and *A Submariner's Life*

'*A gem of concise description.*'
Journal of the Eastern Front Association

Other titles in this series

A BRIEF HISTORY OF

1917

RUSSIA'S YEAR
OF REVOLUTION

ROY BAINTON

ROBINSON
London

Constable & Robinson Ltd
3 The Lanchesters
162 Fulham Palace Road
London W6 9ER
www.constablerobinson.com

This edition published by Robinson,
an imprint of Constable & Robinson Ltd, 2005

A copy of the British Library Cataloguing in
Publication Data is available from the British Library

ISBN 978-1-84119-950-4

Printed and bound in the EU

6 8 10 9 7 5

This book is dedicated to
my friend and companion,
Graham Harrison

Спасибо большое!
ЛЕНИН – *ha ha ha!*

All that holds up thrones is made by workers' hands. Our hands will cast our bullets and fix bayonets to our guns.

Worker's Revolutionary Song, 1917

Quoted by Konstantin Pautovsky in In This Dawn

CONTENTS

ILLUSTRATIONS

Part of the revolutionary frieze on the old Putilov works in St Petersburg
Graham Harrison

Putilov workers demonstrating, led by the factory band, 1917
Graham Harrison / Kirovsky Zavod

Young workers at the Petrograd Putilov works with the first edition of *Pravda*
Graham Harrison / Kirovsky Zavod

Magazine cover, Petrograd 1917, showing Alexander Kerensky
Graham Harrison / Museum of Russian Political History, St Petersburg

Shopping in Petrograd, 1917
Graham Harrison / Kirovsky Zavod

Red Guards distributing bread in Petrograd, 1917
Graham Harrison / Kirovsky Zavod

The cruiser *Aurora*, star of the revolution
Graham Harrison

Helena Matveievna Krapivina, born 1912; Vladimir Abromovich Katz, born 1910; Vavara Vassilievna, born 1913; Prince Andrey Gagarin; Maria Mikhailovna Alexandrovna, born 1915; Nina Petrovna Fedorova & Maria Timoferevna Schlegova; Veterans of the Siege of Leningrad. L-R Vladimir Ivanovich Vuryakov, Antonina Alexeyvna Jurina, Vladimir Fransevich Grunwald, Olga Ivanovna Balunova; Old Communists demonstrating on Victory Day, St Petersburg 2004
All images Graham Harrison

PREFACE

JULIAN AND GREGORIAN
AND CALENDARS

The Bolshevik revolution, already a complex subject, is made more so by the fact that until February 1918 Russia had a different calendar from that used in the West. The Julian (Old Style) calendar was 13 days behind the western (Gregorian). Inevitably, there is a diversity in the sources referred to in this work; many use the new-style calendar to cover the whole period, others use a mixture – old style when referring to original Russian material, new style when referring to western reports. As this work covers events in Russia in the year 1917, I have therefore attempted to stick to the old calendar wherever possible; thus an event occurring on 16 March in the rest of Europe would be 3 March in Russia.

ACKNOWLEDGEMENTS

Having no academic background, writing this book was a daunting project which could only be achieved with the generous help and assistance of a great number of people, both in Russia, Britain and the USA. They were willing to support my efforts in any way possible by pointing me in the right direction and suggesting areas of exploration I may not have discovered without their help.

First and foremost I must thank my utterly reliable friend and companion, photographer Graham Harrison. On our two trips to Russia, first in 2000 and again in 2004, Graham's dexterity in picking a route through the complexities of Russian visa applications and his skill in finding cheap airfares and reliable contacts in St Petersburg made life so much easier. (We'll be back, Graham, when the Neva is frozen . . .)

Mere words will never be enough to thank our good friends and hosts in St Petersburg, Edward and Svetlana Emdin, whose selfless generosity in putting us up in their apartment was far beyond the call of any duty.

Prince Andrey Gagarin, his wife Tatiana and Mikhail Mikhailovich Glinka have taken us under their astute academic wings and supplied many valuable contacts and meetings, as well as providing an everlasting friendship. Our lovely interpreter, the lively and efficient Ekaterina 'Katya' Skorobogatova, made all our meetings with elderly Russians such a pleasure with her speed and utter efficiency.

In America, my thanks go to Professors Alexander Rabinowitch at the University of Indiana and Richard Spence at the University of Idaho for their knowledge and generosity in suggesting source material.

The open-hearted generosity of ordinary Russians always astonished us – such as the time and care taken by Andrey Samatuga and his partner, Sasha, to steer us through archives and even arrange a birthday party for Graham. And to all those sometimes bemused Russian senior citizens and war veterans who were collared at random in the street or invited us into their homes to talk about the past – your names are all in these pages.

For Malcolm Imrie, my agent – one day, Malcolm, your faith will be rewarded. And gratitude to Nicola Chalton and Sarah Moore at Constable & Robinson for her constant effort to keep the thrust of my work on the right track.

To Sue Breese, for her help and generosity, and to H.O. 'Naz' Nazareth of Penumbra Productions – I haven't forgotten, Naz.

Last, but by no means least, I offer my apologies yet again to my wife, Wendy, whose patience with the penury which results from writing history remains on the verge of expiry. One day, love, the ship will come in. To my son, Dr Martin Bainton, and his wife, Jane, and to my daughter Sarah, and her husband,

Ivan, thanks as ever for your continuing enthusiasm for Dad's bizarre obsessions.

There are many others whose omission is not deliberate – you know who you are, and your help is much appreciated.

Roy Bainton

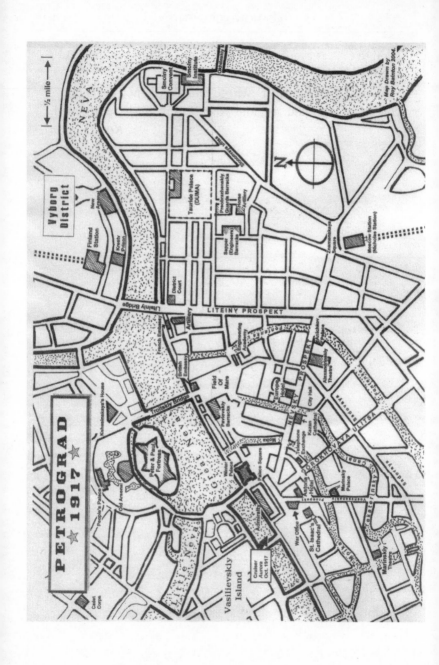

INTRODUCTION

These are signs of the times, not to be hidden by purple mantles or black cassocks. They do not signify that tomorrow a miracle will happen. They show that, within the ruling-classes themselves, a foreboding is dawning, that the present society is no solid crystal, but an organism capable of change, and is constantly changing.

Karl Marx (1818–1883)[1]

The idea for this book arose in St Petersburg one hot afternoon in June 2000. I had paused at a pavement bar on Nachilnaya Street on Vasilievskiy Island for a much-needed cold beer. Within minutes of sitting down, I was joined by a somewhat bedraggled old man.

My uninvited guest had no qualms about taking a mouthful of my ale and begging a cigarette. He looked at the guidebook on the table.

'*Britanski*?' he asked. I nodded. I was surprised as he began to speak to me in faltering English.

'I am eighty-four. My father and my mother were taken away by Stalin. Will you buy me a beer?' It seemed as if his parents' fate qualified him for a drink, so I obliged. I asked him what his parents did for a living.

'My father was Vasily Kolokolnikov. I too am Vasily. He drove a tram in Petrograd. My mother was called Ekaterina. She worked for the Fillipov bakery in the city. My father was involved in the revolution, you know.'

I mentioned the October Revolution. He laughed.

'No, no. *That* wasn't the *revolution*. The revolution was in February. October was a coup d'état.'

It transpired that Vasily had learned English at night class. He had spent his working life as a railwayman, mainly running goods trains between Leningrad and Pskov, but had been injured in a shunting accident and was unfit for service in the Red Army. He told me that during the 900-day siege of Leningrad in the Second World War he had reg-ularly collected bodies from the streets on sledges or carts, and had become so ill himself through starvation that he almost died. After 30 minutes I had warmed to this infor-mative interloper. Being curious about the revolution, I ordered more beer – here was a man with a direct link to the events of 1917.

'Everything was different for my father when the revolution came in 1917. He didn't earn much before that – probably less than forty roubles a week. Driving a tram was a better job than most. Both my father and mother were glad to be that kind of wage earner, and not servants to the rich. We lived in two rooms in the Vyborg district. When I was little I was looked after by my grandmother. These young people today wouldn't believe the conditions. Keeping warm in the winter was the worst. The revolution didn't change that. We were still looking for firewood in 1918. Things only got better after the civil war, but it was still hard. Of course, I was still a tiny child. But my parents didn't have much respect for the Bolsheviks. There was an uprising in July 1917 and my father was driving a tram on the Liteiny Prospekt. A lot of the trams weren't running. After February gangs of workers and soldiers used to fill up the trams and hang on to the outsides. Nobody wanted to pay, either – they said that now Russia was "free" then they could travel where they liked for nothing. Imagine that today! One day when they all got on board they'd broken into a wine cellar in some hotel and the soldiers – they were from the Volinskiy Regiment, I think – were drunk and they insulted a couple of governesses, well-dressed young women who looked after rich people's children. Father stopped the tram and told the soldiers to behave or to get off. In those times, that was a stupid thing to do, but he had good manners. They beat him up. He didn't stay long as a tram driver – he finished before the October coup. I think he was scared. My mother lost her job at the bakery. There was such a shortage of flour and during 1917 a lot of bakeries were looted. She ended up in a laundry after the revolution. My father's experience as a tram driver got him a job on the railway between Petrograd and Moscow. He was a member of the *Vikzhel* – that was the railwayman's union. He was opposed to Lenin's ideas after October. He even wrote some letters while he was in the union. And he never cared what he said about the Communists. Once he'd had enough vodka he would speak his mind. I think that's what happened; that's why he was taken away in the 1930s. Stalin had a long memory. My mother was sent away to work on a collective farm and I never saw her again . . . I was brought up by my aunt.'

He drained his beer glass. I visited the toilet. When I

returned, he had gone, having finished my beer, and had taken my cigarettes with him.

This odd interlude set off a train of thought. The Bolshevik revolution already seemed like a distant historical event, yet there was still an oral connection to that time. Like me, Vasily had spent his life as a worker, but I had been lucky – we'd not had a Stalin in Britain.

I wondered if there were other elderly Russians with similar recollections. If so, then their attitude to the events of 1917 seemed to offer another aspect on the revolution. And his comment about October, the much-vaunted 'Glorious October' being a 'coup' fascinated me. Was this really what Russians felt?

This then is the story of one tumultuous year which changed the world.

With a few exceptions, prior to 1917 we were used to the history of the world as told through the chronicles of kings, emperors, empire-builders and military opportunists. Russia in 1917 was different, for it was, essentially, a chapter written by peasants, workers, soldiers and sailors, hijacked mid-stream by a caucus of determined intellectuals.

Although it is impossible to tell the story of the revolution without the involvement of Lenin, Trotsky, Alexander Kerensky and Stalin, this work will attempt to look at 1917, not primarily through the lens of political leadership, but from the standpoint of the ordinary mass of Russians, without whom the great uprising could never have taken place. First one has to qualify the term 'ordinary' in relation to the Russian people. 'The ordinary people' is a much-loved phrase amongst western politicians. In British political parlance it is meant to signify a mass of common-sense thinkers to whom they wish to appeal. It has proletarian overtones, but can often include anyone whose votes are urgently required. In Russia, as I have learned, one effect of 1917 which continued up until perestroika is that everyone, in political terms, was deemed 'ordinary'. In Lenin's study in the Smolny Institute in St Petersburg one of the many framed decrees adorning the walls issued by the dictatorship is Lenin's on nobility. It wipes away all the old designations on titles. No more dukes, princes, counts, ladies or duchesses. From 1917, everyone officially became a 'citizen' or a 'comrade'. Thus many former 'nobles' were pragmatic enough to take on board this seismic shift and adapt what skills they had to the revolution. It became much safer on the streets if one dressed down a little, and wore a red armband. They had to surrender a salon life of soirées and balls, supported by servants and estates, hide their jewellery and face a new, 'ordinary' existence. Many took the alternative chance – they threw in their lot with the Whites, led by Admiral Kolchak or General Denikin in a bloody but failed attempt to restore the old order.

For the Bolsheviks, society was meant to be levelled out into a proletarian mass. So although I was disappointed in Russia not to come across many surviving horny-handed sons of the soil from the Bolshevik days, one could designate all the interviewees – by their domestic living conditions alone – as 'ordinary' Russians.

In the immediate years after the revolution, the campaign to eliminate the 'propertied classes' – a term which came to encompass almost anyone who, prior to 1917, hadn't earned their living by manual labour – still has overtones of that terrible brutality inflicted upon the Jews by the Nazis when they arrived in Austria. Then, students, professors, stockbrokers, even lowly bank clerks were made to scrub the pavements. In Petrograd in 1918, following a draft law to establish compulsory labour service for 'the possessing classes', thousands of these hapless people to whom Lenin referred as 'bourgeois scum' were to be seen as ditch-diggers, tram drivers, railway guards, road sweepers, building labourers and farm-hands. There would be no more stockbrokers, well-heeled solicitors, idle rich playboys or governesses. When the Russian Civil War broke out, many of those whose delicate hands were used to the feel of a champagne glass now had to get to grips with a shovel as they were sent off to dig trenches. This is what it suddenly meant to be 'ordinary'.

In the decade since the USSR was dissolved, many families, descendants of the old nobility, have felt free to resuscitate their heritage without the fear of a knock on the door at two in the morning.

The twenty-first century domestic lives of people we in the West would call middle class – or in 1917 terms, the bour-geoisie – in Russia, differ enormously from the comfortable suburban existence one might expect for a senior academic in Cambridge or even a redbrick university. One of my friends in St Petersburg, now approaching 70, still refers to himself as 'Prince' Andrey Gagarin. This makes his wife, Tatiana, a princess. Andrey's mother, the spritely, erudite Vavara Vassi-lievna, has spent most of her academic life studying the English language, achieving the post of Professor of English Grammar. Andrey is still Professor of the St Petersburg State Technical University. Like most of the other people I spoke to, they live in city tenement blocks with dank, dark vestibules, stygian un-swept staircases and rickety elevators which often seem to pre-date Stalin. Their lives begin and end behind triple-locked, hefty, double doors. Gardening, beyond the window box and the pot plant, is not a luxury these people have ever enjoyed. If they have a pleasant view from their high window then they are lucky. I felt sorry for one of the sweetest and most artistic old ladies I have ever met, Helena Matveievna Krapivina, whose tiny self-contained room seemed to be denied sunshine on a brilliant Sunday afternoon – all that could be seen through her net curtains was a tall, blank, concrete wall. So these people are indeed 'the ordinary folk'. Attitudes do differ, however, among elderly people who have enjoyed a more manual working life. Whilst the more talkative, reflective types already mentioned offer a steady critique of communism, liberated as they are in their speech since 1991, the more working-class interviewees will still show a slight degree of nostalgic reverence for the days of Lenin – and, indeed, Stalin.

What happened in Russia in 1917 laid the foundations for decades of war, privation, argument and espionage. As with the Nazi period between 1933 and 1945, it has been the inspiration for thousands of books, films, documentaries and the seed-bed of political factions across the globe. What gave this event even more impact is the fact that it took place in a country already at war. It was a fast-moving process, the spontaneity of which, in the first half of 1917, even took the exiled Lenin and Trotsky by surprise. Yet the Russians were already well schooled in rebellion – the debacle of the 1905 revolution had seen to that.

The juggernaut of discontent and the people's desire for change and reform were already in full flow in 1914, but then came the war. A resurgence of old-fashioned patriotism united the Russians behind the monarchy and the motherland, yet this enthusiasm was to be short-lived. Despite initial military successes under General Brusilov, humiliating defeats, such as the Battle of Tannenberg in late August 1914 and the German advance on the Masurian Lakes in February 1915, when the Russian XX Corps suffered 100,000 casualties with a further 100,000 taken prisoner, soon saw reality dawning among the Russian population. By the end of 1914 there were already over 1 million wounded or killed, a figure which would rise to a tragic 8 million by 1917.[2] Defying universal advice to the contrary, the Tsar's almost medieval insistence in 1915 on commanding the armed forces was great, romantic window-dressing. Sadly Nicholas II was an inadequate military leader who squandered the initial passion and patriotism of his armies and frustrated his generals, who in turn, on numerous occasions, frustrated him. The ill-equipped sons of the Steppes were sent on a journey into hell, their only source of sustenance being an outmoded vague propaganda centred on the expired idea of 'Holy Russia'. Having to wait for one's comrade to fall dead in the trenches in order that you could, at last, have his boots or his rifle, was no way to fight a war.

Despite his many other failings, however, Nicholas was not keen to go to war. The monarchies of Europe and Britain were a family. 'Uncle Willy', the Kaiser, had offered the Tsar a last-minute chance to avert conflict, when, on 19 July 1914 he had sent a telegram imploring Nicholas not to let his troops cross the border, informing his rash nephew that it was still up to him whether war could be averted or not. Yet the die had already been cast – six hours earlier the German Ambassador had handed Sazonov, Russia's Minister of Foreign Affairs, a German declaration of war.[3] Nicholas's beloved cousin, King George V, had also sent telegrams to the Tsar asking him to make all efforts to avert war, but Russia's generals and ministers had bombarded their monarch with their fears. The Romanovs were susceptible to such massed influence, yet from the man who had influenced them the most, the monk Grigori Rasputin, came the most prophetic message, as recorded in the memoirs of Ania Vyrubova, lady-in-waiting to the Tsarina:

At this time a telegram arrived from Rasputin in Siberia, which plainly irritated the Emperor. Rasputin strongly opposed the war, and predicted it would result in the destruction of the Empire. But the Emperor refused to believe it and resented what was really an almost unprecedented interference in affairs of state on the part of Rasputin.[4]

And so the stage was set for a desperate drama which, over the next three years, would unravel 1,000 years of Russia's monarchic rule and culminate in the most famous revolution in history.

There are very few working-class survivors today who were old enough in 1917 to recall those portentous events. Like Britain's living veterans of the First World War, who number at the time of writing a mere 35 souls, in St Petersburg today there are probably less than a dozen who can recall what many Russians refer to as 'the October coup'. Some of these feature in this book. For the rest, I have had to rely on memories passed down through Russian families from the period, who now feel free to speak since perestroika. What was striking about my conversations with elderly Russians was their desire not to concentrate simply on their thoughts about the revolution; to them the whole communist period formed the bulk of their lives and it is impossible for them to focus on 1917 without expanding upon the lengthy aftermath. In most cases the Stalin years took up far more recording tape than the revolution. The stories they tell, such as that of Vavara Vassilievna, whose family life was so brutally affected by the purges, are worth inclusion because they act as a sombre counterbalance to the misplaced optimism of 1917.

What few Russian survivors there are from 1917 appear to have had more of what the Soviets would refer to as a 'bourgeois' lifestyle in pre-revolutionary times, rather than a blue-collar, proletarian one. Yet their interesting testimonies create an ambience of the period; even at their advanced years, they can speak clearly with authority because, although small children, they were actually there when the revolution happened. They include Sofia Khvatskaya, 93, whose father ran stationery shops in Moscow and was known as 'The Paper King'. Mikhail Lobodin is 97, and tactfully refers to the Tsar as 'a man of average abilities'. He worked as a lawyer, an economist and a children's writer. His view of the revolution is a dark one: 'the rule of blood'. Ilya Musin is 95. A talented classical pianist, this son of a watchmaker struggled to keep up his daily practice at the St Petersburg Conservatory after the revolution, but the rooms there were so cold he actually damaged his hands permanently, and eventually became a conductor. Vladimir Abromovich Katz was born in 1910 in Odessa, Trotsky's home town. The drama which unfolded in 1917 in Petrograd and Moscow seemed like a distant rumour to the Katz family, yet its repercussions would soon be felt, and Vladimir's future life, like that of his parents, would be dictated by communism. Retired architect Tatyana Dmitrievena Vasilevskaya, now 91, was only nine when the revolution broke. She too sees the period as somewhat grim: 'Since my father was an officer in the Tsarist navy, it was dangerous during the Soviet era to talk about our origins . . . many people we knew were made to suffer because of their bourgeois backgrounds.' Georgy Lugovoi, 99, was the son of a haberdashery merchant who owned five shops in Petrograd. He became a photographer whose work is displayed in the State History Museum in St Petersburg's Peter & Paul Fortress. 'I can't help but feel,' he says, 'that Nicholas II, as a leader, was too weak to protect his country and himself . . . and I think we are still undergoing a revolution – we are still not living in peace.'

Other views often offer a more positive view on 1917 as they were formed at the time of the insurrection by those who had little to lose from the uprising. As to what those same correspondents subsequently thought be to the perversion of their sacrifice under Stalin's iron hand can only be guessed at.

There were other, non-Russian witnesses who found themselves in Russia at that dramatic juncture. Mrs Lilian Nield is a lively 95-year-old who today lives in Manchester. In the first decade of the twentieth century many British companies functioned in Tsarist Russia, where engineering expertise, especially that of Lancashire's mill industry, was at a premium. Lilian's father helped to run a textile mill first in Petrograd and then in Narva, where she spent her early childhood between 1909 and 1917. Like many Britons, with the change of government in 1917 they soon found themselves on their way home – yet Lilian's family saw the revolution coming:

> 'I used to play with Nadewsha Samsonov. She was the daughter of the Chief of Police in Narva. One day we were playing house, as we often did, under the dining-room table. Suddenly Nadewsha said to me, 'There's going to be a revolution, and Daddy says we're going to vanish.' Later that day I asked my Mother what a 'revolution' was. I soon found out; and yes, Nadewasha and her family duly vanished.'

Other first-hand accounts have frequently been utilized to tell the story of the revolution. They include the many diplomats, military attachés and newspaper correspondents who were stationed in Russia during the uprising. Principal among these is the American John Reed (1887–1920) whose book *Ten Days That Shook The World* continues to be the journalistic benchmark on the October revolution. Even ardent right-wingers grudgingly admit that Reed's fact-packed roller-coaster ride through revolutionary Petrograd remains a major contribution to the literature on the subject. Best known as the author of the children's classic *Swallows & Amazons*,

Arthur Ransome (1884–1967) became a correspondent in 1915 for the liberal *Daily News*. His reporting on the revolution has an added dimension, as Ransome fell head over heels for Trotsky's secretary, Eugenia Shelepin. He married Eugenia (his second marriage) and the couple moved to Cumbria. Ransome's reputation as an ardent supporter of Lenin and Trotsky has been somewhat blurred by the recent revelation that he was, in fact, an agent for British Intelligence.

The *Manchester Guardian, Daily Chronicle* and *Morning Post* all benefited from the services over 14 years of a largely forgotten correspondent, Harold Williams (1876–1928). He was also married to a Russian, Ariadna Tyrkova, a very active member of the Constitutional Democrat Party (known as the Cadets). There were other reporters, some with less to say than others, such as *The Times* correspondent, Robert Wilton, who had no time for the revolution at all and reserved his empathy for the beleaguered Russian upper classes.

For almost a century, the Bolshevik revolution has provided politicians, academics, students and social commentators with a political football which is still in the air. Following the dissolution of the USSR, every aspect of this epic event is still shot through with rich seams of potential research. Interpretations of the revolution and its aftermath veer from the unstinting support of a stubborn, worldwide army of left-wing aficionados which divides itself into almost as many political factions as there were in Petrograd in 1917. Lenin continues to be held in reverence, the Trotskyists remain as implacable as ever as they persevere in their championing of the Fourth International, and the more theoretical Marxists continue to point out the dichotomy between the old master's pure dialectics and Lenin's transference of communist theory into action. Russia's twentieth-century past is not the golden age socialists had hoped for. Within a few short years of Lenin's death, the blunt, expedient weapons of terror, mass arrest and imprisonment he had used in the battle against counter-revolution and Allied intervention were honed and polished by his successor to achieve a new historical zenith in organized cruelty. Starvation, murder, millions of needless deaths and a dull, monochrome lifestyle were undoubtedly a giant slap in the face for the hopeful proletariat of 1917. Communism, therefore, has remained as little more than a political swearword. It exists as it always did, as a potent dream transferred into print by Karl Marx. It may have had its spiritual moments, as in the streets of Paris, Marseilles and Lyon during the communes of 1871, or on Chairman Mao's Long March – and still gives off a sporadic spark in Cuba's incessant struggle to live the legacy of Che Guevara – yet these are sparse examples. It has been argued, often to great effect, that Marxism makes too many demands of human nature, which, if we examine the bright and shiny cellphone world we now live in, seems less interested in social equality and philanthropy than we like to imagine. The engines which drive the twenty-first century are powered, as ever, by that age-old motive, greed.

Yet for all this, what the Bolsheviks set in motion in 1917 continued to put the proverbial fear of God into the money markets for decades. To keep Lenin's inheritance at bay required a continual barrage of propaganda which has victoriously equalled anything concocted in the Kremlin.

For the right wing, the life and legacy of Josef Stalin is a powerful gift, a political battering ram to point up that perennial argument that 'revolutions always eat up their children'. The undeniable spectres of the KGB, gulags, forced labour, death and social deprivation have all been used to great effect to keep the icy river of the cold war running swift and deep. From within Russia itself the long-gestating seeds of glasnost and perestroika were planted by the ultimate anti-Soviet cause célèbre throughout the 1970s, led by Alexander Solzhenytsin. For defenders of the USSR, his work made uncomfortable reading. To the philosophical champions of capitalism and western democracy, everything about the revolution was tragic, or worse, just evil. There remains also a more romantic element among the critics of the USSR – a look back through the wrong end of the telescope to something called 'Holy Mother Russia', with all its monarchic pomp and social servitude. This enthralment with a mythical, golden age has a growing army of followers among the Russians themselves. The two-headed Romanov eagle has risen from the ashes of the Soviet system like a phoenix, fed by the Russian Orthodox Church and worn proudly as a lapel badge by émigrés around the globe.

On the outer fringes of this critical mass there lurk darker forces who use the revolution to keep alight the baneful flickering candles of anti-Semitism. The 'white-power' vegetables of the jackboot fringe love nothing better than to suggest that Bolshevism was no more than a global Jewish conspiracy. They seize upon every Jewish participant they can find – with Trotsky as chief villain – and link them with assorted Wall Street bankers, usually with a good dose of that infamous old piece of fakery, the *Protocols of The Elders of Zion** thrown into the vile brew for added flavour. Very few miss the chance to remind us that Lenin did a deal which involved German money to get him back to Petrograd.

---

* *The Protocols of The Elders of Zion* is an infamous anti-Semitic forged document which appeared in Russia in 1905. It purports to be written by the Jews as a blueprint for their world domination, and although frequently shown to be a crude fake, is still popular as a propaganda tool with modern neo-nazies.

Other critics, from plain old libertarians to some international socialists (and many Russians), divide up the two halves of 1917 to declare the March (February, old style) revolution the *real* revolution whilst declaring the October coup to be Lenin's 'counter-revolution'. During the course of writing this book, I have also come to regard the February revolution as the real thing. Its spontaneity, the way it developed overnight – not from the comfortable studies of well-meaning intellectuals but from the workbenches and production lines of Russia's mills and factories, from the barracks of confused and hard-pressed soldiers and the sailors in the mess rooms of ships in the Baltic Fleet – make February 1917 a genuine 'revolution from below'. The tragedy was that the workers in some ways lost their grip on their achievement, so the historical view among the present generation of Russians that 'Glorious October' was, in fact, a military coup, seems to have some validity.

Mao Tse-tung once said that 'Revolution is not a dinner party, not an essay, not a painting, nor a piece of embroidery; it cannot be advanced softly, gradually, carefully, considerately, respectfully, politely, plainly and modestly.' Chairman Mao was correct. Revolutions are the work of focussed, impatient and dedicated men. They are usually not 'nice' people. They can be urbane and witty, like Leon Trotsky, but what drives them is a simmering river of hatred for their opponents. Vladimir Illyich Lenin, as anyone who perseveres with a study of his life will discover, was not a 'nice' man. He could be cruel. His rhetoric is peppered with phrases centred on 'elimination' and 'shooting' with a general thrust of teaching his opponents a lesson. Despite all the subsequent monotheistic iconography the USSR devoted to his memory, no one would have loathed the statues, the banners and the posters bearing his image more than the man himself. He even despised birthday parties. Stalin created a myth and a legend based on the idea of Lenin as a benevolent 'father' of communism. Had he lived on into old age, had the Russian Civil War not happened, one could speculate that the frequently exiled, embittered philosopher may well have softened up and, to use modern parlance, 'chilled out'. Yet if communism was to get a real foothold in the world of 1917, it required organization, intransigence, single-mindedness and a cast-iron will. In these departments, Lenin was well equipped.

Lenin and Trotsky took the Bolsheviks by the scruff of their necks during the late summer of 1917 and this compressed period of control helped to mould the party into the somewhat repressive machine it became. The expedient behaviour of the early Bolsheviks provided fertile ground for generations of western critics.

Like father, like son – here's Martin Amis pulling no punches on the subject of Lenin and his party: 'Seen in terms of freedom and freedom alone, October was not a political revolution riding on the back of a popular revolution (February). It was a counter-revolution.' And he leaves us in no doubt as to his views on the Bolsheviks: 'This was the elephant-trumpeting, snorting, farting mammoth – in the Kremlin living room. Established on an abyss of untruth, Bolshevism was committed to its career of slapstick mendacity, attaining universal and ideal truthlessness under Stalin.'[5]

Somewhere in the middle of this view stand the parliamentarians, who argue that, had Kerensky's 1917 Provisional Government had the chance, then a democratic parliamentary system would have ensued. Yet Kerensky seems in retrospect – despite his histrionics, fiery oratory, his skill as a lawyer and a penchant for dressing as a worker – to fit the dismissive description given him by Lenin as 'a petty braggart', or the more astute assessment by Trotsky: 'His best speeches were merely a sumptuous pounding of water in a mortar. In 1917 the water boiled and sent up steam, and the clouds of steam provided a halo.'[6]

Yet this is all water which has passed under a very distant bridge. The fact remains that in Russia in 1917 one of the greatest spontaneous social upheavals of all time took place, because the ordinary people had had enough. Lenin and Trotsky may well have taken up the reins, but the proletarian horse was already in full gallop by the time they arrived from exile. The sheer political complexity of the situation was not helped by the backdrop of an iniquitous world war, and the fact that the pristine dreams of 1917 had dissolved into a puddle of despair by 1924 seems, with hindsight, hardly surprising.

To say that Russian Communism is dead, despite the remnants of the party still kicking at Vladimir Putin's gates, is an understatement. I recall another afternoon in June 2000 when I first visited the Smolny Institute in St Petersburg. Once the engine room of the revolution, this attractive building, built as a finishing school for the daughters of the landed gentry, today houses the offices of the city's mayor. Lenin's study was, by all accounts, still intact, a fact I have verified with an arranged visit whilst writing this book. Yet today the cockpit of Bolshevism is no longer the revolutionary Disney-land attraction it once was. I had laboured that day in 2000 under the presumption that as a museum, it was still open, but an official in the foyer informed me that to gain access I must write for an appointment. I was intrigued by this new reticence to open a chapter of the city's history to a curious foreigner, especially as Lenin's statue still stood, the sun glinting off the dull bronze, in the centre of a neat bed of geraniums before the Smolny's lofty portico. I pointed this out, and received a curt riposte: 'When the Tsar's bones come back – *he* goes!' Yet four years later, Lenin is still there.

Supporters of the Soviet era are dwindling. In St Petersburg, up until 1993, in the main hall of the Moscow Railway Station at *plóstchad Vosstániya No. 2,* a fine bust of Lenin by the sculptor L. Mess stood. It was removed from its pedestal that year by Mayor Sobchak. There was a huge public outcry over this event and Lenin was replaced with a plaque donated by the protesters which remained for some months, displaying the message 'On this spot, Mayor Sobchak betrayed the people of Leningrad', until this curt proclamation was substituted for the bust of Peter the Great which stands there today. In the Tauride Gardens, a small bronze figure of Lenin seems one of the most vandalized, his head covered by several pourings of thick blue paint. At the legendary Finland Station, the unscaleable polished marble height of Vladimir's plinth is too much of a challenge to even the most determined vandals, who have had to content themselves with some free-market sprayed graffiti around the base. Such trashing of history may seem a sin to old western liberal romantics. But ask any thrusting, entrepreneurial Russian of a certain age who recalls attending school in the 1970s about the way October 1917 and the glories of Leninism were force-fed to a generation, and one can soon understand their dismay at our continuing fascination with their revolutionary past.

On Victory Day, 9 May 2004 in St Petersburg, the 59th anniversary of the ending of the Siege of Leningrad was celebrated in style. It was a beautiful spring day. After moving ceremonies and dedications at the Piskaryovskoye Memorial Cemetery, where thousands of Leningraders, victims of the 900-day Nazi siege, are buried, I encountered a quintet of hard-line Russian Communists who, in their sombre little procession, seemed to hark back to a time even before communism. Each carried an icon – either of Stalin or Lenin. There was no sign of Trotsky, despite his rehabilitation. Middle aged and dour, they stood by the cemetery wall and unfurled a long red banner which outlined their disgust at the break-up of the USSR. Their spokesperson was an intense middle-aged lady called Madredeva Tamara Yurlova. She told us that at the height of Gorbachov's glasnost and perestroika, 73 per cent of Russians had voted against the dissolution of the USSR. Like many such Soviet-inspired statistics, this seemed scurrilous. She handed me a photocopied portrait of Stalin, adding somewhat conspiratorially, 'He never killed *anybody,* you know.'

The rest of this oddball party railed against the state of Russia today, yet apart from we inquisitive foreigners, no one among the thousands of veterans and young Russian servicemen and women passing by took any notice. It is perhaps that adherence to Stalinism which will keep the old communists forever out in the cold. Later that day, at the rear end of the massive military parade along the Nevsky Prospekt, the latter-day communists marched with their banners, followed by a genuinely fearsome sight. It was a group of somewhat thuggish-looking youngsters carrying flags which, from a distance, appeared to bear the red, black and white emblem of the Third Reich. As they drew closer, what had looked like a swastika in that white hole on the blood red flag was in fact the hammer and sickle. I asked a nearby Russian what this strutting group represented. '*Nationalist* Communism' was the reply. Russia, it seems, has more than one version of its own BNP. The appearance of those young, proto-Nazi 'communists' was a reminder that the powerful essence of revolution is not, after all, a fine wine, but nitro-glycerine. When it explodes, in the wrong hands, as it did in Stalin's, it shatters all dreams.

The subsequent tragic fate of most of the original, dedicated Bolsheviks from 1917, and the utter abandonment of all those notions of liberty and fraternity which had staggered into the light in February that year, when examined carefully, produces nothing but bitter disappointment for an enthusiastic socialist. Among the old Russians I spoke to, I had expected slightly rosier views of 1917. There were a few, but most wanted to talk about the long, grim aftermath. Considering just how grim it was, I have included their testimonies at the end of this book as some kind of counterbalance to the exhilaration which shone throughout Russia between February and October 1917.

Capitalism's victory over the Soviet system has not been a magnanimous one. The revolution's shock waves are still felt by the West's cold-war warriors. Today in St Petersburg you can buy your Big Mac, a pair of Levis, drink a Coke and save up a week's wages for a family visit to Pizza Hut. The dollar is the preferred currency, with the euro now running a close second. However, as sporadic, international, anti-capitalism protests continue to make the news, corporate radar screens still show up blips of inspiration around the world which continue to have elements of 1917 as their focal point. This will ensure that the free market's PR men have no choice but to keep on flogging the long-dead horse of the USSR with the same whip which Senator Joe McCarthy, Richard Nixon and Ronald Reagan all gripped so eagerly.

What remains today of the undercurrent of threat posed to the West from the well spring of the Bolshevik revolution and the ensuing Soviet period has been replaced with the far more sinister and archaic intimidation of religious fundamentalism. The odd state, such as the mysterious conundrum of North Korea, still gives the political pundits a focus to provide the perennial socialism vs. capitalism debate with some continuum. Hopefully, therefore, in this brief retrospective on a very significant year, we can side-step the political minefield and take a dispassionate look at the brief hopes, aspirations and fears of a great, long-suffering, yet resilient people – the Russians.

I
FROZEN MINDS

The exasperation of the people is growing by leaps and bounds. Every day more and more of them demand 'Either give us food or stop the war' . . . They have nothing to lose from a disadvantageous peace. Just when the thing will happen and how, it is hard to tell. But events of the greatest importance and fraught with the most dangerous consequences are most certainly close at hand.

Report from the Russian State
Police Department, January 1917.[1]

Sergei Kravchinsky, an 86-year-old Red Army veteran, is amused when westerners ask questions about 'those old days'. Like a lot of Russians today, the mention of the name Lenin is usually followed by a somewhat mysterious, knowing laugh: 'Lenin . . . *ha ha ha.*' It is hard to say if this is an affectionate chuckle or a mask for embarrassment. But before Lenin's arrival in 1917, there were other Petrograd characters who remain in the collective memory. Above all, literature in Russia is still today a passion matched only by football in the West, and as Sergei pointed out, for the workers it wasn't always Pushkin and Gogol:

> I remember my mother telling me that in the years before the 1914–18 war, she was one of the early telephonists in St Petersburg who worked in the telephone exchange just off Gorokhovaya Street. There weren't too many telephones in the city back then. The wages were terrible, but she got by. She said her hobbies included reading – mainly *Pinkertonovshchina* – detective stories. They were very popular among the workers then.

Within a few short years, however, the working population of the city, like Sergei's mother-to-be, would discover that the clandestine behaviour of the upper classes of Petrograd could outstrip anything they might find in a cheap novel.

The average temperature in Petrograd between January and March 1917 was a bone-chilling minus 12.1 degrees Centigrade, compared with minus 4.4 degrees in 1916.

The darkness, the frost, the brittle ice on the Moika Canal and the encrusted, trampled snow on the pavements in the early hours of 30 December 1916 formed the perfect scenario for a murder. But this was no ordinary killing. The victim was a man of such immense influence in the affairs of Russia that his death was bound to have momentous repercussions. His demise was a long-drawn-out, unpleasant affair involving ineffective poison and, ultimately, a fatal gunshot. The body was removed from the scene of the crime in the dead of night to be tossed from a bridge on the Neva, where it sank through a hole in the cracked ice below. The mysterious nocturnal goings-on surrounding the event were fully detailed in a report from Petrograd by Robert Wilton, the correspondent for the London *Times*:

> Suddenly from the direction of the Blue Bridge a motor car drove up to the palace. The servants assisted by the chauffeur, in the presence of an officer who was wearing a long fur cloak, carried out what looked like a human body and placed it in the car. The chauffeur jumped in and putting on full speed made off along the canal side and also promptly disappeared. Almost at the same time General Grigorieff was informed from the Prefecture that Rasputin had been killed in the palace of Prince Yusupov.[2]

Rasputin's death had been anticipated among Petrograd's upper classes for some time. That it should have come not at the hands of some ragamuffin revolutionary but those of Prince Felix Yusupov – an Oxford-educated transvestite in possession of an immense fortune, 38 palaces and some of the Crimea's richest oilfields – only demonstrates just how much Grigori Rasputin's malevolent influence in Russia's politics and war effort was acknowledged throughout every class in the land. The Russian royal family's lack of credible leadership over their people was also brought into focus by the isolation of the Tsar himself. Perhaps he still had faith in Russia's 'Old Fundamental Laws' laid down in 1716, which had decreed: 'God himself commands that all men must bow to his supreme power, not only out of fear but also out of conscience.' If this was the case, then by 1917 the starving masses were having none of it.

After fathering three daughters, Nicholas had longed for a male heir, but when one arrived, the life of the young

Tsarevitch, Alexi, would be blighted by haemophilia. To the Tsarina, Alexandra, Rasputin seemed to be a genuine 'holy man' possessing occult powers which could stem the young boy's attacks of bleeding. Yet Rasputin soon earned a reputation as an opportunistic charlatan, not only among the ordinary population but among the Tsar's loyal ministers and every titled personage of influence. The monk's weird personal doctrine of 'redemption by sin' helped to satisfy his own prodigious sexual appetite and fuelled many a salacious scandal. However, he had crossed the Rubicon when he began to issue his supernatural guidelines on the conduct of the war. When Nicholas was not present, Rasputin would proffer his advice in private sessions with Alexandra, who would include a range of handy tips in her letters to her husband, such as:

> Now before I forget I must give you a message from our Friend prompted by what he saw in the night. He begs you to order that one should advance near Riga, says it is necessary, otherwise the Germans will settle down so firmly through the winter that it will cost endless bloodshed.[3]

This disturbing reliance on a hard-drinking peasant monk with a taste for crude depravity did nothing for the reputation of the Romanovs. His death, therefore, came as no surprise. Rasputin had once scrawled across the bottom of one of his photographs: 'Nobody knows what's going to happen to us in the morning.' How right he was.

The Browning revolver which pumped that fatal bullet into the mad mystic was the starting pistol of the revolution. Yusupov and his rich, aristocratic friends simply had the one strategy – kill Rasputin – but they appear to have had no contingency plan to cover the aftermath. Their vain hope was that Rasputin's demise would bring the Romanovs to their senses and save the dynasty. It patently did not. Nicholas, an autocrat to the end, would remain oblivious to the gulf between himself and public opinion – if the upper classes could commit such a deed, then anything could happen.

Sofia Khvatskaya, born in 1909, had an idyllic Russian childhood. Her father ran stationery shops in Moscow and was known as 'The Paper King'. Her mother was a dressmaker, an occupation which Sofia would eventually choose. At their country home in the Yaroslavl Oblast, Sofia enjoyed a rural life with her sisters. The family had four hectares of land, with pigs, sheep and horses – her childhood was spent feeding chickens, digging for potatoes and carrying water from the river. They ate well, with eggs, buckwheat and butter. But then came the war, and with it, the Bolsheviks.

> At that time there was terrible chaos. Things were in a real mess. One day you heard the Tsar was in one place, another day he was somewhere else. We all prayed that he would go abroad, because that was the only place he could save himself and his family. He had a soft character, as we would call it.[4]

If that 'soft character' had listened more carefully to his people, then the coming fate of Sofia's family may have been avoided. After the revolution, when the countryside was pillaged for every scrap of food, the Khvatskayas would lose everything, with Sofia's husband, Alexander, doomed to a decade of imprisonment in labour camps.

The news of Rasputin's murder rumbled on throughout the sombre, ice-bound days of January 1917, but the ordinary people of Petrograd had other things on their mind – bread, firewood and the daily tragedy of news from the eastern front. Urban electricity supplies had been cut drastically. Keeping cold and near starvation at bay had become a full-time occupation, yet this constant strain and daily grind had pushed the workers beyond endurance. Petrograd's population, doubled since the turn of the century, had soared to two and a half million. The massive industries – textiles, automobiles, armaments and chemicals – seemed to have an insatiable demand for labour. It arrived in the city from around the country – simple peasants looking for a different way of life, men and women from less industrialized towns and cities who thought that Petrograd might be the answer to their acute poverty. They would soon be disappointed. The work was long, hard and grim, the wages poor, and the cramped living accommodation a far cry from the fresh air of the tundra or the steppes. At least in the country there had been bread, the occasional egg and some meat; in Petrograd these commodities were luxuries.

Day by day more trains arrived at Petrograd's Warsaw Station to disgorge their tragic cargo of wounded soldiers from the front. What hospitals there were overflowed with bloodstained patients. Medical supplies were dwindling. Yet even these foul conditions were preferable to going back to the trenches. Many men made their injuries last as long as possible rather than be sent back to the misery of the front. In the Baltic and on the fortress island of Kronstadt, the Tsarist navy was teetering on the brink of mutiny. Hunger and a longing for peace had united everyone behind a red banner of impatience and anger. Since the start of the war there had been a rise in bread prices of over 300 per cent[5]. The average factory worker or tradesman was earning less than 50 roubles per week, a sum which would hardly provide one with the necessities of life. The war had seen the Russian rouble slump from 94 to 155 for 10 pounds sterling; and it would plunge much further than this. Bread alone, that staple of any diet, was costing anything from 12 kopeks upwards for a loaf of inferior black bread, with white bread at over 20 kopeks. Many foodstuffs which, even before the war, had been rarely enjoyed by the working class, had faded into golden memories; veal, pork, herrings and cheese had suffered a staggering 700 per cent increase in price since 1914. A new suit of clothes would cost a factory worker the equivalent of five months' wages, a pair of shoes almost three months. And things were about to get much worse.

Yet, this was still a city of contrasts. Directly across the street from St Isaac's Cathedral, just ten minute's walk from the Winter Palace, stood the lofty splendour of the seven-storey Astoria Hotel. Built between 1910 and 1912 in the art nouveau style, the Astoria bustled with a clientele of smartly-uniformed Allied officers, journalists and assorted international business entrepreneurs. Here the wine flowed, the aroma of pork and veal still wafted from the extensive kitchens, if not as regularly as it had done in better times. From the windows of the Astoria the military men could watch the sad tragedy of a decomposing society as it made its daily parade between work and home. Those who could afford it clambered aboard the crowded trams, while the majority, the less well off, trudged through the snow keeping a keen eye open for any edible bargain along their route.

The first tram had appeared in Petrograd in 1880, having been built and tested by an engineer, Fiodor A. Pirotskiy. The trams of Petrograd would become an important factor in the political history of the city. Even today, in twenty-first century St Petersburg, the people claim proudly that it was Pirotskiy who invented the concept of the tram, only to have his idea snatched from him, developed and marketed around the world by the mighty Siemens company. Prior to trams the population – those who could afford it – travelled the length and breadth of the city by horse-driven cars called *konka*. In 1906 the *konka* were carrying 106 million passengers per year, a trade which kept thousands of drivers, coach builders and stable hands in work. Thus the rise of the tram would spark yet another of Petrograd's many protests as the new rails were laid along the city's main thoroughfares. By 1907 there were 150km (93.8 miles) of track in the city when the electric tram service opened on 16 September 1907. Soon the horse-drawn *konka* vanished, and by 1917 the city's tram system was operating 710 cars. Although they often had reason to strike – and did – many of the drivers of these tough, resilient vehicles stood by their posts and kept the service running throughout the bitter struggles of the revolution and the ensuing civil war.

Along the Nevsky Prospekt opposite the City Hall there still stands another grand hotel. A popular watering hole with the rich and titled, the Grand Hotel Europe was Petrograd's finest. Behind this lofty eclectic façade a world of elegance and plenty existed, far removed from the ragged life of poverty outside. Here the diplomats dined, served by a staff as famous for their servile excellence as the reputation of their wine cellars. In this city of paupers and palaces the talk among the wealthy and the poor was of the war. For the supporters of the Tsar the war against Germany was a grand crusade, another huge chapter of sacrifice and suffering in a country whose history was shot through with penance and anguish. Many of the Army's peasant conscripts, however, had little idea of what the war was about. One day they would be chopping wood, planting crops and feeding the cows, the next, startled and disorientated, they would find themselves in a rough, ill-fitting uniform, crammed into a troop train bound for the front. To the peasant soldier, the war was often just one big puzzle. Yet the call of Holy Mother Russia had always been answered. When it came, they had to go.

In the big factories such as the Russki Renault plant in the north of the city across the Neva in Vyborg, and among the huge, 30,000-strong workforce at the massive Putilov arms factory, the talk was different. Here, where hungry workers had regularly worked up to twelve hours a day or more, they were agitating for a 50 per cent pay rise, shorter working hours, better management, more food – and peace. Among the working class the notion of revolution, although a regular topic, was way down on the agenda. Revolution was the loftier aim among the intelligentsia who led the more radical elements in the plethora of political organizations which met daily in Petrograd. Within the main political parties there was still some appreciable support for the war. The proletariat at this stage would have settled for a decent pay rise, three square meals, an eight–hour working day, some sugar for their tea and the return of their loved ones from the front. Yet no-one was listening, especially their autocratic monarch and his equally insensitive wife.

Nicholas II had come to the throne in 1894 as a reluctant Tsar who claimed he 'knew nothing of ruling'. He saw his accession to the throne as 'the worst thing that could have happened to me, the thing I have been dreading all my life'.[6] Two years later, in May 1896, at a military training area in the Khodynka district of Moscow, where Nicholas's coronation was to take place, panic broke out among the huge crowds in a stampede for free beer, gifts and sausages. The gifts and food were scheduled to be distributed at 10 a.m. – with Nicholas arriving at midday to enjoy a range of open-air entertainment – from special booths, but their location was unfortunate as the ground was rugged, and dotted here and there not only with trenches but occasionally with wells. The 500,000 people who had assembled for this attractive act of munificence needed some form of stewardship and policing, yet the authorities had failed to make adequate plans and 1,400 people were killed. This was a ghastly tragedy yet the new Tsar appeared to carry on celebrating regardless of the disaster. Although Nicholas and Alexandra did spend their time during that fateful day visiting hospitals, they nevertheless pressed ahead with their evening attendance at a grand ball given by the French Ambassador, whose government were celebrating a new alliance with Russia. And so, among the poorer people, the image of the last Tsar and his wife as a crassly insensitive couple was sealed. Whilst families mourned, Nicholas and Alexandra danced, a grim paradox that would haunt the Romanovs to the end.

His reign was punctuated by a catalogue of disasters. The ignominious destruction of Russia's Baltic Fleet at the hands of the Japanese at Tshushima in 1905 was a catastrophe which had fuelled the first failed Russian revolution of that year. The barbarous act of shooting down a crowd of defenceless demonstrators outside the Winter Palace in January 1905, a grim event known as 'Bloody Sunday', was another indelible stain on Nicholas's character. Strikes had gripped the whole of Russia in 1905 as industry and the railways ground to a halt. The Tsar eventually conceded that some concession must be given to the people. It came in the form of his 'October Manifesto', when the First Duma, an elected parliament, was created, without whose approval no law could be passed and which ostensibly would provide Russians with some civil liberties. Its Prime Minister, Sergei Witte, made enough political changes to avoid further violence. The October Manifesto of 1905 provided a constitution which divided the revolutionary groups. In the confused lull which followed, Nicholas acted quickly, sending in troops to break up the hopeful Soviets which had been formed in St Petersburg and Moscow. The most prominent revolutionaries were hunted down, exiled or imprisoned – 1905 had been, for the Romanovs, a close-run thing. But as Trotsky (who, unlike the then unknown Lenin, was a prominent Menshevik organizer in the 1905 uprising) would say later, 1905 was just a dress rehearsal.

Duma or no Duma, the Tsar was still in charge. Witte, who had done so much to industrialize the country and save his monarch's skin, was dismissed by Nicholas in 1906. Nicholas now regurgitated Russia's old Fundamental Laws which, in essence, gave him total control over the Duma, which on two occasions between 1906 and 1907, he dismissed. It had dared to criticize him. Soon the rich, the Tsar's greatest supporters, benefited from new voting legislation which gave them a two-thirds majority in the assembly. Nicholas now had his own pet parliament which would support him without criticism. Despite this situation, the Duma's new Prime Minister, Peter Stolypin, knew that the lives of the country's poor and dispossessed required some improvement, but Stolypin, who came from the rich landed gentry, also had his dark side. As governor of the province of Saratov in 1905 his ruthless suppression of the peasants had been legendary. As Prime Minister he continued this policy, ordering the execution of over 1,100 victims between August 1906 and April 1907. Such brutality, despite his success in bringing capital into Russia and his efforts to increase agricultural production, would not be forgotten. Even Nicholas's supporters had little time for Stolypin and his reforms and in 1911, he was duly assassinated.

Within three years of Stolypin's murder, the revolutionary movement was back in business. Only weeks before the outbreak of the First World War strikes raged throughout industry and the streets of St Petersburg were awash with a sea of red flags. Yet the age-old soul of traditional Russia was about to reassert itself.

When the First World War broke out the people laid down their revolutionary banners and massed in front of the Winter Palace, where they fell to their knees in fealty and subjugation to their 'Little Father', and in great reverence sang the national anthem. Russia's problems had been set aside in the face of a common enemy, the princes, dukes and speculators could relax – war had come to their rescue.

By 1917 that patriotic fervour had evaporated. Almost 8 million men had died at the front, many without even weapons or ammunition. Men were deserting from the trenches in droves; those going home on leave failed to return to the front; thousands languished in German prison camps. There was a huge shortage of farm workers as male peasants were conscripted into the Army in their thousands. Horses had been requisitioned for the front, and what food there was was not getting through to the urban population as the railway network was constantly in military use. The lack of coal and fuel had closed many factories and businesses, adding unemployment and poverty to the people's burden of misery.

Meanwhile, Nicholas had another problem – his wife. Alexandra Feodorovna was a German princess, the daughter of Grand Duke Louis of Hesse-Darmsradt and Alice Maud Mary, the daughter of Queen Victoria. She was aloof, spoke poor Russian, and, like her husband, appeared to remain oblivious to the tide of discontent which was lapping at their feet. By 1917 her constant disastrous meddling, in tandem with Rasputin, in Russia's political affairs had earned her a dubious although inaccurate reputation as a German spy, intent on bringing Russia to defeat. She was already being generally referred to as 'the German Woman (*nemka*) – she who has come to us behind a coffin'. Patriotic ardour and the negative sensitivity the Russians had towards all things German during this bitter war had been there from the start, when, in 1914, the name of St Petersburg had been diplomatically altered to become Petrograd, the former sounding far too German for public taste. Yet without doubt Nicholas loved his wife dearly even though she did, at times, drive him to distraction.

To the workers the Nicky and Alex show was nothing but a bizarre source of prurient rumour and gossip. Whatever reserves of dignity and prestige the Romanovs had once possessed were utterly expired. The Duma, struggling against all the odds to form some semblance of a government, was still dominated by argumentative factions of titled landowners, assorted gentry and political opportunists. Frequently, on the impulse of Alexandra, they had been dismissed on the smallest whim and replaced with even greater incompetents. A bizarre example was the Minister for the Interior, Alexander Protopopov, a man whose sanity was in some doubt. As the head of the Tsarist secret police, the Okhrana, he had often dismayed his agents when, in conference, he would hold much of his conversation with an icon on his desk. Protopopov, rumoured to be suffering from syphilis, had now been given the task by the Tsarina (following Rasputin's advice) of overseeing the country's food distribution. Yet far from being a humanitarian mission, he saw the job as an extension of his police duties, not a tool for relieving hunger. If he held back food supplies, he knew riots would ensue, and riots meant that he could introduce repression on a grand scale, thus drawing potential revolutionaries into his net.

As a source of government, the Duma seemed to offer little in the way of hope or progress. All the workers could do was to agitate and organize themselves, and they were becoming fairly adept in both departments.

Since 1917, throughout western culture, the term 'Bolshie' has become synonymous in day-to-day working life with anyone in the workplace who stuck their heads above the parapet to express contrary views. Although the Russian working class were no more or less rebellious or antagonistic than their British, French or German counterparts, it was their tough working culture, forged against a background of rigid autocracy, which, in some ways, set them apart.

A great number of workers in urban industry came from rural backgrounds. In the city they began to abandon many of the religious observances they had grown used to in the countryside. Many of these peasant workers still looked the part in their belted, rustic, *rubashka* tunics, with their trousers tucked into high boots. As they became urbanized their style changed and the peasant haircut, usually a pudding-bowl style, was adapted to the more popular coiffure of their industrial workmates. Despite poverty and deprivation, the way you looked was important, particularly as some poorer workers had on occasions been stopped by the police from entering Petrograd's Summer Gardens because of their scruffy appearance. In the city they also had more opportunities for education. In the period between the first revolution of 1905 and the uprisings of 1917, a whole range of institutes and Sunday schools sprang up, such as the Central Workers' Circle of St Petersburg. Evening classes became popular and many workers enrolled at institutions such as the Smolenskaia, where lessons on Sundays could include anything from literature to chemistry. It was within many of these institutions, and those run by the more progressive factory owners, such as that set up by the industrialist N.A. Vargunin and the well-run educational classes at the Putilov works, that the nature of politics was revealed. Understanding of the wider cultural world through education could only bring into sharp focus the workers' own sorry plight. Union organizers and party cadres in the factories helped to expand this interest. By 1917, once the initial patriotic fervour for the war had begun to evaporate, Russian industrial workers had developed an interest in progressive politics and a healthy appetite for shop-floor debates and meetings.

Russia was a late-comer to industrialization. In the late nineteenth century the status of a great power was based on her level of industrialization, not, as had previously been the case, on the extent of her territory. Apart from having a monarchy, the country differed vastly from western Europe. The Tsar's empire covered one-sixth of the globe, being 2,000 miles from north to south and 5,000 miles from west to east. Only 44.4 per cent of this vast empire were Russian – 17.8 per cent were Ukranian, there were almost 8 million Poles, 13 million Turkic Muslims and nine other diverse nationalities.[7] Among Russia's population of 129 million there were dozens of different languages and cultures which, to the populace of Moscow and St Petersburg would have seemed as alien as that of the Plains Indians had been to the first American settlers. In the first Russian Census in 1897 Her urban working class accounted for a mere 4 per cent of the working population.[8] Peasants and rural workers made up 82 per cent. By 1913, as more and more peasants flocked to the cities to find work, this figure had dropped to 67 per cent[9].

In the countryside, serfdom had only vanished with emancipation as late as 1861. In 1917 the economy was still in many ways a peasant, or rural, one. The peasantry were largely superstitious, religious, illiterate and conservative, although it would be a mistake to translate illiterate as stupid. These were tough, resilient people whose distrust of educated townsfolk was matched only by a simmering hatred for their titled landlords. By the time the war started, they were also developing a mistrust of priests, and in many villages the quest for knowledge and education was on the rise.

Despite the emancipation of 1861, and a reduction in their taxes in the 1880s, the peasants were in many ways Russia's second-class citizens. Extreme poverty was a burden they continued to carry, and their backbreaking workload, where the wooden plough was still in use, had changed little over the centuries. Meanwhile there was a new, rapidly developing barrier in the countryside between them and a better life. Another kind of rural landlord, a class of wealthier peasants, the Kulaks, had become avaricious middlemen between the poorer peasants, the estate owners and the gentry. Kulak is a Russian word for 'fist' – and as the Kulaks were generally regarded as 'tight-fisted', this has a degree of resonance in our own language. Another popular contemptuous name for these enterprising peasants was *miroyed,* which translates as 'commune eater'.[10] Sometimes referred to as the 'Prosperous Russian peasants' they have become one of the most demonized groups in official Soviet history, and one could argue, even from a socialist point of view, that the broad sweep of the historical put-down of the Kulaks is in some ways unfair. For instance, here's the rather vitriolic Stalinist entry for Kulaks from the Soviet Encyclopaedic Dictionary (1964) Volume 2:

> **Kulaks:** rural bourgeoisie, the most numerous of the bourgeoisie layers in a capitalist village. The Kulaks enrich themselves through the cruel exploitation of farm labourers, the village poor and other layers of the working rural population. The Kulak class is the result of the corruption of small goods production.

In Tsarist Russia in 1913, the Kulaks were 12.3% of the population. They produced 50% of all bread. The Kulaks concentrated on their farms a large portion of agricultural machinery and instruments of production, also owned commercial-industrial enterprises and ruthlessly robbed working peasants by practising usury. Along with capitalists and landed gentry, the Kulaks are the most rabid, the most unappeasable enemy of the proletariat revolution. During the period of the foreign military intervention and civil war 1918–20, the Kulaks, the owners of surplus bread, tried to strangle with hunger the young Soviet Republic. The Kulaks organized gangs, viciously dealt with workers and rural poor, helped the interventionists. Under the direction of the Communist party the working class and village labourers undertook a ruthless struggle against the Kulaks.

Until 1929 the Soviet government pursued policies of restricting and displacing the Kulaks, decisively suppressing all their attempts to fight the Soviet authority, spoil state bread procurements, kill village activists, etc. As a result of forced collectivization, the Kulaks were liquidated as a class. With the victory of the *kolhoz* system (collectively owned farms) the conditions that gave rise to the Kulak order disappeared. In Soviet villages, the bourgeois ownership system has been forever liquidated and the socialist system created.

In nations with people's democracy, in conditions of intense class struggle, after World War II agrarian reforms were carried out, undermining the basis for large-Kulak ownership; the special weight of the village socialist sector continues to grow and conditions are being created for its total victory.[11]

One cannot help but shudder at the words 'liquidated as a class'.

Many aspects of the official Soviet description of Kulaks

may well have been appropriate in 1917. Yet when it came to feeding Russia, as Lenin soon came to realize, the Kulaks were important.

If, even in Stalinist propaganda terms they 'produced 50% of all bread', then at least they were producing something valuable. Their economic rapacity since 1861 had grown as capitalist production had increased. Before then the peasants had been regarded as a single feudal mass. Following emancipation new factions began to form, with 45 per cent progressing to becoming wealthy landowners – or as Lenin had it, the rural bourgeoisie, with the remaining peasantry divided into the smaller landowners the petty bourgeoisie, and those with little or no land, the rural proletariat. Yet despite the momentous events which took place in 1917, by 1921, by which time he was facing a peasant rebellion, Lenin was forced to go easy on his rural bourgeoisie when he instigated the New Economic Policy (NEP). As for the *kolhoz* system, on a scale of misery and hardship this mass enforced collectivization of the countryside resulted in a system which far surpassed any of the iniquity experienced by the peasants prior to 1921. Converting the peasants to their way of thinking was also no easy task for the Mensheviks and the Bolsheviks. The rural population liked to do things their own way. They distrusted town-dwelling intellectuals, and stubbornly held on to their faith in the Tsar, believing forlornly that at some future golden dawn he would indeed give them the land. In the 1870s the Socialist Revolutionaries, for example, were a party with a strong membership of student drop-outs who saw it as their revolutionary duty to work among the peasants (the *narod*). Their idea was simple: to work alongside farm workers and villagers and eventually convert them to a belief in the violent overthrow of the monarchy. Known as the *narodniks,* these often naïve yet dedicated revolutionaries were also greatly distrusted by the peasants. Many of the *narodniks'* ideas seemed incomprehensible to them, and with their respect for the Church, the Tsar and their own traditional ways, they utterly disappointed the young missionaries of violence. When the terrorist group, People's Will, assassinated Tsar Alexander II in 1881, the iron-fisted aftermath saw the *narodniks* ruthlessly hunted down, killed, imprisoned or exiled.

In the first half of the nineteenth century, agricultural land in feudal Russia was laid out field by field in pairs of long, narrow strips. These were tended by the serfs side by side, the produce of one section going to the landlord, the other to the serf.

After their emancipation of 1861, the land the peasants had once cultivated for themselves now became the property of a peasant commune, the *Mir,* formed by those serfs who were at one time servants to a common landlord.

The old landlords held on to the rest of the land not used to maintain the serfs. This was the majority of any acreage, and was still divided into strips alongside the communal land. All the forested and pastoral land upon which, during feudal times, the serfs could graze their livestock, was now owned by the landlords. This had a devastating effect on the so-called 'liberated' peasants after 1861 – with no legal access to the forests, they no longer had the product they most needed in the winter: firewood.

Into this economic gap, as they would in any growing capitalist society, stepped the opportunistic Kulaks who imposed a tax on the peasants to use the pastoral lands. Some peasants decided to leave some of their productive land fallow and turn it into pasture, but the Kulaks would not be cheated of their profits. As peasant lands still had long strips of the landlord's lands running through them, the Kulaks devised a toll system with a fee payable for each animal which crossed the landlord's soil.

As for their supply of firewood, the peasants had no other choice but to work the Kulak's lands for them in return for access to the forests to cut timber. This profiteering from the land and the forests was one of the main reasons Russia had so many revolutionary parties.

By 1914 the Kulaks had even bribed their way via local officials to prevent themselves being conscripted into the Army, knowing that when neighbouring peasants were called up, their land would be going cheap. Whilst hundreds of thousands of peasants died in the Russian trenches, the Kulaks enjoyed a land-grabbing free-for-all.

By 1917 the Kulaks owned 90 per cent of Russia's arable land. Throughout the war the most valuable commodity was grain. Naturally, the Kulaks were well aware of this profitable fact as food prices began to escalate. In 1916 food prices accelerated three times higher than wages, in spite of hugely successful harvests in both 1915 and 1916. The price of grain in 1916 had reached two and a half roubles per *pud* and was anticipated to rise to 25 roubles per *pud*.[12] To push prices up, the Kulaks decided to hoard grain and other food surpluses as their lands continued to increase. A number of Russian and international banks also held vast stocks of grain which, as prices rose, appeared to represent a sound investment.

Throughout 1916 the average labourer in the cities ate between 200 to 300 grams of food per day. The bread ration was 2.6lb per person per week. By 1917, this was down to just 1.8 lb per person, and would get even lower – yet the grain silos and storehouses in the country were bursting at their seams. The queues for bread along Petrograd's Nevsky and Liteiny Prospekt often stretched for angry miles and many workers went for two to three days with no food at all. The one thing these ragged and hungry thousands – unemployed workers, mothers, newly-arrived peasants and recuperating soldiers, who stood for hours in the cold each day – had was time to exchange views, to speculate on their situation and exchange information. Like the patrolling police and the agents of the Ohkrana, who kept a steady eye on the breadlines, they knew that something was coming; something big, something terrible. The only question was – when? In January 1917, no one knew.

Many of the labouring traditions well known in the remote countryside had been brought to the urban workplace as peasants flocked to the cities to seek out new work. To the refined and educated Russian, temperance was considered a mark of cultural development, a view shared by the growing number of consciously advanced workers who had undergone a political awakening. For the rest, however, vodka and collective fist fights were the two pastimes which established their identities. In industry, the arrival of a new worker on the shop floor signified a free drink. New male employees were expected, by tradition, to take their workmates to a tavern and buy a bottle of vodka. The custom was known as *prival'noe'* and, particularly in the textile industry and among metal workers, any semblance of comradeship was on hold until *prival'noe'* had taken place.[13]

One worker, A.S. Shapovalov, recalled in his memoir:

> If a new worker refused to offer *prival'noe'*, even if he were to starve or die, other workers made him unable to remain in the factory by various harassment: on the gear of his machine a nut was put, his machine got broken, and he would be fired. Or they enjoyed the following activity: they secretly attached tails made of a piece of cloth or dirty dust cloth to the worker without noticing his own tails. Sometimes they set these tails on

fire. When the worker was surprised and took the tails off, burning his hands, everyone threw ridicule upon him.[14]

Considering the privations factory workers were suffering then there is no doubt that such a custom was hard on a worker's pocket. Yet no matter what his financial situation, the routine still had to be faced. One way of financing a vodka-driven evening was to resort to *peregonka,* whereby the struggling newcomer bought what goods he could, on credit, from the factory shop. He would then hawk these around various shops and sell them at a discount until he had enough to pay his way through this tough bonding ritual.

As far back as the sixteenth century young Russian men had indulged in collective fist fights, a brutal pastime which had died away somewhat by 1917. These violent scraps were usually carried on between two factory teams from opposing companies, or by gangs of men from one neighbourhood against another. Winter time was the favourite season. Sometimes as many as 500 took part, forming two opposing 'walls' (*stenka na stenku* – 'a wall against a wall') of men, many of whom would go home with broken noses or black eyes, although any form of weapon was forbidden. (A British school playground game, still played in the 1950s, 'British Bulldog', had many similar, if far less violent elements.) Behind all this primitive and brutal competition was a search for mutual respect. A tough and fearless opponent, despite his locality or place of employment, could become a local hero. After moving from the countryside into the urban environment, these fights often helped the peasant immigrant in his quest to establish a sense of community.

With such tough cultural activity as a training ground, perhaps the fearless enthusiasm for taking to the streets on demonstrations and, later, manning the barricades, was a natural progression. However, although the coming revolution needed muscle and bravery, it also needed education. By 1917 many of the country boys who came to town could at least read and write, and there was a developed keenness for knowledge and education, much of it spurred on by the 1905 revolution. One of the favourite socialist revolutionary claims, as a criticism of capitalism, has always been 'an uneducated workforce is a pliable workforce.' As the quality of their day-to-day lives during the war had sunk to an all-time low, and with an uncertain future ahead, new ideas were at a premium. They came in the form of the many political leaflets, posters and publications which were always studied in detail.

Catherine Breshkovskaya was born in 1844, the daughter of a serf-owning landowner. After various arrests and periods of exile in Siberia for her socialist activities, in 1901 she had helped to form the Socialist Revolutionary Party with other revolutionaries such as Alexander Kerensky. In 1907 she was arrested again and exiled for life to Siberia, but like many of her kind, she stood steadfast in her beliefs and carried on campaigning. She was no Bolshevik, and even supported the war, yet like Lenin, she realized that the country's huge peasant population would be a key factor in bringing about change. So even in exile, she wasted no time in disseminating information.

In one of the villages I gave away my last illegal leaflet and then decided to write an appeal to the peasants myself. Stephanovitch made three copies of it. I did this because when I spoke to the peasants they always said, 'If you would write down these words and spread them everywhere, they would be of real use, because the people would know then that they were not invented.'[15]

By 1917 there were many like her in the seething political underworld of Petrograd and Moscow. These dedicated activists could not supply bread, fuel or clothing – but they did a roaring trade in offering hope for a better life. Yet who could turn this hope into reality?

The Social Democrats were a Marxist group formed by George Plekhanov in 1898, to whom, the proletariat were the key to the forthcoming revolution. In 1903 they had split into two factions. The Mensheviks (minority), led by Trotsky and Martov, believed in a slow change towards socialism and were prepared to wait. The second faction, the Bolsheviks (majority), asserted, under Lenin's leadership, that an educated revolutionary elite could bring socialism sooner. Meanwhile the peasants were represented by the Social Revolutionaries, whose policies centred on the collective ownership of land. They were led by Victor Chernov and Alexander Kerensky. On the liberal side, the Constitutional Democratic Party (known as 'the Cadets'), led by Pavel Milyukov, believed in western-style constitutionalism.

In January 1917 the Bolshevik membership was less than 25,000. The party's leader, Vladimir Illych Lenin, still largely unknown among the peasants or the rebellious ranks of Petrograd's striking factory workers, was languishing in exile in Zurich in cramped rooms above a cobbler's shop at 14 Spiegelgasse. Keeping control of his party and its publications from halfway across Europe made for a dispiriting life. During that freezing start to what would be a momentous year, Lenin had addressed a meeting of young Swiss workers at which he had announced that 'I may not live long enough to see the forthcoming revolution.'

Little did he know, that within a month, everything he had so far devoted his life to would suddenly have great meaning and focus. In Petrograd, the flint of autocracy had struck the metal of discontent one time too many – the ensuing spark was about to ignite an explosion which would reverberate around the world.

2

ACROSS THE RUBICON

Our pleas for bread they would not abide
And instead sent bayonets, lead!
In sacrifice too many comrades died . . .
But they tore the crown from the despot's head.
Demian Semyanov, metalworker at the
Viazma Railroad Depot, Smolensk Province[1]

Although there would be a slight but welcome thaw in February, in January 1917 the ice still maintained its grip on Petrograd. Beneath a dull, iron-grey sky the people thought of only one thing: bread. Their hunger fuelled their growing anger as throughout the streets of the city the queues of patient, starving women stretched for miles. Many would wait for up to eight or even twelve hours only to be disappointed. Of course, there was bread if one could afford it, elusive though it seemed. Bakeries were still working, some more than others. The Army had its own bakeries, like the bakery of the First Artillery Brigade or the one overseen by the Technical Committee of the Chief Quartermaster's Administration. There were commercial bakeries such as Fillipov, Poiman and others, whose products were leaving the shelves as fast as they left the ovens. Yet for the mass of workers, there was never enough to go round. Somehow the rich seemed to be able to carry on eating. For the hard-pressed steel worker on 8 roubles a day, a good meal remained a dream.

Despite all this misery, the court jeweller, Fabergé, celebrated the fact that business had never been better. The Empress Alexandra's lady-in-waiting, Ania Vyrubova, was delighted to note that the recent season had been one of the most memorable for gowns, and the sale of diamonds in higher circles was flourishing.[2]

At the other end of the social scale, watching the crowds, the secret police, the Okhrana, were becoming increasingly nervous. Their reports to the government were now frequently peppered with grim warnings of an impending, inevitable uprising, a typical example being:

The proletariat of the capital is on the verge of despair . . . the mass of industrial workers are quite ready to let themselves go to the wildest excesses of a hunger riot. The prohibition of all labour meetings, the closing of trade unions, the prosecution of men taking an active part in the sick benefit funds, the suspension of newspapers, and so on, make the labour masses, led by the more advanced and already revolutionary-minded elements, assume an openly hostile attitude towards the government and protest with all the means at their disposal against the continuation of the war.[3]

Few people were ignorant of the fact that something was about to happen. Whatever it might be, it wasn't going to be

pleasant. Yet there were others in Russia who stood inno-
cently between the destitution of the workers and the
detached pleasures of the rich. The growth of Russia's
industry had been contributed to in no small way by many
Europeans and Americans, their expertise in the fields of
engineering, construction and transport proving invaluable
to the Tsar.

Now 95 and living in Radcliffe, Manchester, Lilian Nield
(née Wallwork) was born in Lancashire in 1909. Her father,
Joseph Arthur Wallwork, was involved in the thriving cotton
industry and was employed by Platt Brothers of Werneth in
Oldham. Together with his wife Annie, he had set out with
many other Lancastrian mill experts on the adventure of a
lifetime, helping to establish Russia's textile industry. Little
Lilian was just over six weeks old when she arrived in St
Petersburg, where she grew up.

We lived at 54 Slononvaya Prospekt in a large granite building
with an English community in the east of the city. 'Slononvaya'
means elephant, because that was the street where the Tsar's
elephants used to pass along on their way to drink from the
River Neva. Today the street is called Suvorovskiy, after Field
Marshal Suvorov. The building opposite us, the Smolny Institute, was at that time a finishing school for the girls of the
rich and titled. It became Lenin's headquarters in 1917. By the
time I was five I had no idea what England was like, because all
I knew was St Petersburg. It was a magic place for a little
Lancashire lass. Palaces, shops full of jewellery for the rich,
exotic porcelain, furs. The poor people were at the very
opposite end of the scale: badly dressed, hungry and very,
very impoverished. I suppose we, as foreigners, were somewhere in the middle. We had servants. Father was working for
the Coates Cotton Mills in St Petersburg. All the textile mills

had a lot of people from Lancashire working in them. We had quite a good status in the community.

Lilian remembers skating on the frozen Neva, riding in the snow, muffled up in blankets on a *troika,* listening to the bells on the horses and staring up at the Milky Way between the scudding snow clouds. At Easter the servants would take her to the Russian Orthodox Church. There would be hard-boiled eggs in all colours, and *blini,* small pancakes. At night she could hear the servants in the room upstairs praying aloud and banging their heads on the floor in supplication to God.

When the Romanovs celebrated 300 years on the throne, Lilian watched:

> Thousands of people crowded into the Palace Square to pay homage and cheer their Little father of all the Russias and his Tsarina. I remember because it was on July thirteenth and my father had accepted a post at Kranholm Mills in Narva, and we left for there nine days later.

There were no English schools in Narva so Lilian had an Estonian governess, Ella. Away from the resplendent boulevards of the capital, Lilian came to understand her Russian hosts. Even though not quite seven in 1917, she began to realize that the ordinary people of Russia had been carrying a bitter burden of fear for generations.

> My best friend was Nadewsha Sansonov. Her dad was Narva's chief of police. The Sansonovs had an old aunt living with them. She was dumb. She had had her tongue cut out whilst still young for bearing false witness. I began to realize that for the poor, life was very cheap. For them, cruelty and beating were a way of life. On more than one occasion I saw prisoners stripped

naked in the snow and tied to a post to be whipped whilst big
guard dogs snapped at them. Mr Sansonov didn't think he was
being cruel, just 'firm' – which everybody seemed to accept.
Everyone seemed to live in fear of being sent to Siberia. One
night the servants were screaming in our kitchen. My father
rushed in and found a demented working man brandishing a
knife – he wanted to kill Father. A furious fight followed and
Dad overpowered him. The man's name was Baraban, and he
seemed to imagine that Father was responsible for his son being
exiled to Siberia for committing some crime at the mill. Once
Father had explained in detail that he had nothing to do with
this, the man flung himself at his knees, sobbing and begging
for mercy. Father never reported the incident, but we gave the
man a warm meal and sent him on his way.[4]

In the freezing cold of 9 January the streets of Petrograd
were filled with 145,000 strikers. They were commemorating
the tragedy of Bloody Sunday in 1905, when the priest Father
Georgi Gapon had led 200,000 men, women and children
through the snow to the Winter Palace. The people he led had
wanted political rights and an end to the war with Japan.
Dressed in their Sunday best they had carried aloft pictures of
the Tsar but he rewarded their protest with bullets – among the
1,240 casualties 370 were killed. And now, 12 years on, the
people at least knew where they stood. Their banners read
'Down With The Romanovs!' – gone were the portraits of 'the
Tsar of all the Russias'. Now the red flags fluttered in the bitter
breeze.

Yet there seemed no sign of a shift in the government's
continuing inertia. Throughout January the strikes increased.
Now it was not only the big factories from Petrograd's more
militant, working-class Vyborg district, and the huge workforce of the Putilov arms factory – many lesser industrial

centres and other businesses were suffering strike action too. More women were also becoming involved in industrial walk-outs and demonstrations, a fact which would figure prominently in the stormy months ahead. Demonstrations were becoming more regular, and their nature had become defiantly political.

Huddling in the working-class *traktirs* (tea rooms) the talk among the workers had gone beyond the war, wages, working hours, conditions and even bread. Revolution was in the air.

Yet no one had particularly planned a revolution. How and when it would happen, and who would lead such an insurrection was still far from clear. Various plans for some kind of advancement of society were scattered across the complicated political spectrum in the capital. In the Duma the ineffectual liberals and moderate conservatives, led by Pavel Milyukov, continued their squabbling. Yet at least Milyukov understood the failings of the Tsar's government. In November 1916 he had made his famous speech dealing with the crass misman-agement of the war effort, breaking his invective down into various points which he highlighted with the repeated question 'Is this stupidity or treason?' However, despite such boldness Milyukov would continue to oppose any revolutionary action, arguing that the only weapons the Duma had were still 'the word and the vote', neither of which seemed to be having much effect.

Sadly, the Duma's futile pleas to the Tsar to allow the organization of some kind of government which the people might respect were directed at a man who still allowed his Minister of the Interior, Alexander Protopopov, to consult his horoscope as to when he could dismiss or convene the Duma. It had been a method good enough for the Emperor of Japan, so it seemed entirely acceptable for a Russian monarch. In the Tsar's insulated, autocratic little world, liberal politicians of

any hue were simply a distant irritation. On the left outright
calls for an immediate armed revolt echoed around the hundreds of political gatherings in Petrograd. There had been talk
among Duma members in late 1916 of a possible palace coup
d'état but Mikhail Rodzianko, the Duma President, was having none of it, although many would have responded favour-
ably had the Duma had the courage to wrest control of the
country from the Romanovs. Such a move might well have
steered Russia along a very different historical path in the
twentieth century, but Rodzianko could not divest himself of
his ill-placed regard for the Emperor (who had jovially referred
to Rodzianko as 'the fattest man in the empire') saying,
'Legislative bodies cannot occupy themselves with coup d'état.
I am neither able nor willing to arouse people against the
Tsar.'[5]

It didn't need a Rodzianko to turn the population against
the monarch. Nicholas was already doing a pretty good job at
making himself unpopular, not only with socialists and revolutionaries, but among many of his closest supporters who
populated his court, and especially the hard-pressed generals
who were vainly trying to fight the war. The time had long
passed when military leaders were prepared to remain silent.
Although there had been some military successes during 1916,
and for a while the retreats and the discontent had seen a
temporary reverse, by 1917 the generals were caught in a trap.
It was created from above by Nicholas's confused and ineffectual leadership, much of it the result of his wife's erratic
meddling in the affairs of state, and from below by the
dissipation of morale which, in turn, was turning into a wave
of spontaneous rebellion in the ranks. Victories against the
determined, well-equipped and focused armies of the Kaiser
were nigh on impossible in such an atmosphere.

As General Krimov's train brought him back to Petrograd

from the front in January 1917 this weary soldier bore a heavy burden of ill tidings as he travelled through a frozen, blighted landscape where the sinister rule of Rasputin, Nicholas and Alexandra had been replaced by that of an even darker triumvirate – poverty, hunger and death. Upon his arrival in the capital, the General made his way to Mikhail Rodzianko's private residence where various industrialists with war interests, members of the Duma and others had gathered to hear Krimov's report on the state of the war. What they heard that night would not have sent them home to a peaceful sleep. Rodzianko's reluctance to support a palace coup d'état would have found little sympathy with this beleaguered senior soldier. Already another great military leader, one of the few who had successful campaigns in this war behind him, General Brusilov, had declared, 'If it comes to a choice between the Tsar and Russia, I will take Russia.' Krimov was no less assertive, telling the gathering at Rodzianko's house that the Army would welcome the news of a coup d'état, claiming that the Army were ready to participate in such an event. At the front, he said, the men and their officers no longer had any faith in Nicholas's command. Politics had entered the trenches, and soldiers now felt that victory was impossible unless a new and decisive government took over Russia's affairs. Among the assembled Duma deputies the debate raged, with Shidlovsky declaring that if Nicholas was ruining Russia then there could be no point in wasting pity on him. Another deputy, Shingarev, boldly asserted that Krimov was right, and that a coup was indeed necessary. And yet they did nothing.

Outside in the razor-edged frost the people scavenged for food. No animal was safe. By now even some of the more upper-middle-class apartments were hardly heated above freezing. Fences and furniture were demolished for firewood, valuable heirlooms were traded for the luxury of a loaf of black bread. Children, weakened by constant hunger, had lost even the energy to cry. Shops closed early. Meat had become a rare luxury, as had many other provisions, such as fat, oil and sugar. Desperate people had begun looting bakeries, yet even the looters were often disappointed.

Out in the countryside things were slightly better as the peasants produced what they could for their own consumption. Whilst the cities starved, in other parts of Russia, on the surface, life seemed at odds with Petrograd's desperation, as one British correspondent reported:

> There are towns in the south and east where it is still possible to buy any quantity of bread at peace prices. But difficulties of transport and defects in organisation cause constant jerks and jolts in the mechanism which supplies the larger towns and on the present occasion the jolt is more acutely felt in Petrograd than usual. Long queues before bakers' shops have long been a normal feature of life in the city. Grey bread is now sold instead of white, and cakes are not baked.[6]

Yet what surplus there was often stood a poor chance of making it into Petrograd or Moscow. The rail system was dogged by strikes and breakdowns, and when it was operational, it was usually in full use by the military, moving men and equipment. Against this background in the capital the dispossessed looked towards the workers' councils, the Soviets, wherein the Bolsheviks appeared to be the one organization speaking the language the people wanted to hear.

Since the failed 1905 revolution the Mensheviks ('member of the minority') had looked to the workers' movements for a sign – but Julius Martov, their leader, continued to insist that the revolution could only take place when the workers were ready for it. The exiled Bolshevik leader, Lenin, offered an uncompromising contrast. Although he was anxious to start a revolution as soon as possible, even he had conditions – firstly, it must be led by professional revolutionaries, and secondly, the conditions and the timing must be right. A spontaneous rising without a planned sense of direction and lacking skilled political helmsmen at the wheel could only result in another 1905. Striking, although it gave the working population's disaffection a voice and visibility, had in some ways become ineffective. Wage demands for 50 per cent increases were disregarded, and in any case, with the sporadic supply of fuel, many businesses were forced to shut down, the result being that angry workers were often faced with lockouts. Political activity had reached new heights. Weaving their way skilfully through all this massed discontent the Bolsheviks saw their support steadily increase. Anti-war propaganda was the order of the day. At the front, morale had ceased to exist, with many soldiers having no idea what the war was about. One peasant conscript, F. Starunov, typified the sense of dismay and confusion in the trenches:

> Where was I going and why? To kill the Germans! But why? I didn't know . . . I thought who really is my enemy; the Germans or the company commander? I still couldn't see the Germans, but here in front of me was the commander. The lice bit me in the trenches. I was overcome with dejection. And then as we were retreating I was taken prisoner.[7]

With the death toll rising, many of the army's more able officers had perished, to be replaced by new young officers of educated peasant and lower-class stock who arrived at the front without the heavy baggage of an upper-class background. They had much more in common with the beleaguered men in the trenches than the bristling young career officers of 1914. Both in private and often openly, they expressed their distaste for the country's leadership whilst displaying sympathy for their comrades of lower rank, crimes which in previous decades would have been an instant passport to exile in Siberia – or worse.

The Tsar, and particularly his wife, Alexandra, still regarded all this trouble as 'the work of hooligans'. As in the past, they perhaps felt comforted by the fact that in Petrograd in January 1917 the highest number of troops in the city's history were stationed there, numbering some 170,000 men, with a further 152,000 men in the regions closest to the capital. Nicholas was used to unflinching loyalty – if things became too out of control, then surely, all he had to do was to issue an order. But the secret police, the Okhrana, knew the truth about these soldiers, conscripts of a different breed from the old Tsarist armies of the past. It would be the Okhrana who would have to call on these men on the monarch's command should their services in quelling rebellion be needed, yet police reports about these troops made uncomfortable reading. Many of the drafted men were known troublemakers who had been heavily involved in inciting strikes; some were malcontents from the Donets coal mines. Many of the usually fiercely loyal Cossacks in Petrograd at this time, men who were traditionally part of a volunteer tradition, were now conscripts, from villages in the Kuban where the population badly needed every fit and active male.[8] Being called up rather than volunteering was a source of resentment, and their absence had begun to have a devastating effect on their home communities.

Attempts to sway Nicholas and make him see sense had come from all directions. On 12 January the British Ambassador, Sir George Buchanan, had an audience with the Tsar. Buchanan's daughter, Meriel, recalled the event, stating Sir George:

implored him to consider what he was doing, telling him that
he had come to the parting of the ways, and that it rested with
him either to lead Russia to victory and a permanent peace or
to revolution and disaster. The Emperor replied that my father
very much exaggerated the seriousness of the situation, and
that he could count on the army to support him in any crisis. At
the end of the meeting he, however, shook my father's hand
and thanked him for all he had said; but apparently again
falling under the Empress's influence, he continued to allow her
full power, and the situation grew daily more acute.[9]

Poor old Rodzianko had also kept up his desperate barrage
of pleading. Being closer to events as he was in the Duma, he
was well aware of the growing organization of the Soviets and
the support for the Mensheviks and Bolsheviks. Not long after
his meeting with General Krimov, Rodzianko was faced on 3
February by the Tsar's brother, Grand Duke Mikhail, who
issued the stark question: 'Do you think there is going to be a
revolution?'

Rodzianko expressed his hopes that the country could be
saved, conditional on dislodging the Empress from her place in
politics, plus the installation of ministers in whom the population could have confidence. He unwittingly repeated Buchanan's dark foreboding with a personal coda: 'We shall have a
terrible revolution which will carry away the throne, the
dynasty, you and me.'

Mikhail seemed to have taken this on board, replying, 'Sir
George Buchanan said the same thing to my brother. Our
family realizes how harmful the Empress is. She and my
brother are surrounded by traitors; all decent people have left
them. But what to do?'[10]

Although Mikhail made a promise to try and sway his
brother, nothing seems to have come of it, which seems hardly

surprising. Only two months before, in November 1916 the Tsar's uncle, Grand Duke Nikolai Nikolayevich had made a similar attempt. In a private conversation wherein he tried making his nephew see sense, Uncle Nikolai discovered that the silent Nicholas seemed impervious to logic, still preferring, at that time, to take his advice from Rasputin, via Alexandra. By February 1917, still in mourning for her departed mystic, the Empress had begun to resort to taking advice from the sinister and half-crazy Minister of the Interior and head of the Okhrana, Alexander Protopopov, who claimed to be in touch with the murdered monk's ghost every night. Maurice Paléologue, the French Ambassador, recalled in his memoirs for 12 January 1917:

> Old Prince Kurakin, a master of necromancy, has had the satisfaction of raising the ghost of Rasputin the last few nights. He immediately sent for Protopopov, the Minister of the Interior, and Dobrovolsky, the Minister of Justice; they came at once. Since then, the three of them have been in secret conclave for hours every evening, listening to the dead man's solemn words.[11]

Even Nicholas had, as early as November 1916, expressed his doubts over Protopopov to Alexandra, saying, 'he jumps from one idea to another . . . it is risky to leave the Ministry of Internal Affairs in the hands of such a man in these times.' Alexandra thought differently and wrote back to him at his headquarters: 'It does not lie in the name Protopopov but in your remaining firm and not giving in – the Tsar rules and not the Duma.'[12]

Thus the Empress's continuing grip on her husband's decision making was demonstrated to all yet again, with another disastrous result being the resignation of the Prime Minister, A.F. Trepov, who had threatened to go if Protopopov was not removed. With Alexandra in control, any audience with Nicholas was met with impatience. Others who attempted to puncture his stubbornness were met with petty complaints that 'they went on too long' and that other guests were kept 'waiting for tea', or that these irritating, despondent visitors from the Duma or the Army were making him late for vespers.

The delivery of flour to Petrograd had dropped dramatically as heavy snowfalls had closed many railway lines, leaving almost 60,000 wagon loads of food stranded. On top of this, with the temperature over 20 degrees below zero, many locomotives were stranded with burst boiler tubes. Finding over 1,000 Polish-manufactured replacements for these had now become almost impossible, as the Germans had taken Warsaw. Even the small luxury Russian workers enjoyed – and an important one for providing energy – drinking tea through a cube of sugar, was now denied as sugar became increasingly scarce. The humble potato had almost taken on the characteristics of solid gold. Yet still the women queued outside the shuttered shops.

As the drama of disaffection in Petrograd was about to unfold, many miles away a man whose time would soon arrive was having troubles of his own. Like Lenin in Zurich, Leon Trotsky, apart from receiving the regular communiqués from the Bolsheviks and Mensheviks back home, was not fully in the picture as to the currently volatile state of politics in the Russian capital. After a life of exile and expulsion, he had been thrown out of France, and had ended up in Spain, where, in Cadiz, as a suspicious foreign revolutionary he was as usual accompanied on his daily outings by detectives. Having tried to secure permission to go to Switzerland, but to his dismay receiving no response, he was disturbed to be told that, as the Spaniards wanted to get rid of him, his next exile could well be in Havana, Cuba. He told the Governor of Cadiz, 'I won't go voluntarily.' The Governor replied that if that was the case, he would be compelled to place Trotsky in the ship's hold. Eventually, with various helpful gestures from liberals and socialists he discovered that he could go to New York instead. He spent his waiting time brushing up on his English, ready for his sojourn in the New World.

Together with his family, Trotsky sailed on the Spanish Transatlantic Company's steamer *Monserrat* on Christmas Day, 1916. The future founder of the Red Army's fellow passengers included the artistic and commercial dregs of Europe. There was a boxer and novelist, who claimed to be the cousin of Oscar Wilde, a billiards champion, an artist, and many others from all walks of life: 'deserters, adventurers, speculators, or simply "undesirables" thrown out of Europe. Who would ever dream of crossing the Atlantic at this time of year on a wretched little Spanish boat from choice?'[13] The accommodation on board was cramped and uncomfortable, and the food appalling. But 17 days later the Trotskys arrived in the United States, where Leon could witness first hand the churning, vibrant, capitalist society which he sought to destroy, the diametric opposite of the system he would help to lay the foundations for in just a few short months. As Trotsky plunged back into his daily round of revolutionary writing, meetings, speeches and debates among New York's European exiles and various American socialist groups, back home in Petrograd the tension continued to mount.

Throughout February, in his meetings with Nicholas, Rodzianko had become ever more exasperated, but on 13 February, despite the huge danger staring him in the face, Nicholas issued a stubborn counterblast: 'The information I have is quite contrary to yours, and as to the Duma . . . if it permits itself such harsh speeches as last time it will be dissolved.'

In the face of this, Rodzianko appears to give up the ghost, telling the Tsar that he feared that this may well be his last audience with him. However, Rodzianko's cautious respect for his monarch was about to be eclipsed in a hot wind of reality.

On 14 February the Duma was convened in which the fiery Alexander Kerensky, a leader of the Trudoviks (a labour-affiliated group in the Socialist Revolutionary Party) would make a speech which would soon bulldoze the procrastinating Rodzianko aside.

Kerensky was a 36-year-old lawyer who had studied in St Petersburg and earned a reputation as a defence lawyer in a number of celebrated political trials. As an important link in the confusing period between the two revolutionary periods of 1917, he would, as we shall see, briefly hold the fraying political reins of the country between Lenin's return in April and his ascendancy to power in October. Kerensky, however, despite all his hot revolutionary rhetoric, was a 'defencist' – he would continue to support the war against Germany.

Lenin called him a 'petty braggart', and Leon Trotsky, in his usual ornate and colourful style, would later write of Kerensky:

> He personified the accidental in an otherwise continuous causation. His best speeches were merely a sumptuous pounding of water in a mortar. In 1917 the water boiled and sent up steam, and the clouds provided a halo.[14]

Nonetheless, that halo shone among the factory workers in the Vyborg district, in the ironworks and the shipyards, and among many in the Petrograd Soviet, in which Kerensky was a deputy. Whatever the policy or directive of the day might be, the workers would always ask, 'What will Alexander Fyodorovich say?'[15] Kerensky was a bold, dramatic speaker, who assembled his image as a man of the people with care. Not for him the politician's frock

coat, the black tie and starched collar; he wore a neutral black
tunic. With the removal of one of his kidneys, many imagined he
had only months to live. Wherever he went, to palaces or workshops, everyone's hand was shaken – even doormen and cleaners.
This was the kind of politician the people were looking for. What
he had to say on 14 February as the Duma reconvened was a
stirring example of playing to the Soviet gallery.

> The country now realises that the Ministers are but fleeting
> shadows. The country can clearly see who sends them here. To
> prevent a catastrophe the Tsar himself must be removed, by
> force if there is no other way . . . If you will not listen to
> warning now you will find yourself face to face with the facts,
> not warning. Look up at the distant flashes that are lighting the
> skies of Russia.[16]

Even as Kerensky was delivering his broadside, outside a
massive demonstration of over 90,000 striking workers
stormed along the Nevsky bearing aloft anti-war and anti-
government banners. In the windows of the bakeries in Petrograd and Moscow the handwritten, whitewashed signs were
becoming painfully familiar: 'No Bread Today – And None
Expected'. At the Tsar's palace in Tsarskoe-Seloe, Alexandra,
incandescent at Kerensky's oratory, called for his arrest and
execution. But no one was listening.

The week commencing Monday, 13 February would deliver
a shower of sparks which would soon light the coming bonfire.
Protests rumbled on until, on Saturday, 18 February the
Putilov men struck again. Although initially there were only
486 of them out of a workforce of 26,700, men working in the
gun-carriage workshops at the huge arms factory walked out
on strike demanding a pay rise. Their boldness was soon
bolstered as the strike rapidly spread through the sprawling

plant, affecting the assembly shops and the shrapnel works. Four days later the workforce faced a lockout.

There was a distinct shift in the mood of the people on Wednesday, 22 February, when the freezing temperature suddenly released its grip and rose to a comparatively comfortable 8 degrees Centigrade. In many ways, the future of Russia would be decided the following day.

Thursday, 23 February was International Women's Day, and to the thousands of women workers in the Vyborg textile factories, it seemed as good a time as any to give vent to their anger, particularly as there would already be parades of various women's organizations along the Nevsky Prospekt, demanding rights, which would be formed from groups of women from many classes.

The institution of International Women's Day was a recent one in 1917. Its history had its roots in the labour movement. It was first proposed by a representative to the 1910 Socialist Women's Conference in Copenhagen, and inspired by an 1857 demonstration of women garment workers in New York who had protested against their working conditions. The first IWD took place in 1911 in Denmark, Germany and Austria. The chosen date (11 March, new style calendar) marked a day in Germany in 1848 when the King of Prussia had faced an armed uprising after making unfulfilled promises of reform which included votes for women.

The Bolsheviks in common with other socialist factions were keen to see the female population as politicized as possible. Women revolutionaries too worked hard at this task.

Concordia Nikolayevna Gromova-Samoilova was born in Irkutsk in Siberia in 1876.[17] Her father was a priest. By the time she had gone through high school and finished her education in St Petersburg, she had already become one of tsarism's most hated enemies – a seditious student. During the spate of strikes which raged through the capital in 1896, Samoilova was already known as an organizer by the Okhrana. In 1914 she became involved with the launch of a new journal, *Woman Worker*. Funds for the project and subscriptions came from the readership of the fledgling *Pravda*. As the first issue was about to go to press, along with the rest of the editorial board, Samoilova was arrested and imprisoned. Whilst she languished behind bars, the work was carried on by a woman comrade who had escaped the police, Elizarova. Subscriptions for *Woman Worker* had continued to drop through her letterbox – the working women of St Petersburg seemed to like the idea of having their own paper. Samoilova was eventually released and in a piece which has echoes in the women's movement during the miners' strike in Britain seven decades later, wrote of International Women's Day in *Pravda*:

> When women went into the factories and worked at the same machines as men, they discovered a new world, new relations of people in the process of industry. They saw the struggle of the workers for the improvement of their conditions. And every day, more women workers became more and more convinced that the conditions of work united them with the men workers of the factories, that they have all one common interest, and the women workers began to feel that they were part of one industrial family, that their interests were linked to the whole of the working class.[18]

International Women's Day in 1917 would be one to remember. There was one constant chant among the women who paraded around the streets of the Vyborg area – 'Give us Bread!' As the female crowds grew, the spontaneity which would characterize the rest of this momentous day became evident. As they came across factories and other workplaces where men still laboured, many women made snowballs and threw them at the windows, challenging the workers within to lay down their tools and come out to join them. This they did in their thousands, and soon, from the outlying districts, the columns of angry people began to head towards the centre of the city. Many anticipated the worst. Expecting, from previous experience, that the Cossacks, police and the Army would be turned out against them. Thus many had brought along knives, pieces of wood, anything which might be used as a weapon.

The commander of the Petrograd Military District, General Serge Khabalov, had issued an order on 10 February throughout the capital prohibiting public gatherings and meetings, the warning being further hammered home with a paragraph which made it clear that martial law was in force, and that the Army and police were ready to put down any resistance. Yet the confidence of the crowds was bolstered this time with the appearance in their ranks of soldiers and young army officers, who appeared to be as hell-bent on heckling the police as the rest of the mob. Yet despite their growing organizational grip, the Bolsheviks in the Petrograd Soviets were not ready for this sudden, huge surge. Having reserved 1 May for their big day of demonstration and protest, this premature explosion of angry disapproval, the biggest so far, was quite unexpected. To the Bolshevik deputies this wasn't revolution as such, this was mass disorder, and although it was a genuine expression of the people's discontent, it lacked direction and control. The people's problems could not be resolved in this way – only further death, tragedy and injury could be the result. Yet the angry behemoth grew and rumbled on. A sea of red flags and banners clogged the main thoroughfares, chanting, singing rousing versions of the banned 'Marseillaise' and revolutionary songs such as 'Comrades, Boldly In Step'. Now it included clerical workers, students, teachers, all united in a common rage. Along the Liteiny Prospekt and the Nevsky, shops, including Petrograd's large bakery, Fillipov, were broken into and looted. Policemen tring to intervene were set upon by the mob and in some cases were brutally beaten to death. Eventually, as predicted, the Cossacks appeared, and the Army – yet this time there was a marked reluctance on behalf of the soldiers to open fire.

One old woman, following a group of red flag-bearing young men, was chastised by the mounted Cossacks as they rode their mounts along the Nevsky pavements: 'Old crone! Why are you following those men?'

The old woman turned angrily on the Cossack officer: 'Not an *old crone* but a mother of sons at the front – I follow these men to bring them back!'

A member of the Bolsheviks, a worker named Kayurov, threw off his cap and approached the Cossacks. 'Brother Cossacks, help the workers in a struggle for their peaceable demands; you see how the pharoahs [slang for the police] treat us hungry workers. Help us!'

Others took off their caps. The Cossacks threw glances at one another, and dashed into the fight on the workers' side.

Later, the scene which had been so threatening before was transformed as the crowd of workers tossed a Cossack in their arms who had just run a policeman through with his sabre.[19]

On Saturday, 25 February the massive crowd was swelled further by 14,000 workers from the Obukhov factory, and many more joined the strikers, men who made the big guns and mortars for the Army from the Pipe Plant on Vasilievsky Island. More soldiers were brought onto the streets, and the bridges across the Neva, ringed by policemen and troops, seemed no longer to be a barrier to the angry crowd. They had previously ignored the heavily guarded bridges by risking crossing the frozen Neva on foot to unite with other workers, but now nothing was going to stop them. Although shots would ring out they would cross the bridges, push confidently through the mounted ranks of cavalry. A feeling of resignation was beginning to run through the military ranks. There had even been several almost light-hearted confrontations between the Cossacks and groups of women demonstrators.

As a mobile riot squad, the Cossacks (from the Turkish *quzaq* – adventurer or outlaw) armed with their lances, whips, sabres and rifles were the most feared force in any confrontation. Colonizers of lands along the Ural, Don and Dnieper rivers, their history went back to the sixteenth century, when they formed into bands of young men fleeing from serfdom. Their form of self-government was conducted with a free annual vote around the camp fire to elect a chieftain, known as a *hetman*. Fishing, hunting and plundering formed a Cossack's life, and this existence was supported by the Tsar after the Cossacks had contained the Crimean Tartars, their reward being an annual subsidy of grain, arms and clothes; a Cossack who married was given a plot of land on the banks of the river. Peter the Great showed his admiration for their superb horsemanship by forming them into regiments of irregular cavalry. Under the reigns of the Tsars Alexander II and III, and Nicholas, they had obeyed orders with a ruthless efficiency, and would mercilessly cut down any resistance to the regime. These were men who lived in the saddle – they would even carry a bale of hay on their mount's back in order to stay on duty for 12 gruelling hours.

However, in this new, serious and volatile uprising, a wave of pragmatism had overcome these fierce and colourful riders. Often seen in a romantic light, the Cossacks had a softer side for the opposite sex. Ringed in the streets by female demonstrators during these difficult days, a new phenomenon had developed, as somewhat benign and sometimes frisky banter had broken out between the women and the Cossacks. The women would make friendly appeals. One such meeting was reported where a woman asked, 'Why don't you attack the police instead of the people?' The reply was a mark of the Cossacks' growing awareness of the situation: 'We'll deal with the police eventually.' Such a response would usually be met with a loud, rousing cheer from the crowds. However, these were still early days and many pockets of Tsarist discipline remained among the police and more loyal army units.

By the afternoon of Saturday, 25 February the two mile length of the Nevsky from the Admiralty right along to Znamenskaya Square and the Moscow Station was a solid, black river of people. The trams were no longer running, and passengers arriving at the head of this grim procession at the Moscow Station suddenly found their way blocked; with no cabs or trams, they were going nowhere. Later that afternoon, a crowd of well-dressed shoppers had been forced off the Nevsky onto Mikhail Street, running for their lives to escape a hail of bullets from machine-gun nests which had been posted by the police on various rooftops. In the confusion a car ran over a woman and a sledge overturned, killing the driver. All around people were huddling in doorways and alleys to shelter from the constant deadly barrage. Some lay dead in the snow. Along the Nevsky the more dedicated police squads still saw it as their duty to select the more prominent demonstrators from the crowd and make arrests. Yet when they tried to hold prisoners temporarily in houses along the street, the crowds soon discovered where they were and broke in, releasing the captives.

Behind the upper classes' closed doors, the raging storm outside was viewed through the gaps in the curtains with growing alarm. Yet in many ways, those with faith in the Romanovs clung on to the normality of their daily lives in the confident hope that this nightmare would pass, crushed by the forces which had always crushed such events in the past. From the comparative safety of their comfortable rooms in the Europe and Astoria hotels, visitors and foreign guests also watched history unfurling below, written in blood across the broad, snowy street. Among the hotel guests were members of the Allied forces who had picked the wrong time to spend a spot of leave in the capital. One was a British Royal Navy rating, John Eastman.

We had been into the Opera House. It was nice and peaceful when we went in. But when we came out later on, we were amazed to find hundreds of thousands of people, all swarming down the Nevsky Prospekt, shouting, screaming as the Cossacks on their horses charged them, using whips. These people were making for the other side of the city, trying to keep out of the way, but some were also heading for the gates of the Palace, shouting 'Down with the Tsar!'

It all came as quite a surprise for us. We escaped around the back streets and eventually found a policeman. He told us that the people had revolted. There were plenty of bodies laying about – whether they were all dead or not is hard to say. Back at our base in Estonia, the day the revolution broke out the people broke into the local vodka factory and got drunk. Our own sympathies? Well, we did feel that the peasants had a very poor deal. They weren't allowed to walk on the same pavement as the middle, upper or officer classes. They weren't allowed into a restaurant if those classes were in there, and in a theatre they were only allowed into a certain part and had to stand during the interval.[20]

A short walk from the Anichkov Palace on the Nevsky, on this same Saturday, at the Alexandriskiy Theatre, Mikhail Lermontov's classic play, *Masquerade,* had gone through a dress rehearsal for the opening performance that night. In the audience was a 19-year-old student from the Petrograd Institute of Engineering called Sergei Eisenstein. Fate would decide that this talented and earnest teenager, who was also a competent cartoonist, would forever be associated down the decades with the great events which were unfolding in Russia through his directorial skill with films such as *Battleship Potemkin* and *October.* There was no mistaking Eisenstein's revolutionary credentials. His first attempt at a cartoon was a drawing of the guillotined head of Louis XVI, wearing a halo, suspended over the bed of Nicholas II with the caption 'He got off lightly!' When young Sergei submitted this to Arkady Averchenko, the editor of the magazine *Satirikhon,* the work was rejected with the words 'Anyone could produce that.'[21]

By Sunday, 26 February Nicholas had issued a stern order that the Petrograd garrison must take full control of the situation. Soldiers from the Volinsky Regiment and Cossacks were turned out and this time, much to people's dismay, many deaths ensued. Yet this tragedy was another turning point. Many of the Volinsky soldiers realized that the huge, surging crowd of easy targets could well include their parents, brothers or sisters. About 200 people still were gunned down that day. When the soldiers of the Litovsky Regiment took sides with the crowd, a number of policemen had donned Litovsky overcoats as a disguise and opened fire. Robert Wilton, the London *Times* co-respondent sent a telegram home:

> Shortly after 3 p.m. orders were given to clear the street. A company of Guards took up their station near the Sadovaya and fired several volleys in the direction of the Anichkov

Palace. Something like 100 people were killed or wounded. On the scene of the shooting hundreds of empty cartridge cases were littered in the snow, which was plentifully sprinkled with blood. After the volleys the thoroughfare was cleared, but the crowd remained on the sidewalks. No animosity was shown towards the soldiers. The people shouted 'We are sorry for you, Pavlovsky! [Pavlovsky Guards Regiment] You had to do your duty!'[22]

When the Volinsky and Pavlovsky men returned to their barracks that night after the bloodshed, heated debates and arguments broke out among the troops. By Monday morning, 27 February, mutiny had spread throughout the Petrograd garrison. It began with 600 men, but within hours 170,000 had mutinied. Rodzianko was outraged. Writing to General Nikolai Ruzky, he demonstrated a more simplistic view of the mutineers:

Unexpectedly for all, there erupted a soldier mutiny such as I have never seen. These were not soldiers of course but *muzhiks* [peasants] taken directly from the plough who have found it useful now to make their own *muzhik* demands. In the crowd, all one could hear was 'Land and Freedom', 'Down with the Dynasty', 'Down with the Romanovs', 'Down with the Officers'.[23]

Elsewhere in the country the news of the insurrection had formed a wave of inspiration for other workers. In Narva, Lilian Nield recalls how the comfortable world of the British émigré was about to end:

'I woke up in the middle of the night because I could feel something was wrong. I went into my mother and father's bedroom and they were staring through the windows. We could see an angry crown assembled outside the prison. They'd made a bonfire by the doorway. They had released all the prisoners and locked the policemen in the cells. The young lads in the crowd had taken the policemen's guns and were firing indiscriminately. The world seemed to have gone mad. No-one seemed to be in charge. Our position as foreigners was awkward. Britain had become Russia's ally in the war, and many Russian workers now wanted Russia to come out of the conflict. So some were against us and some weren't. A party of these rebels raided our house and took what food they could find. When I went out in the streets after that, I had to wear a red arm band – it was to show I was with the revolution – a safety measure. They had imprisoned Nadewsha's father, and the only people who were allowed to visit him were me and Nadewsha. We used to take him black bread, dripping and black peas. Very soon that was also to become our family diet, too.

Soon we received an instruction from the British Embassy that we had to pack to go home. Father had to stay behind to fight the Germans. Mother and I packed and we had to wait in Petrograd (they had by then chosen that name instead of St. Petersburg because that sounded too German). There was fighting on the streets between the various political factions. It was dangerous to go out. But eventually our travel papers came and we were moved to a lovely summer house on the Finnish border which belonged to an aristocratic family. There were a number of British families sharing the house who, like us, were waiting to go home. I had to share a single bed with my mother. One night an angry mob surrounded the house and we all hid under the beds until morning. We then found out that the aristocrat who owned the place had been murdered that night. A month passed and we were sent to Sweden, then by train and boat to Norway. Eventually we arrived in Aberdeen. It was another year before Dad got back. He travelled from Murmansk after spending time fighting the Germans. Everything we had, our money, our valuables, had been left in Russia, and I had to cope with a new life in England. But it was an adventure which has stayed with me throughout my life.[24]

At his military HQ at Mogilev, Nicholas read the latest letter from his beloved wife. As usual, Alexandra's opinion of the continuing social earthquake seemed nonchalantly carefree:

It's a hooligan movement, young boys and girls running about and screaming that they have no bread, only to excite – then the workmen preventing others from work – if it *were* very cold they would probably stay indoors. But this will all pass and quieten down – if the Duma would only behave itself – one does not dare print the worst speeches.[25]

Enraged by events, and quite wrongly blaming the Duma for the disturbances, Nicholas lashed out on the 27th and prorogued the assembly. The ever-faithful Rodzianko dutifully complied, but not without a parting shot via a telegram to the Tsar: 'By your Majesty's order, the sessions of the Imperial Duma have been adjourned until April. The last bulwark of order has been removed.' Rodzianko then pleaded for the reopening of the Duma, outlined the seriousness of the mutinies, and gave a warning that if this spread through the Army:

Germany will triumph and the destruction of Russia along with the dynasty is inevitable. I beg your Majesty to carry out the above recommendation. The hour which will decide your own fate and the fate of Russia has arrived. Tomorrow may be too late.

Nicholas was unmoved. He now sought to handle the problems in Petrograd with the aid of a man whom the British Ambassador, Sir George Buchanan, would refer to as 'the Tsar's military dictator', General Nikolai Ivanov. Ivanov was now ordered to assemble loyal troops to march on Petrograd and restore order.

At this most crucial point in his reign, Nicholas had shut down the one official centre of debate which could at least act as a political focus point which might keep the lid on the cauldron. But the situation, which both he and the Empress had unwittingly helped to create, was far more desperate than he could imagine.

Rodzianko and the other Duma members, however, being closer to the epicentre of the uprising, knew that someone had to keep on talking. Bending the monarchy's law by not using the main debating chamber at the Tauride Palace, the Duma members met privately in a side hall. What transpired from that meeting would be one of the most important acts in the revolution. Reports from the various deputies tumbled forth. Dismay was expressed at the Cossacks – they appeared to be siding with the people. Something was happening among the Vyborg workers – they appeared to be holding an election of some kind of their own. The Volinsky regiment had mutinied, killing their commanding officer. Barricades were being erected in the street. The catalogue of breathtaking reports continued.

Alexander Kerensky was quick off the mark, warning that, even as they spoke, the deputies were facing the expected arrival of an army of workers numbering some 25,000, who would soon be at the Tauride. He demanded that this new ad-hoc committee should take over the uprising and immediately assume leadership, but he was voted down. Instead, a committee was formed whose aim was 'the re-establishment of order in the capital'. Kerensky, however, did not come away empty handed, being voted on to this new committee and immediately elevated to the position of vice-chairman of a new Petrograd Soviet, organized by the city's factory workers, and led by Nikolai Chkheidze, the Duma delegate for the Social Democrats. Kerensky was, as the Liberals knew, one of the few political firebrands who could step in successfully between them and the angry crowd. In forming the Soviet the Mensheviks were to the fore, with the Bolsheviks complaining bitterly that, although they were the driving force behind the workers' street demonstrations which had ultimately brought them to this historic crossroads, they were being left out.

The leaders of the Duma then assembled in Rodzianko's office, now fully aware that if the royal order proroguing the Duma was disobeyed, and they decided to assemble, this would be an act of revolution. Should they declare a Constituent Assembly? As they argued, the advancing workers' 'army' Kerensky had warned of arrived at the Tauride Palace gates, stormed and overcame the guards. Kerensky boldly went outside and addressed the crowd, paying special attention to the soldiers, referring to them flatteringly as 'the first revolutionary guard'.

Nothing could stop the revolution. Prisons were emptied of their political inmates. Delegates and members from various revolutionary groups now felt free to flock to the Tauride Palace. There was a feeling of liberation, a sense of no turning back.

On Wednesday, 1 March all caution was finally thrown to the wind when the Provisional Committee, now dominated by Pavel Milyukov, formed a Provisional Government. The Petrograd Soviet was also keen to flex its substantial muscle, as radical members began to argue that they were in a strong position to form their own revolutionary government, a move which was supported strongly by the workers and soldiers. Despite Milyukov's ascendance, the Soviet went ahead and the soldiers issued the famous Soviet Order Number One, which stripped away most of the authority held by their officers, sanctioned the election of soldiers' committees – who would have control over weapons. The Soviet would only act on the Provisional Government's orders providing those same orders did not conflict with Soviet policy. Any orders issued by army officers would now need to have the approval of the Soviet.

At that first historic meeting of the Soviet, suddenly freed from the chains of repression, the atmosphere was one of unbridled jubilation as workers took to the floor to speak. When the soldiers of the various regiments – those who had turned their guns away from the people – rose to their feet, there were deafening cheers as each man shouted the name of his regiment. They declared their brotherhood with the workers and the ordinary people, against whom they had no desire to serve, as in the old days so recently past. Each contribution was terminated with the cry 'Long live the revolution!' to even louder applause.

The new Provisional Government, however, had the support of the Soviet's Executive Committee as there was still a residue of respect for what were deemed to be worldly, professional politicians, despite the fierce opposition of the Bolsheviks. A cabinet was formed. The Premier would be Prince George Lvov, respected for his work as chairman of the *Zemstvos*, the organs of local government in the countryside. Kerensky – the only socialist member – would be Minister of Justice, Miliukov Minister for Foreign Affairs, with Alexander Guchkov as Minister of War. Now many of the popular demands, previously paraded through the streets on banners and yearned for by underground news-sheets, could be satisfied. The death penalty was abolished. The Church could no longer meddle in the affairs of the state – it would be separated. Discrimination based on race, religion or class was outlawed. Democracy would be extended to local government, and to tackle the thorny subject of land distribution, a special Constituent Assembly would be set up. Equal enfranchisement with a secret vote would be brought in. But in the ecstasy of these well-earned hours as they celebrated the birth of their new state, many had forgotten that at that moment they still had a Tsar, and the Tsar still had his would-be military dictator, General Ivanov.

For Mikhail Rodzianko, all his nightmares had come true. He had tried one last telegram to his beloved Emperor, but as usual, Nicholas wasn't listening. Satisfied that he would soon have order restored by General Ivanov, he had decided to return in his train from Mogilev to the bosom of his family at Tsarskoe Selo, where his children were suffering with measles. But the railway workers had other ideas and the route of his train was blocked. He was dismayed to find that it would be diverted to Pskov, which was over 100 miles (160km) south of Petrograd. Whilst the Petrograd Soviet was basking in its new power, Nicholas sat in his sumptuous railway carriage belatedly discussing the possibilities of constitutional reform, a pointless exercise, oblivious as he was to what was happening 100 miles away.

Meanwhile the mood of many previously loyal members of the High Command had shifted, as fear, respect and loyalty for the Romanovs evaporated. As his train arrived in Pskov, Nicholas's Palace Commandant, Voeykov, who was travelling with him, was met by General Ruzky, who was in no mood for pleasantries, eyeing Voeykov with contempt. 'Look what you have done,' he spat, 'all your Rasputin clique – what have you got Russia into now?' Through his contact with Rodzianko, Ruzky knew the full extent of what was happening. Those few remaining members of Nicholas's inner circle seemed to bask in the same misplaced confidence which emanated from the Empress – all this trouble was simply a blip in Russia's history which could be ironed out with a show of force.

That evening Ruzky tried his hand with the Tsar. He knew of Rodzianko's failures in such meetings, yet tried, as respectfully as he could, to outline the facts to Nicholas, and explain that if he made concessions to establishing parliamentary rule, perhaps based on the British system, then all might still be saved. The essence of his argument was that 'The monarch *reigns* – but the government *rules*.' Although he reluctantly agreed to some form of responsible ministry headed by Rodzianko, Nicholas still failed to comprehend, replying, 'I am responsible before God and Russia for the country's fate.' In any case, it was all too late. He stated that he could never place his trust in the Duma – to do such a thing would have deadly consequences. As he would soon discover, the consequences of not doing such a thing were far deadlier.

General Ivanov, who was now in Mogilev on the River Dnieper, set about his mission to restore order in Petrograd with gusto. His first task was to open up a dialogue with the Duma using a primitive telegraph apparatus called the Hughes wire. This provided a laborious, slow question-and-answer process, with the answers he was receiving not the ones he expected. He asked what food supplies were available. None. How many of the railway stations in the capital were secure? None. Were the police reliable? No, the police force had all but evaporated. He then discovered that several of the Duma's ministers had been arrested by the revolutionaries. Although dismayed, Ivanov still held the hope that the promised 'loyal troops' would be waiting for him at Tsarskoe Selo. Boarding his train at Mogilev, he set out, stopping at Dno, where he found a lack of discipline and an atmosphere of truculence had spread among the troops there. Ivanov, with his huge beard, still possessed a Russian general's fearsome aura. Barking and shouting he moved among the men at Dno and, for a short while at least, restored a little military discipline. Yet he was wise enough in using his military brain to have another locomotive coupled to the rear of his train in case he needed to make a hasty retreat.

When he eventually arrived at Tsarskoe Selo, any hopes he had of finding those loyal troops he so needed were crushed. The only troops who set out to meet him, the 15th Cavalry Division, had also had their train stopped en route. By this time the revolution had taken a firm hold. News had circulated of the huge naval mutiny at Kronstadt. Throughout the Baltic Fleet 200 officers had been imprisoned and 100 murdered. Their Commander-in-Chief, Admiral Viren, had been killed, his body sliced into small pieces and thrown onto a bonfire.

Even the Tsar's soldiers at Tsarskoe had mutinied, and many officers had been murdered. Ivanov was disturbed to see truckloads of soldiers and armoured cars passing by, their occupants' rifles garlanded with strips of red bunting. He met the Empress briefly, and as their conversation convinced him that his mission was doomed, he made a quick exit and returned to his train, relieved that he'd attached that second locomotive. He headed south again, this time to Vyritsa.

Mikhail Rodzianko, who had planned to travel to Pskov by train for one last session of pleading with the Tsar, had been unable to make the journey. He found the new controlling rabble, whom he referred to as 'dogs', utterly distasteful. When he urged the Soviet to carry on the war in order to save the country, the fearless and newly empowered revolutionaries challenged him, saying to the crowd that what this man was asking them to do was lay down their lives for a land which 'belonged to princes and barons'. One delegate made the position clear: 'The real question is this – would Rodzianko be so keen for them to fight on for "the land" if it belonged to the *people?*'

Kerenksy, now joined by General Brusilov, whose early campaigns in the war had provided such hope, and the Chief of Staff, General Alexeev, united in their call for Nicholas to abdicate.

Late on Thursday, 2 March 1917, Nicholas II signed the act of abdication on board his train in Pskov station in the presence of two Duma deputies, Guchkov and Shulgin. The Tsar had hoped to abdicate in favour of the young Tsarevich, Alexi, but earlier that day the Romanovs' doctor, Serge Fedorov, convinced Nicholas that his young son's haemophilia was incurable. Nicholas decided, therefore, to abdicate in favour of his brother, Mikhail.

To the Grand Duke Mikhail, his brother's transference of power seemed nothing more than a poisoned chalice. After what must be one of the shortest kingships in history, within 24 hours he had refused the post, knowing his safety could not be guaranteed. So came to an ignominious end over three centuries of Romanov rule. Russia was no longer a monarchy.

One day in March, in a cramped room above Herr Kammerer's cobbler's shop at 14 Spiegelgasse in Zurich, Vladimir Illych Lenin was, as usual, crouched over his small writing table poring over various political documents and manuscripts. The window was closed to keep the awful smell from the butcher's shop next door at bay. His wife, Nadya, had just finished washing the pots from their lunch when the door burst open and a Polish Bolshevik, M.G. Bronski, dashed in, breathlessly exclaiming, 'Haven't you heard the news? There's been a revolution in Russia!' After the excitement died down, Lenin's fertile brain went into overdrive. A revolution – and he wasn't there. Some way, somehow, he had to get back to Russia.

Seven days after the abdication of Nicholas II, on the night of 9 March 1917, an engineering officer and a small platoon of soldiers armed with spades and shovels marched into the grounds around the palace at Tsarskoe Selo. Behind the fairy-tale edifice, the Romanovs, no longer rulers, slept, prisoners of the new regime.

Working in silence by lamplight, the men exhumed the body of Grigori Rasputin and carried the coffin through the dark-ness to the forest of Pargolovo, where a huge pile of logs awaited. They broke open the casket and manhandled the decaying corpse with sticks onto the pyre. It was drenched in petrol and set alight; the fire burned for six hours. Around the perimeter of the orange glow from the fire, a circle of several hundred peasants, *muzhiks*, stood like silent ghosts in the flickering shadows, their faces set in horror. This was the real end of the *Bojy tchelloviek* – Alexandra's 'Man of God'.

As the cold dawn pushed its dull fingers through the pines, the peasants dispersed and the soldiers began to bury the ashes beneath the snow. To the superstitious *muzhiks*, these bold, determined young men in their red armbands had not only incinerated Old Russia, they had hidden its very history beneath the soil.

3

THE PRODIGALS RETURN

My parents supported the Bolsheviks but
said they'd never heard of Lenin or Trotsky
until they came back in 1917. They wondered
what all the fuss was about because they thought
they'd already had the revolution when the Tsar went.
They soon found out that they were wrong.

Ekaterina Victorovna, retired
textile worker, St Petersburg[1]

The sudden wave of liberation and hope which resulted from
the dramatic events of February and March expressed itself in
many ways. Despite the continuing hunger and deprivation,
something approaching a gala atmosphere developed among
the workers as people garlanded themselves with red ribbons
and took time off work. Servants decided to take whole days
off from their masters' service. There were smiles to be ex-

changed on every street corner and eager discussions began around the wonderful promises the future might hold. The Tsar had gone. It seemed like a dream. Red flags and banners appeared everywhere. They fluttered from passing cars, and hung from windows and balconies. Yet not everyone was as happy as the workers. As the police and the dreaded Okhrana now faded into the political shadows, the old laws of the Romanov regime lurched into impotence. Parallel to the boundless joy among the workers ran a river of revenge and retribution. Shops were being looted, and the more dedicated policemen, their recent power now dissipated, were targeted for severe beatings. Many of these encounters with angry crowds resulted in grisly and brutal deaths. Along the main thoroughfares such as the Nevsky and Liteiny Prospekts, the hi-jacking or commandeering of vehicles became common-place. Armouries had been broken into, with weapons and ammunition being distributed. Now it was not only the servicemen who were carrying rifles – many workers were armed too. Trucks and cars careered along the broad streets loaded with shouting, victorious men, both civilians and in uniform. From a distance their rifles seemed to point skywards in a cluster like the quills of a porcupine, their blackness punctuated by strips of red bunting fluttering from their barrels.

Men at arms, the soldiers and sailors who were, in effect, the peasants in uniform, and the working class, had stored up centuries of resentment against the indignities foisted upon them by the nobility and the bourgeoisie. To many foreigners, such as the British and Americans in Petrograd and other urban areas, no matter what their politics, what they had witnessed of these indignities seemed almost medieval. It was common, for instance, that Russian naval ratings on leave with their girlfriends would be stopped in the street by an officer and put through a ritual humiliation. This usually involved a sneering inquiry as to what ship the sailor was serving with, followed by a slap in the face, and in some cases the rating had to turn about to be kicked in the bottom by the officer – resistance was a near guarantee of a trip to Siberia. Spitting in a serviceman's face by a superior was common. In the cinema, officers were allowed to sit in the auditorium facing the screen, whilst the rank and file had to sit in a specially designated area *behind* the screen, so that those who could read soon learned to read captions backwards. Many venues and hostelries were off-limits to the lower ranks. Now, all this would change – the better-off classes had to accept that the once accepted status quo had gone forever.

There are few survivors alive today who can recall the atmosphere, but for those who can it often has a less than joyful feel. Helena Matveievna Krapivina was born in Petrograd on 16 November 1912.

Although I was very young I do recall some of the events of 1917. My family had a dacha in the Crimea near the Black Sea. My father was a lawyer in Petrograd. My mother was from Siberia. She was from a noble background. Her family had some connection with Admiral Kolchak, who led the Whites in the Civil War. One of my ancestors went to fight with Napoleon.

Mother stayed at home when I was a child. We had servants at that time. We lived at the dacha in the Crimea for the whole summer. In 1917 my father had sent us a telegram asking us to urgently return to the city of Petrograd. Everybody seemed to be heading back and it was very difficult for us to get train tickets to return. There were huge queues at the stations and many trains weren't running. But we did get back eventually. It is difficult to know what to expect when someone says that there has been 'a revolution'.

When we got off the train in Petrograd it was very dark in the city. There was broken glass on the pavements and shadowy groups of men standing around with guns. There were no lights in the windows. It was difficult finding transport, and when we finally arrived back at our apartment we were forbidden to go near the windows. There was shooting going on all around the city. From that moment of returning our lives suddenly became very difficult. To begin with there was no food. Many shops had been looted and closed down. Eventually we were given some ration cards. It was difficult to get the food. We got fish and some soup. We had a decent sized apartment in Petrograd but one of the results of the revolution was that we could only live in one room, as the rest of the apartment wasn't heated. We kept warm by sitting around the gas stove. 1917 was the most difficult year. The following year we managed to eat a little better when my father managed to get some food rations which were only supposed to be given to university professors. This consisted of frozen horse meat and some frozen soup. I re-member he brought it to us on a small sleigh. Sometimes we went to a village just beyond the suburbs because there we could change some of our household goods for eggs and butter. Our lives were quite difficult until Lenin introduced the New Economic Policy at the beginning of the 1920s. On the Nevsky Prospekt before this the windows of the shops were all broken and many places had closed down. Things never returned to how they were before 1917, but there was a period when a few of the commodities we had missed seemed to re-appear. After the NEP things began to improve.[2]

In the factories in the Vyborg district the workers' committees met regularly with a new confidence and boldness. There was so much more to discuss now that the unprecedented rising had taken hold. Meetings of groups of workers and soldiers became a regular fixture on street corners, in doorways, in any open space. 'Going to a meeting' was the answer most people gave as to how they might spend their evening or afternoon. With their right to assemble in this way forbidden for so long under Nicholas's regime, the freedom to gather together, debate and discuss the revolution was sheer intoxication.

In the city's tea shops men and women gathered around tables in animated groups and discussed the various qualities of one political faction or another. Some cafe owners, perhaps acting in a spirit of self-preservation as much as revolution, their windows draped with red flags, threw open their doors to the workers and offered free drinks and snacks. Better to feed the rebels than lose one's business. This was a time, a brief window in a dark history, when the lowest of Russia's oppressed classes could finally see the light.

But of course this euphoria could not be maintained. Organization was an obvious imperative if the revolutionary wagon was to be kept rolling. This unprecedented and successful uprising had caught the Mensheviks and the Bolsheviks on the hop. But when it came down to organization, it was the workers who led the way.

The workers' councils wasted no time. Freed from the threat of Tsarist oppression, new committees were formed and began to spread rapidly. One of the main spurs to this rise in activity was the threat of closures and the new hope that the changing social scene might finally bring about one of the workers' main goals – the cherished eight–hour day.

The workers in each business or industrial base directly elected their own committees and as confidence grew, their demands would soon extend beyond working hours and closures – now the workers could plan for the taking over of their employers' businesses. They would run the factories themselves. With the monarchy gone, and the Provisional Government in place, Moscow and Petrograd's businessmen and industrialists, in the form of the Manufacturer's Associations, had little choice but to listen to the new committees, although actually recognizing them would take some time. However, on 10 March the eight–hour day was granted, although not everywhere. Other problems, such as the seemingly insurmountable issue of food supplies and high prices could not be tackled overnight. Six days later, out in the countryside, all the farms and land which had been directly supplying the Romanovs were taken over by the new government, and on 17 March the same thing happened to Nicholas himself – his possessions and land were no longer his, becoming the property of the people.

The emboldened peasants – *muzhiks* – now threw caution to the wind. If the urban workers could run their factories, then the agricultural workers felt that their greatest cause – owning the land – was about to be achieved. Despite warnings from the Provisional Government that violence and sheer robbery were not the path to liberating the land, the *muzhiks* pressed on, attacking landowners with German names, invading their houses and estates. Now they would have firewood by the cartload, and the prime beasts in their erstwhile master's herds became fair game. Over at Tsarskoe Selo, where the Tsar and his family remained under house arrest, Red Guards were shooting the tame deer in the palace park and were at last dining in style. The spiritual appetite for radical change had, for the moment, been satisfied, but despite butchered cows, pigs and deer, the hunger pangs would rumble on for some time.

In the Duma, Alexander Kerensky was still the man of the hour. As head of the new government, Prince Georgy Lvov, despite his liberal stance, was still regarded by the Soviets as a suspicious representative of the old gentry. Foreign Minister Pavel Milyukov had no time for Lvov's procrastinating style, yet Milyukov lacked an understanding of the possibilities the revolution presented. He was at heart still a monarchist, and the Soviets knew it.

At the War Ministry, an even more rabid monarchist still held sway – Alexander Guchkov. At this early stage, despite their influence among the urban workers, the Bolsheviks were still a very small minority. Of the 242 workers' Soviets formed by April 1917, the Bolsheviks controlled a mere 27. The main Petrograd Soviet, undoubtedly the most radical assembly acting for the workers, had 600 deputies by the end of March, out of which only 40 were Bolsheviks.[3] Yet the militant stance of the Bolsheviks on the war, and the composition of the Provisional Government, was shared by many workers.

On 26 March a worker signing himself as A. Zemskov wrote a long and detailed letter which he hoped would be read by the government, sending his missive for the attention of the senior Menshevik in the Duma, Nikolai Chkheidze. Its ultimate destination was intended to be Kerensky's desk. Zemskov admitted to being a deserter who had been working in the fields of the Kuban steppes under an assumed name. The quality of his expression and his grasp of politics belies the misapprehension among many foreigners at the time that the Russian proletariat were an illiterate mass. At almost 3,000 words, this document is too large to reproduce here. However, a few extracts from this broadside fired at the Provisional Government amply demonstrate the working classes' views on what needed to be done to advance their cause:

> You have probably forgotten the words of your great prophet, Marx, who said that 'the emancipation of the workers is the

task of the workers themselves'. The bourgeoisie is striving for democratic forms of governance because in them it sees the most convenient method of oppression and exploitation. If you want happiness and freedom for the working people, then climb down off their back and stand next to me and do my peasant work; take up the plough with me.

He goes on to discard nobles, priests, scholars, merchants and poets as 'nothing but greedy predators making off with the products of our labour'. He dismisses the idea of setting up a new state as 'an organ of oppression of the working classes, created to protect bourgeois property' and rounds off with:

I am a proletarian free of prejudice. I ask you to excuse me for my rudeness and form of exposition, for I have been writing not in a study with unlimited free time but in the field on a cart, when I could take myself away from my fieldwork.[4]

Such passion would become a regular outpouring among many workers who now felt free to express their thoughts in writing. In fact, the scale of literacy in the country in 1917 had improved impressively over the three decades up to 1917. In 1881, compared to a literacy rate in Britain of 84 per cent, the figure in Russia was a mere 11 per cent, with only 2 per cent of the population attending school, compared to 15 per cent in Britain.[5] By 1917 in Petrograd 89 per cent of male workers and 65 per cent of women workers were literate. Throughout Russia, the figures were 79 per cent and 44 per cent, so letters such as Comrade Zemskov's are not surprising.[6]

It would be down to Kerensky to keep up the revolution's momentum, and this he did with an energy and panache which impressed the radicals. Kerensky was no newcomer to the cut and thrust of fundamental politics. Before being elected to the Duma in 1912, he already had a worthy reputation as a defence lawyer. When workers were massacred at the Lena gold mines in 1912, his detailed investigation into the event sealed his reputation as a 'man of the people'. He would come to be referred to as the revolution's 'first love', however, like most first loves, this would be a short-term affair. He abolished the dreaded Okhrana and brought into force an amnesty for all those charged with acts carried out for political purposes. There would be freedom of the press and expression. The regime in prisons was to be overturned. Shackles, chains and straightjackets would be abolished, and the more brutal Tsarist prison officers would lose their jobs, to be replaced by disabled ex-soldiers. Flogging would be stopped. Political prisoners, along with hundreds of criminals, were released from their cells. Courts, such as the Supreme Criminal Court, were abolished. Most importantly, the death penalty was scrapped, and hot on the heels of this would come legislation to prevent discrimination based on sex, nationality, race or religion. Women would be able to vote – and even volunteer to join the Army as combatants.

Thus for a while, what had been one of the most oppressive autocracies in the world seemed to become the most radically free society. This had all been achieved with a degree of death and injury, but those critics who had expected a bloodbath on the scale of the French Revolution had been disappointed.

Abroad, reactions to the uprising were mixed. Pacifists in Britain – and there were a sizeable number, no matter how unpopular their cause – saw what had happened in Russia as a confirmation of their ideals. Bertrand Russell was quick to comment in March that 'The Russian Revolution has stirred men's imaginations everywhere and has made things possible which would have been quite impossible a week ago.'[7] While workers and other supporters from the Labour Party and various anti-war groups flocked to Russell's celebratory rally at the Albert Hall, Ramsay MacDonald was prepared to wait and see. Unlike many of their European counterparts, the Labour Party was not a revolutionary organization. It would be the following year, 1918, when the famous Clause Four would be adopted:

> To secure for the producers by hand or brain the full fruits of their industry, and the most equitable distribution thereof that may be possible, upon the basis of the common ownership of the means of production and the best obtainable system of popular administration and control of each industry and service.

A far cry from the relative simplicity of 'All Power to the Soviets!', but prior to the rigours and tragedy of the war, in Britain the country's workers had begun to organize in earnest long before the Bolsheviks and Mensheviks achieved success. For instance, the Miners Federation of Great Britain had already won the eight–hour day Act in 1908 along with district minimum wages in 1912.[8] Yet although many Russian workers and the liberal intelligentsia had an abiding admiration for the British parliamentary system, it is worth noting that British women would not get their vote until 1918 – and even then, only if they were over 30, with another decade to wait before this would fall to 21. Also, due to the war, many thousands of British workers, despite the eight-hour day, were working much longer than this. Russians also enjoyed as many as 30 more religious holidays each year than the British, which made the Russian working year over three weeks shorter.[9]

In America the US government proclaimed recognition of Russia's new Provisional Government on 9 May. In retrospect, it seems paradoxical that the cradle of capitalism should be the first foreign nation to recognize a government which would, within a few short months, declare an implacable stance against almost everything the United States stood for. However, even in a world where revolutions take place, money will always oil the machine, as both the exiled Lenin and Trosky knew.

Much has been made over the years of the fact that both these architects of the new Russia took money from wherever it was offered to further their aims. If there can be any room for the notion of morality in war, then what has rankled the critics has been the suggestion that the Bolshevik triumph came about due to funds from Germany. This paradox is brought into stark relief when one considers that Kaiser Wilhelm's resolute forces had already killed millions of Russians by the time Lenin planned to go home. 'Peace, Land and Bread' may have been the banner of the revolutionaries, but the main platform of thought in the new Provisional Government, including that of Alexander Kerensky, was that the war should continue to be fought in defence of the motherland – Tsar or no Tsar. For Trotsky and Lenin, who would without doubt be pilloried as agents of the enemy, it would be their preference for dollars and deutschmarks rather than bullets which would bring peace, albeit a very costly one.

In March 1917 many of bolshevism's greatest players had been living abroad for years. Sverdlov, Stalin and Kamenev were in Siberian exile. Some were in London or Paris. Zinoviev, Lunacharsky, Litvinov and Chicherin were scattered around Europe. Another comrade, Alexandra Kollontai, was strategically positioned in Oslo. Kollontai was an important link for Lenin in Zurich, who was unable to communicate directly with Bolsheviks in Petrograd. She, however, was in touch with the Central Committee from her Norwegian base, and although a cumbersome channel of communication, at least she could receive and despatch information.

By the time Comrade Bronsky had brought Lenin the news of the revolution, Trotsky was in New York with Bukharin working on an émigré newspaper, *Novy Mir*. Now the revelation of the momentous events in Russia had suddenly become like a huge magnet exerting an irresistible pull on socialism's waifs and strays.

In his pokey room above the cobbler's shop in Zurich, Lenin refused at first to believe Bronsky's breathless news. The whole idea that a proletarian uprising could take place at this time seemed too incredible. He waited until later that day when the newspapers came out. Feverishly reading the reports from Russia he now knew that only one thing mattered – getting back to Petrograd. All around the globe Russian liberals, socialists, anarchists and intellectuals who had thought that they might never see their homeland again began making plans – the amnesty issued by Kerensky had opened a previously locked gate. Some way, somehow, they had to find a way home.

One of the first beneficiaries of the amnesty to arrive back from exile was Josef Stalin, together with fellow Bolsheviks Lev Kamenev, Jacob Sverdlov and M.K. Muranov. The latter was a metal worker who had been elected to the Fourth Duma by his Kharkov Gubernia constituency. Suddenly repatriated back to their natural political habitat, this determined quartet, with Stalin at the helm, soon took over at the offices of *Pravda*, the party paper which, with the abdication of the Tsar, was now back in business. Casting a sinister foreshadow of his years ahead, Stalin immediately went against the anti-war stance which both Lenin and Trotsky had taken up in Zurich and New York. In his editorial, Stalin decried the slogan 'Down With The War' as 'impractical'. He picked his way through the demands for peace issued by the Soviet of Workers' and Soldiers' Deputies with semantic cunning, stating that:

> Our slogan is pressure on the Provisional Government with the aim of compelling it to make an attempt to induce all the warring countries to open immediate negotiations . . . and until then every man remains at his fighting post![10]

This did not go down well among the workers and their Bolshevik representatives in the factories of Petrograd – indeed, it was an embarrassment because the party's hard anti-war line had suddenly been inexplicably breached. The Bolsheviks were known for their implacable attitude towards the Provisional Government. To be suddenly regarded by the likes of Prince Lvov and even Kerensky as 'reasonable' put them in danger of seeming to make a u-turn on one of the major revolutionary demands. Stalin pressed on with another idea which ran counter to Lenin's thinking, calling for a unification of the leftist elements of the Mensheviks with the Bolsheviks. This was all something he, Kamenev and Sverdlov would have to answer for when Lenin and Trotsky arrived home.

At this time Trotsky was still a Menshevik, but his views on the revolution, although written over 3,000 miles away from Zurich, in New York, echoed Lenin's. By 3 April Lenin's first 'Letter From Afar' was printed in *Pravda*. In it he saw the success of the February uprising as attributable to the devious machinations of the French and the British, who would have used any methods they could to prevent Nicholas from bringing about a separate peace with Germany. The thrust of his message was diametrically opposed to Stalin's outbursts. Meanwhile, across the Atlantic Trotsky was of the same mind, warning his countrymen that, now that the Tsar had gone, the Provisional Government was in effect saying:

Now you must pour out your blood for the all-national interests . . . In other words, Russia now takes her place in the joint ranks of imperialism with other European states, and first of all with her allies, England and France.[11]

Both men were now busy making plans to return to Russia, where some heads needed knocking together.

Some of Lenin's own ideas on how to get back were faintly ridiculous. One involved paying smugglers to get him through Germany and into Russia, but when told that no smugglers could get him any further than Berlin, this plan was dropped. Another scheme involved him flying into Russia. Despite his obvious political and organizational skills this idea demonstrated just how little he knew about aviation as it existed in 1917. Although he insisted on this plan for some time, he would only become dissuaded when presented with two desolate facts – firstly, that he stood every chance of being shot down, and secondly, the aeroplanes available even at this late stage of the war could never cover the distance. It was his practical and astute wife, Nadya, who poured water on his other hot plan – to kit himself out as a Swedish deaf mute, catch a train to Denmark and then somehow make his way to Finland. Only Lenin's spouse could have fully outlined the stupidity of this idea, sharply reminding him that he talked in his sleep and would inevitably start ranting over his major obsession – the Mensheviks.[12]

Oddly enough, it would be a Menshevik who would ultimately put the wheels in motion to get Lenin back to Russia. Julius Martov had been disregarded by Lenin as 'too intelligent to be a first-class revolutionary', yet it was Martov who now came to his aid. Lenin's attitude to Martov by 1917 offers an example of the rigid code of discipline the Bolsheviks took upon themselves. Sentimentality and what must have been regarded as the bourgeois notion of friendship had little room in Lenin's world – political expediency was everything. He had little time for art and music, although he had shown early artistic talent, admired the music of Wagner and could play the guitar.

Lenin and Martov went back a long way. The two men had met in what was then St Petersburg in the 1880s, at a time when the young Lenin was still in awe even of social democrats. Martov, whose grandfather had been a well-known editor and publicist, came from a prominent Jewish family. His real name was Tsederbaum. In the bleak period following the execution of Lenin's brother, Alexander Ulyanov, who had been hanged in 1887 for his involvement in the assassination of Tsar Alexander II, Lenin had eagerly taken up the revolutionary baton and formed many bonds with others who sought the downfall of the Romanovs, Martov included. The two young men would meet clandestinely in the St Petersburg public library, always shadowed by the ever-present Okhrana. The daring duo had planned to publish their own radical newspaper, but as they prepared the first proofs of this, Lenin was arrested in December 1895, with Martov following him into custody a month later. After two years in jail Lenin was banished to Siberia. By the early 1900s Martov and Lenin had fallen out over their interpretation of what a party member should be. The more passive Martov lacked Lenin's tactical cunning and in many ways disagreed with the latter's obsession with discipline and leadership. Thus the two men, prominent figures in the Russian Social Democratic Worker's Party split in 1903 to form the two factions – Martov leading the Mensheviks (minority) and Lenin the Bolsheviks (majority). Over the ensuing decade their differences would grow. But in 1917 Lenin's old comrade would figure prominently in bringing him back to the heart of the revolution.

The Allies would certainly not issue Lenin and his exiled comrades with any kind of documentation which might allow them back into Russia. They were aware of Lenin's ultimate aim – to unseat the Provisional Government and take Russia out of the war. For the Germans, this was a path worth following. Martov, who had returned to Petrograd, made the proposal that a deal could be discussed with the Germans – in return for safe passage of Lenin and other exiles, the Russians would release a number of German prisoners of war. The idea was supported by one of Switzerland's Social Democrats, Robert Grimm, who volunteered to negotiate with Berlin on behalf of the exiles. However, back in Petrograd, the Provisional Government's Foreign Minister, Milyukov, stood in the way of the scheme. It was only when the power of the Petrograd Soviet intervened that things began to move.

Dismissing the efforts of the Social Democrats, Lenin looked to the left of Swiss politics for his next support, finding it in the socialist Fritz Platten. Platten went to see the German consul in Bern, and came away with the blessing of the German Foreign Ministry, who issued their support for the plan to send a train across Germany. It suited the Germans to have as many exiled revolutionaries heading back to Russia as wished to go, no matter what their thoughts were on the war. As Germany's supreme commander General Erich Ludendorff later wrote of Lenin's expedition: 'From a military point of view, his journey was justified, for it was essential that Russia should fall.'[13] So keen were they that they even disposed of the immediate idea of having prisoners of war in exchange, suggesting that the émigrés should campaign for the release of Germans once they had returned to Russia.

Lenin and Grigori Zinoviev planned the trip, which would take 32 revolutionaries over the border into Germany, up to

the Baltic coast and then on by sea to Sweden, and ultimately
Russia via Finland. The decision was that everyone would
have to pay their own fare to avoid any accusations of
German help. In retrospect, considering the accusations
and discussion over the years over Lenin's acceptance of
German assistance, the fact that the passengers on this trip
paid their own fares fades into insignificance. Travelling
unhindered across enemy territory in an enemy train supplied
willingly by Russia's foe would be ammunition enough for all
of Lenin's critics to brand both him and Trotsky – whose
return from New York would take him nowhere near Germany – as traitors and enemy agents. As later research has
revealed, there was significant German involvement in getting
the exiles back to Russia.

At the centre of this support was the suitably named Dr. A.
Helphand, known as 'Parvus'. Parvus was well known to the
comrades in Zurich, and especially to Lenin's close Internationalist confidante there, Karl Radek. Parvus was a Russo-
German Social Democrat with a significant weakness for
corruption when it came to women and money. The German
Social Democratic Party had expelled him after he had misused
party funds for his own advantage. By the time the First World
War was in full flow, Parvus had become an ardent German
patriot who worked on behalf of the German Army. His
faithful servant was another wheeler-dealer named Fuersten-
berg-Ganetsky. Ganetsky was important in Lenin's life as an
exile for it was he who had arranged with the Austrian
Government in 1912 for Lenin, Zinoviev and Kamenev to
be able to live in Cracow. At the time of Lenin's planned return
to Russia, both of these men would be important links in the
exiles' route back to Petrograd.

Even as the plan unfolded, Europe's socialists were appalled
that Lenin had accepted this German offer; his own country-

men living in Switzerland denounced him. In an attempt to calm things down and rally some genuine support from other radicals, Lenin sent a telegram to the French pacifist writer Henri Guilbeaux, who was also in Switzerland. In it Lenin asked if Guilbeaux and the socialist Romain Rolland could be at the station when the revolutionary train was due to leave, but Rolland was having none of this, and told Guilbeaux that he should use any influence he had with Lenin and his comrades to stop their trip through Germany.[14]

By the time the big day arrived, however, 27 March 1917,[15] Lenin had made what peace he could with the Swiss workers he had so carefully lectured and nurtured in Zurich. Upon leaving their lodgings at Herr Kammerer's cobbler's shop, Lenin parted from his landlord with the remark, 'So, Herr Kammerer, now there's going to be peace.'[16]

The genial cobbler wished him luck, adding, 'I hope, Herr Ulyanov, that in Russia you won't have to work so hard as here.'

Lenin pondered for a moment, then replied, 'I think, Herr Kammerer, that in Petrograd, I will have even more work.'[17]

The group of eager travellers met at Zurich's Zähringerhof Hotel for a celebratory meal and to offer their farewell to a number of Swiss and Italian socialists. Then it was on to Zurich railway station where their train awaited. Lenin had laid down the conditions of their journey: they would not speak to any Germans along the route; the German officers who were to accompany them would keep their distance at the back of the carriage, and across the coach's floor a line was drawn in chalk, denoting Russian and German territory. If anyone came on board the train at any time during the journey, Lenin's instructions were that no conversations or meetings should take place. Fritz Platten and the Polish so-cialist Karl Radek would travel with the party. On the station platform, however, two opposing factions had assembled. Italian and Swiss workers were singing the 'Internationale', yet many others hissed and booed the party, accusing them of being spies.

It is easy to imagine how the European working-class supporters viewed this impending departure. Like many of their Russian comrades, they too would have been swept up by the tide of patriotism during the war. Although they were keen to listen to Lenin's speeches and gained much inspiration from these hard-line Russian revolutionaries, the workers' view of the war, as held in countries like Britain, bordered on 'my country – right or wrong'. Many had lost members of their families in the trenches, to them Germany was an unforgiving enemy and a force of darkness to which they should give no quarter. Socialism could come later. Yet now, here were the very men and women whose meetings they had attended, who spoke of a better world to come, treading heavily on their war efforts and accepting help and succour from the enemy. Perhaps what the angry workers could not fully grasp was Lenin's absolute imperative – he was a Russian, exiled for years, and now everything he had planned for in his own country had happened without him being present. For him to get back meant any means possible – they could argue the finer points of his perceived treachery later. Lenin, the unsentimental, the pragmatist, firmly believed that he should be at the centre of this historical epoch.

And so, fearless, he brushed through the crowds and climbed on board the waiting train. As he entered a compartment he saw a man who professed to be a socialist yet was suspected of being an informer. Lenin grabbed him by the collar and removed him unceremoniously from the train. As Lenin watched the warring factions on the platform cheering and booing simultaneously, accusing the party of 'going home at the Kaiser's expense', he was tempted to disembark, perhaps to argue his point, but was dissuaded from doing so.

With a blast on the whistle the locomotive, shrouded in steam, lurched forward, taking this trainload of revolutionary brains, or, as Winston Churchill would later refer to it, 'a plague bacillus', on into history.

Lenin's train has often been referred to in a sensational way as 'the sealed train', but this is gilding the dramatic lily. Although three of the compartments in the carriages were sealed, a fourth was left unlocked for use by the accompanying German officers. Thus the melodramatic impression gained by many who have briefly delved into the history of the revolution, that the returning Lenin and his comrades were in a locked, impenetrable carriage for the whole journey is incorrect. The 'sealed train' was anything but.

The train's first stop was at the border post of Thayngen. There the punctilious Swiss customs men exerted their authority over the party when they discovered that Lenin and his friends had exceeded their official allowances of goods such as chocolate and sugar. The confiscated contraband would be sent on to friends. Once through the mountains they arrived at the German border at Gottmadingen, where they disembarked whilst the German officers steered their way through the efficient Teutonic documentation which would ensure the continuance of this epic journey.

When the train arrived in Frankfurt, Fritz Platten went into town to buy newspapers and beer. Contrary to Lenin's wishes, Platten enlisted the help of some German soldiers to carry the goods back to the train. They were joined by some interested German railway workers, and when the beer and news-carrying group arrived at the train the irrepressible Radek wasted no time in attempting to convince them that when they departed they should spread the doctrine of revolution amongst their workmates. So much for no contact and no conversation.

In Stuttgart, Lenin stuck to his guns when one of Germany's prominent trade union leaders, Wilhelm Janson, came on board. Fritz Platten had to tell Janson on behalf of the party that Lenin would not meet him. One could imagine that such a journey for these dedicated, homeward-bound politicians would be one full of joy. For the ebullient, wise-cracking Radek and the other émigrés, including Inessa Armand, an attractive woman for whom Lenin had an abiding yet controlled affection (a fact that his wife Nadya was well aware of), the trip would indeed be filled with singing, joking and laughter. For the never less than dedicated Lenin, however, any form of buffoonery at such a time was extremely irritating. As he tried to concentrate on his writing in his own compartment, the waves of jollity seeping through the wall became an annoyance. Lenin had long given up smoking himself and discouraged it in his presence. Many of the party therefore sought solace from their nicotine in the carriage's toilets. Yet even such a simple pleasure would fall under his passion for control. He cut a sheet of paper into 'tickets' – one kind for the regular use of the toilet and one for smoke breaks, so that anyone visiting the lavatory for either purpose had to apply for the right ticket. No one complained – this was only further proof to the travellers of their leader's supreme sense of organization.

The train reached Berlin where to everyone's frustration it remained in a siding for a whole day, but by 1 April they at last steamed into the Baltic port of Sassnitz. Here Lenin's belt-and-braces approach to secrecy, developed after years of subterfuge whilst crossing and re-crossing borders, took on a ridiculous turn. With this journey already one of high profile with the German authorities, he suggested to the party that they all change their names before the ferry crossing, a futile and pointless idea, because the Germans knew full well who these emigrants were. They bought their tickets for Sweden and embarked on the ferry *Queen Victoria,* bound for Trelleborg. Legend has it that most of the party succumbed to seasickness, apart from Zinoviev, Lenin and Radek, who endured their journey on deck with animated discussions on politics. At last they were out of Germany; Russia seemed ever closer.

In Trelleborg they were met by one of Lenin's old comrades, the Polish socialist Jakub Hanecki, who had organized a welcome which included a splendid meal. Whilst his hungry comrades tucked in, Lenin commenced to put Hanecki through an animated inquisition over events in Russia.

From Trelleborg, the next day they all arrived in Stockholm. En route to Sweden's capital, at Malmö, Lenin was greeted by an emotional Ganetsky, whose joy at meeting Lenin was pushed aside as the helpful German was interrogated over events in Petrograd.

At Stockholm a generous, celebratory breakfast awaited them, provided by the city's mayor, Karl Lindhagen, the local press making much of these important guests. Radek, however, realizing the diplomatic demands this sense of occasion demanded, became acutely aware of how scruffy they all seemed compared to their reasonably turned-out hosts – the ill-kempt Lenin was wearing hobnail boots and was in bad need of a new suit – so Radek took his leader on a shopping trip around Stockholm. If Lenin was to take control of the revolution, then at least he'd do so in a decent suit and a good pair of shoes.

Thus, better sartorially equipped for his important role, Lenin set off on the train north from Stockholm to the Finnish border. At the Finnish town of Tornio another train was taken for Helsinki. On this journey Lenin finally got hold of some recent copies of *Pravda,* and what he read threw him into a rage. Stalin and Kamenev's support of the Provisional Government was bad enough, but he also discovered that a prominent Bolshevik in Petrograd, the trade union organizer Roman Malinovski, had been uncovered as an agent of the Okhrana. What must have made this grim news more painful was that, unlike many leading Bolsheviks, Malinovski, a metalworker, was a genuine product of the working class, and had even been a member of the Fourth Duma. Over the years he had been under suspicion, and in 1912 had almost been exposed by the Marxist writer Nikolai Bukharin. Yet on that occasion Lenin and Zinoviev's spirited defence of the trade unionist had won the day. But now that the secret files of the Okhrana had been opened, Malinovski's treachery as a paid informer was exposed. By Christmas 1918, Malinovksi would be dead, shot by a Bolshevik firing squad, his death witnessed, as requested, by a gathering of Bolshevik workers.

As the train arrived in Helsinki the excitement mounted. There was now one final stage of the journey to face – one more train, pulled by locomotive number 293, which would take Lenin from Helsinki to Petrograd. The train to Petrograd plodded along at an agonizingly slow pace into the night. Twenty miles outside Petrograd, it stopped at the small station at Beloostrov, where Lev Kamenev, representing the Bolshevik Central Committee, came on board. It had been a long time since the two men had met, yet there was to be no cosy reunion, as Lenin ripped into Kamenev about the editorial calamity he and Stalin had perpetrated at *Pravda.* Just after 11 p.m. on 3 April 1917, the locomotive puffed away from Beloostrov for the final 30 minutes of this long, frustrating expedition. The thoughts among the party suddenly changed from the elation they had enjoyed since leaving Switzerland to genuine worries that what lay ahead might not be revolutionary heaven but the more familiar prison cell. Yet their concerns were unfounded.

All around the concourse outside Petrograd's Finland Station crowds of workers and soldiers had gathered in the dark. The street lights weren't working, but the Bolsheviks had purloined some searchlights from the Peter & Paul fortress, and in addition had driven an armoured car down to the station entrance. To many workers this man, this 'Lenin', remained an enigma. Some knew through reading his pamphlets and editorials that he had their interests at heart. They had heard of his strengths as an organizer and a potential leader, but as to who he actually *was*, what kind of a man he might be, remained to be discovered. Few even had any idea what he looked like – in fact the first publicly available photograph of him had only been printed that week, in the Swedish newspaper *Politiken*.[18] Yet someone needed to take the Bolshevik helm, and, by all accounts, the man for the job was heading into Petrograd at that moment.

On the station platform two ranks of sailors from the Baltic Fleet had lined up in their smartest uniforms as a guard of honour. Suddenly the gloom along the track was pierced by the white eye of the locomotive's headlamp. Into the station the train rumbled and hissed, its bell clanging, and drew to a halt.

Outside the station the beams of the searchlights flickered across the building's façade, occasionally glancing off the many waving red and gold banners held aloft by the workers, sailors and soldiers. The light from the carriage windows filtered through the clouds of steam which slowly dissolved. The carriage door opened, and onto the platform stepped Lenin, in Russia at last after ten years of exile.

He immediately addressed the sailors, who were standing to attention, and wasted no time in telling them that the Provisional Government had duped them into carrying on with the war. This was not what the waiting crowds – and especially the Bolsheviks – would be expecting. He was presented with a bouquet of flowers and carried shoulder high by jubilant comrades to what had recently been the Tsar's personal waiting room at the station, which had now been renamed the 'People's Room'. There the Menshevik Nikolai Chkheidze greeted him in the name of the Petrograd Soviet and the revolution with a brief speech which culminated in a poorly concealed hope that Lenin might support the war effort 'to defend our revolution against every attack both from within and without'. But all this washed over Lenin. Still holding his incongruous bouquet, he made his position clear – that of calling for a world socialist revolution and an end to the war.

The massive crowds lining the blocked streets outside took him and Nadya by surprise. The searchlights picked him out as he clambered onto the turret of the waiting armoured car. There he repeated his message, claiming that capitalism must be defeated, and that as socialists, those who believed in this cause must cease any support for the Provisional Government.

Although there were cheers, the majority of the gathered crowd found his attitude little more than confusing. Hadn't they just got rid of the monarchy? Hadn't the workers wrested control from their bosses? Had not the secret police been defeated and disbanded? They had brought about a total change of Russian society, and where had Comrade Lenin been? Their belief was that Germany, with a new wave of Russian inspiration, would be defeated, and the Allies would bring about the peace. What was this man saying – that they should lay down their arms? There were mutterings among many workers and sailors that they had invited a German spy into their midst. Nevertheless, he was here, and soon they would come to understand his strange ideas more clearly.

The armoured car rumbled off along the streets, strafed every now and then by searchlights from the Peter & Paul fortress. The gathered workers, clutching their red banners and flags, craned their necks to see the revolution's prodigal philosopher. Soon Lenin's entourage proceeded over the Neva across the Troitskiy Bridge to the new Bolshevik headquarters which were now in the recently commandeered house of the prima ballerina, Ksheshinskaya, not only a Romanov favourite but rumoured to be a mistress of a Grand Duke and perhaps even Nicholas himself.

From the second-floor balcony he addressed the waiting workers, telling them that revolutions such as theirs would soon take place in Britain, France and Germany. The time had come for the world's toiling masses to rise up. The rest of his speech that night spread alarm among his old comrades, who imagined they had achieved so much in his absence. Soldiers and sailors displayed their irritation with Lenin's anti-war stance; some called him a madman. The tough Kronstadt sailors, the uprising's shock troops, muttered among themselves, 'Let him come down here and say these things. Who does he think he is – sitting in Switzerland whilst we've been fighting.'

As he settled in to this new palatial residence, everyone imagined Lenin's first port of call the following day would be to the Tauride Palace where the Provisional Government were no doubt expecting him. Instead, the human being behind the iron mask of organization appeared. He visited his mother's grave, where he stood, cap in hand, in contemplative silence. For Lenin, this driven, focussed revolutionary with a bottomless capacity for hatred of his opponents, this was a rare moment of meditation.

As spring blossomed in New York, temporary resident Leon Trotsky had dubbed it 'the city of prose and fantasy, of capitalist automatism, its streets a triumph of cubism, its moral philosophy that of the dollar'.[19] That said, he was nonetheless impressed by the place, and so were his children, who would be loath to leave this exhilarating metropolis, so different than any of the cities in which their father had so far spent his exile. But Trotsky, like Lenin, was a revolutionary, and a Russian – he too had to get home. As a revolutionary socialist, he had declared this sole occupation to be 'no less reprehensible than that of a bootlegger'. Lenin had been kept fully informed of what Russian revolutionary émigrés – including Trotsky – were up to in New York by the ultra-left Alexandra Kollontai, who would, in years to come, join the massed ranks of Trotsky's enemies under Stalin's leadership.

He had spent his time assiduously reading American history, travelling from meeting to meeting, lecturing in German and Russian – by his own admission, his command of English left much to be desired. But now all efforts were dedicated to getting the necessary paperwork which could free the Trotskys and send them on their way home. When the news had come of the uprising in Petrograd, Trotsky had begun a round of visits to embassies and consulates. After some argument at the Russian embassy, he was finally issued with the papers needed to return home. From the Russians this meant an entry permit. Oddly enough, he would be entering his native land bearing a US passport, courtesy of President Woodrow Wilson.[20]

Next stop was the British consulate, where he was required to fill out a questionnaire and be issued with a transit visa. It appeared that there would be no opposition to his returning to Russia.

There was a carnival atmosphere on the quayside on 25 March when the Trotsky family and several other returning exiles boarded the Norwegian ship, the *Christianiafjord*. Eager socialists had gathered to present the passengers with flowers. They were the joyful recipients of speeches and good wishes.

Yet Trotsky's joy and excitement at the prospect of going home would be short lived.

Once clear of America, the *Christianiafjord* called at Halifax in Nova Scotia, where Britain held sway, and the Royal Navy had been instructed to board and inspect the *Christianiafjord*. In addition to the homeward-bound Russians, the passengers included a number of Americans, Dutch and Norwegians, all of whom had their passports and papers examined by thoroughgoing British bureaucracy. The Russians, however, were subjected to a more sinister degree of scrutiny which angered Trotsky and his comrades, being closely questioned about their aims and their political convictions. He was having none of this. 'You may have all the information you want as to my identity,' he said, 'but nothing else.' This played into the hands of the two British detectives, Westwood and Machen, who had failed to get Trotsky to talk. After discussing the truculent passenger with others, Machen and Westwood came to the conclusion that Trotsky was 'a dangerous socialist'.[21] A number of his comrades fired off a vigorous broadside to the British Government, which Trotsky saw as futile and refused to participate, commenting wittily, 'I did not join with them because I saw little use in complaining to Beelzebub about Satan.'

The result would be a month-long interruption to the journey, as on 3 April British officers boarded the ship and demanded that Trotsky, his family and five other Russians accompany them ashore. When he refused the family were manhandled by British sailors and taken ashore. With his wife and two boys, aged nine and eleven, placed in the house of a pro-British Russian agent, Trotsky was taken to a disused former German iron foundry in the town of Amherst. This had been converted into a concentration camp for various international enemies of the King, mainly German U-boat crews.

The British Army commandant at Amherst was an irascible Boer War veteran, Colonel Morris, to whom Trotsky's continuing refusal to toe the line was a constant irritation. Morris outlined Britain's reason for detaining the Russians – they were, according to Whitehall, dangerous to the Russian Government. The argumentative Trotsky managed to confuse Morris by telling him that it was the same Russian Government who had issued them with documents to go home. Morris then argued that Trotsky and his party were dangers to the Allies – an obtuse argument, considering that at this time British forces were still fighting alongside the Russians in the war.

Trotsky was never one to let the grass grow beneath his feet. He utilized his time at Amherst in the most political way he could – converting the German submariners to socialism. After a month of this, during which the whole camp was turned into a series of revolutionary meetings and debates, it soon became obvious that this star prisoner was even more dangerous here than he might be in Russia. More muddy propaganda was set up to defend Britain's case – that Trotsky's trip home had been subsidized by the German Government. Back in Petrograd, Lenin railed against the Allies from the pages of *Pravda* and it did seem obvious in Bolshevik circles that the Russian Provisional Government's Foreign Minister, Milyukov, knew full well of Trotsky's detention and was reluctant to act for his release – he and Trotsky had been bitter political enemies since 1905.

It was the Petrograd Soviet which finally brought the Provisional Government to its senses and finally, on 29 April Trotsky, his family and comrades, were finally released and booked to sail home on a Danish ship. His send-off from Amherst was every bit as lively as his departure from New York, with his new German converts to revolution cheering

him on as a makeshift band played the future founder of the
Red Army through the camp compound.

For Trotsky, the trip home, first to Sweden, and then
through Finland, would not be crowned with spectacular
ceremony upon his arrival as had been the case with Lenin.
On the Finnish border at Belöostrov, a party of revolutionaries, including representatives from the Bolsheviks, came on
board the train. Yet although he was still officially one of their
number, no one came to greet him from the Mensheviks. More
emotional and human in his behaviour than the icy Lenin,
Trotsky found time to embrace Mosei Uritsky, an old comrade
from his exile days in Siberia. Uritsky, who was eventually to
become head of the Soviet version of the Okhrana, the Cheka,
in Petrograd, would die the following year, assassinated by a
Social Revolutionary. Like Lenin before him, as Trotsky's
train trundled on towards Petrograd, he devoured the news
from the Russian newspapers and became dismayed by the fact
that so many former political allies had given their support to
the Provisional Government. Trotsky could see that his days as
a Menshevik were numbered; at least the Bolsheviks wanted
out of the war.

Finding somewhere to live in Petrograd wasn't as straight-
forward as it had been for Lenin. The family first moved into
the Kiev Hostelry. They were then invited to share the apartment of a man who, posing as a blacksmith in 1905, had called
himself Loghinov and joined Trotsky in street battles with the
police. Loghinov now revealed his true identity as Serebrovsky, an engineer. The apartment was just what the Trotskys
were looking for, but Serebrovsky's politics were not. After
some violent arguments wherein the generous engineer
accused Lenin of being a German agent, Trotsky packed his
bags and took his family back to the cramped hostelry. Within
months his living conditions would improve when the Trots-

kys would have an apartment across the corridor from Lenin on the second floor of the Smolny Institute.

But for now, any roof would do. The spring had arrived, and with the sun came another rise in temperature – the battle lines between the Bolsheviks and the Provisional Government were being drawn.

It would be a complex fight, with many pitfalls. The ideas of the exiles would be difficult to sell to a population which already believed it had achieved the impossible. History would interpret their efforts.

> the ones who stuck to their hopeless principles got success as an un-looked for bonus. Lenin achieved supreme power; the German Social Democrats never got anywhere. The more ruthless, extreme, and uncompromising your politics, the greater will be your reward in this world as well as the next.[22]

Together, Lenin and Trotsky would forge ahead in one of the most ambitious political struggles in Russian history. No war, no prissy notions of western-style liberal democracy would stand in their way. The spontaneous joy of February was already a distant memory.

4

RED DAYS, WHITE NIGHTS

And when the sun darkens and the prospect is war,
Who's given a gun and then pushed to the fore?
And expected to die for the land of our birth
Though we've never owned one handful of earth.'

Worker's Song[1]

By mid-June in St Petersburg the sun remains above the horizon until midnight. With the slush and the cold finally gone, the weather becomes perfect for staying outdoors, perfect for meeting and talking. These are the 'white nights' which offer so much delight to tourists.

In the Petrograd spring of 1917, all this seemed to be an extra bonus to the bright air of unlimited freedom which had descended upon the population since the fall of the Tsar. But some western correspondents saw things as they were.

The frank joy of the early state of the Revolution has given place to bitter party strife, and growing resentment against the extremists and disturbers of order. The desire for order is becoming a passion with the crowd, and the national instinct, at first baffled and stunned by the vehement outcry of preachers of immediate social revolution, is beginning to reassert itself. I sometimes begin to fear the reaction may be too violent.[2]

This 'desire for order' reported by British reporter Harold Williams may well have been strong among the newly liberated workers and soldiers, but the route to satisfying this lay ahead like a bloody obstacle course.

The workers at factories such as the A.M. Ouf machine, metal and engineering works, Trubochnyi zavod (the Petrograd Pipe Factory) the Old Parviainen machine works, and that vanguard of workers' action, the Putilov plant, the mill and railway workers, were all becoming a little confused.

Anna Gromov, who spent her younger years as a gardener in Leningrad, is today a lively, 86-year-old survivor of the Nazi siege. She recalls her father's concern following Lenin's return.

My father worked as a junior clerk at the Russo-Asiatic Bank in Petrograd. There was a lot of worry over Lenin's speeches when he got back, because one of the things he spoke of was nationalising all the banks in Russia to make them into one national bank. The family were already struggling – they lived on horsemeat when they could get it, black bread and sunflower seeds – and the idea of all the banks being amalgamated could mean that many jobs may be lost. It was unusual for people like my parents, but they supported the Mensheviks, and I know my father thought seriously about joining the Bolsheviks before any nationalisation might happen – he thought that this might secure his job. But it didn't matter in the end. The following year, when I was born, he caught pneumonia and died. But that wasn't exactly the fault of the revolution. It could just as easily have happened under the Tsar. My mother was a good cook and eventually got a job in the kitchens in a hotel. I can't remember which one, but she used to smuggle little bits of food home in her coat pockets. I was only a kid, so I can't say much about what really happened. I grew up under communism so for me I never knew anything different, but looking at my country's history from that time makes me realise one thing – the revolution had to happen. There was no other way, and as for Nicholas, well, perhaps a nice man, but a useless leader.[3]

Lenin, and now Trotsky, back in Russia, were the victims of a vicious smear campaign – that they were agents of the Kaiser and Germany's General Ludendorff. A hard core of the Bolsheviks, the one tight minority party whose power base would be built on proletarian support, still clung doggedly to their policy of peace at any price. Following Lenin's auspicious return, many workers involved in armaments production, and thousands of soldiers and sailors, had attended his speeches, given from the balcony at Ksheshinskaya's mansion, only to come away with growing incredulity. Men like the colourful Kerensky and his assortment of ministers in the Provisional Government seemed to see things from the soldiers' point of view too – Germany must still be defeated to assure the honour of Russia, Tsarist or Socialist. Lenin's insistence on pulling out of the war appeared to reinforce the accusations that he was a German spy. Hadn't he accepted German money to pass through the enemy's territory in order to return and foist his dishonourable ideas upon his countrymen? And how did this Trotsky return? Was he too the recipient of German money?

The discontent was hammered home when one demonstration of wounded servicemen, many without limbs, passed along the Petrograd thoroughfares with banners proclaiming 'Our wounds deserve victory'. The hurt felt by servicemen was understandable. Since 1914 they had fought some hard and bloody battles; families were in mourning; millions were dead. Many men had begun to think of an early peace as the only solution to the problems of their wives and children back home. Yet seeing your fellow soldiers die under a hail of German bullets could in many cases feed the desire for victory against the foe. It would be this remaining spirit which the Provisional Government would hope to capitalize upon in the summer of 1917.

Although the bulk of the military rank and file came from the same stock as the workers and peasants, their political organization differed in some ways to that of their comrades in industry. Scattered throughout the country and across the front line in various regiments, their thirst for knowledge and enlightenment has been made obvious from their many outpourings of pleas and in letters to members of the Provisional Government, the Petrograd Soviet and political parties, which have been unearthed since the dissolution of the USSR. As an example of this, following the February revolution, even men stationed well away from the front still demonstrated a hearty solidarity with their trench-bound comrades who were facing the German onslaught. The workers of Petrograd, well schooled in the art of industrial strife, were closer to the source of Bolshevik pro-peace propaganda. Their strikes and disputes continued, and when it came to interrupting the production of armaments and goods for the war effort, this inevitably caused concern in army ranks. On 24 March 1917, the Garrison Soldiers' Committee at Tsarskoe Selo, only 15 miles away from the capital, showed their frustration in an appeal to Petrograd workers:

> Comrade workers! According to information in our posses-
> sion, work has still not resumed at several of Petrograd's plants
> and factories. Among the many reasons for this (the shortage of
> fuel, the simultaneous dismissal of a large number of experi-
> enced supervisors and others the workers disliked), your de-
> mands for very high payments for your work have been far
> from insignificant here. We know that you are right, comrades:
> the entire people groaned under the lash of the autocratic-
> capitalist regime, but in this year of great nationalist calamity,
> of war, then the salvation of the Homeland depends upon the
> productivity of the factories, their work cannot slacken or halt.
> It pains us, it pains us terribly, to think that you, whose blood
> has mixed with our soldier blood on the pavement of Petro-
> grad, to the firing of the Tsar's machine guns, have forgotten us
> so quickly . . . The enemy is just as close and just as dangerous,
> assembling his regiments for a crushing blow against Russia.
> Our defenders need bread to gain the strength to repulse the
> enemy, they need clothing to keep from freezing in the cold
> damp earth of the trench, they need weapons and ammunition
> to defend the homeland. Think about this, comrades.[4]

Among the political parties the Social Revolutionaries and the Mensheviks were pressing for an early end to the war with no contributions or annexations in favour of Germany. There was also a smaller Menshevik faction, led by George Plekha-nov, which sought Germany's defeat.

Plekhanov and Lenin had a long history together as revo-lutionaries, but following the split at the Second Congress of the Social Democratic Labour Party in 1903 which had created the two warring factions, the Bolsheviks and the Mensheviks, their paths diverged. Plekhanov remained as editor of the radical journal he and Lenin had brought into existence, *Iskra* (the Spark), a platform from which he would continue to attack Lenin's ideas. His arguments ran counter to many of Lenin's – for example, Plekhanov did not believe that a small group of dedicated revolutionaries could wrest power from the Tsar, and he rejected terrorism. Even as late as 28 October 1917, he wrote:

> No, our working class is far from ready to grasp political power with any advantage to itself and the country at large. To foist such a power upon it means to push it towards a great historical calamity which will prove the greatest tragedy for all Russia.[5]

As history has shown, when it came to political in-fighting, especially in 1917, Vladimir Illyich Lenin was the last person you wanted to cross swords with – his hatred of opposing theories to his own meticulously worked-out beliefs even extended to their authors. To Lenin, the term 'comrade' had little to do with the bourgeois notion of friendship. You were either on the Bolshevik bandwagon, or you were beneath its wheels; there was no room for kerbside commentators.

Plekhanov made every attempt to appeal to the workers as he believed that the new freedoms gained by the revolution could only be assured if Germany was defeated. The Bolsheviks stood out on a limb. Their stance at this time was summed up starkly by the British Ambassador, Sir George Buchanan:

> The Bolsheviks . . . were out and out 'Defeatists'. The war had to be brought to an end at any means and at any cost. The soldiers had to be induced by an organised propaganda to turn

their arms, not against their brothers in the enemy ranks, but against the reactionary bourgeois Governments of their own and other countries. For a Bolshevik there was no such thing as country or patriotism.[6]

Buchanan's bitter coda to his assessment fitted well the stance taken against Lenin and his party by Alexander Kerensky. But despite their lowly position in the Petrograd Soviet, it was the Bolsheviks whose flair for organization was having increasing success among the workers. For the advancement of their political agendas, the parties who met regularly at the Tauride Palace needed the working-class masses every bit as much as the industrial barons needed them to make profits.

Although the Russian revolution has, by its very nature, been trumpeted down the decades by subsequent Soviet chroniclers as the great 'proletarian' revolution – which the February revolution undoubtedly was – any writer scouring the mass of literature on the subject will eventually notice that the lives of the revolutionary leaders were not, in the main, an existence where one's hands were dirtied by honest toil. Lenin was a trained lawyer, so was Kerensky. The urbane Trotsky enjoyed a good education at his parents' expense in Odessa. Others were disaffected students with a laudable social conscience. None of this is to say that being a revolutionary theorist or activist was an easy option in Tsarist Russia. Far from it. Many revolutionary exiles from better-off families soon discovered what the words 'hard labour' meant when they arrived as exiles in Siberia. Yet to find real, blue-collar workers among the revolutionary intelligentsia who knew the rigours of the factory shift system, or the pull on your muscles behind the plough, one has to dig pretty deep. They existed, yet their individual stories have often been obscured behind the banners they carried.

Throughout Russia's race to become a credible industrial giant in the second half of the nineteenth century thousands of new businesses opened up in urban areas, many of the larger concerns relying on foreign expertise for their establishment. The textile industry saw hundreds of mill technicians and engineers leaving their native Lancashire to set up in Russia. Industry became an international crossroads in the land, with French concerns such as Renault, British construction and railway experts, American automobile designers and many electrical advisers who would assist in keeping public transport moving and the cities illuminated. With the war, foundries, metal and iron works became more important than ever. As an example of the growth of organization among the Russian urban working class, the history of the Putilov plant gives some insight. Although the Vyborg district on the northern banks of the Neva would always retain some of the most militant workers and Bolshevik supporters, Putilov often led the way when it came to making demands and striking. Not only was this plant the hub of the war effort – as indeed it would be under Stalin's rule – it was also a veritable college for revolutionaries. To have a massive, pliable workforce in one location working a shift system meant that the urban, industrial proletariat could be seen as a working, living mass, not just some theoretical page in a Marxist tract. Here was a keen and ready electorate for revolutionary theory and practice, and the union organizers and political cadres at Putilov were some of the most skilled in the revolution. In modern parlance, one could say that they 'walked the walk' as well as 'talking the talk'.

This massive complex still exists today as the Kirovsky Zavod (factory) named in honour of Sergei Kirov, the popular head of the Leningrad Communist Party from 1926 to 1934, reputedly murdered by Stalin. Although it employs a workforce which only represents just 30 per cent of that in 1917, this is still, at 10,000 people, one of modern-day St Petersburg's largest. From this massive site in the southern reaches of the city the many thousands of tanks, locomotives and ships which have seen the Soviet Union through revolution, civil war, the Second World War and the Cold War have rolled out, the product of decade after decade of political and economic pressure to meet the demands of war and Stalin's draconian Five Year Plans. Everything mechanical, from trucks to tractors and many household goods, has at one time been produced here, including the famous armour-clad trains ordered by Lenin for the Civil War, huge, iron behemoths sprouting guns and bearing such names as 'Victory or Death'.

In the twenty-first century, as a joint stock company, the factory continues to turn out turbines for the gas industry and products for construction, agriculture and transportation. Today the main administration building looks somewhat neglected and run down. Nearby you can still see a bronze bust of the site's famed strike leader and revolutionary organizer, Ivan Gaz. Halfway up the exterior walls of the building an elaborately-carved frieze runs along beneath the rusting window frames. It tells the story, in the style of Trajan's column in Rome, of the factory's immense influence on the Bolshevik revolution. Sadly, unlike its Roman counterpart, the Kirovsky frieze lacks the obvious durability of Italian marble. Bits of Lenin and his adoring proletariat are falling away, a somewhat poignant sign that this elaborate sculpting of Russian revolutionary history is being eroded by neglect.

Yet inside the Kirovsky Zavod building, on the first floor, the past is preserved in a large and fascinating museum spread over three rooms. In today's new, market-driven Russia, where the introduction of Bolshevik history at any conversational gathering of young Russians is usually greeted with a broad yawn, this respect for the past is heartening for a dewy-eyed western romantic. In western terms, it seems almost the equivalent to having a museum of militancy at Fords in Dagenham, or the old British Leyland plant, to celebrate the strike movements of the 1970s, complete with a statue of strike leader 'Red' Robbo.

The constantly changing history of the Putilov works goes back 200 years. In 1789 Russia was at war with Sweden. For the Russian Army, the manufacture and supply of ammunition was a constant problem. A small iron-casting foundry was set up on the island of Kotlin, close to the naval base at Kronstadt, but this became strategically unsuitable. In 1801 Tsar Paul I had the new Chugoliteiny (Cast Iron Foundry) established on the site which would become today's Kirovsky plant. He gave the job to an expert in the field of foundry work, an industrious Scotsman, Charles Gascoine, who had already established a similar foundry which he had run at Olonetsky, after his arrival in Russia in 1786. During the first ten years, what was produced there, with just under 400 workers, were munitions for the Russian Army and Navy. Soon the range of production broadened to include ironwork for St Petersburg's bridges, naval fixtures and fittings. The workforce steadily increased, but in 1824 disaster struck when the city suffered the greatest flood in its history and 150 Putilov workers drowned. The plant was all but destroyed and remained empty for over five years.

It came back to life as a venture overseen by the Russian Association of Miners. Russia had begun a serious expansion of her railway network and rails were needed, but even with the help of Nicholas I, the business floundered, and a British company, Richter Day & Co., took over. It seemed that the plant was cursed, as by 1864, still massively in debt, the British were turfed out and the Russian Government took it over.

Four years later, it was sold to Nikolai Putilov, who was just the man to make it work, being a good engineer and an able businessman. Putilov set about reorganizing production methods with great effect. The timing was right. Russian heavy industry was on the rise. He installed the first open-hearth furnace in Russia to produce steel and by 1874 the plant was turning out railway carriages as the range of products continued to expand. But in 1874 the worsening economic crisis in Russia caught up with Putilov and, with debts soaring, he appeared to be teetering on the brink of bankruptcy. It was to be a significant increase in military demands which saved him. When Putilov, much respected as the man who had brought Petrograd's heavy industry into the European big league, passed away in 1880, following his lead, the directors pressed on.

By the 1890s the economic crisis had receded, and the manufacture of artillery, gun carriages, ammunition and rolling stock for the railways soon led to massive expansion. Patrol boats and torpedo boats were built here for the Navy. By 1910 the factory had the largest single workforce in Russia, and one of the biggest in Europe.

Surprisingly, despite the history of militancy at the plant, Nikolai Putilov was not the archetypal nineteenth-century hard man to his workforce. The shift system in operation then seems rigidly austere today: workers worked a 12-hour day shift from 6.30 a.m. to 6.30 p.m., with no meal or lunch breaks; the night shift took over at 6.30 p.m. until 6.30 in the morning with the same conditions, and staff finished at 5 p.m. on Saturdays. There were minor rebellions in the plant under Putilov's rule, yet he had a healthy benevolent streak, and was a skilled mediator who could usually settle most disputes. Much of the agitation in the plant was instigated by the political struggles in Russia as a whole.

Legend has it that Putilov knew each worker by name. A

highly educated man himself, he also insisted that his work-force were educated. He established a college on the site for his workers, and one of the conditions of taking a job with the firm was that you accepted this opportunity for learning. This included not only the basics of reading, writing and arithmetic, but geometry, painting and technical education which would be valuable on the production line. Each successful student received a coveted education certificate. Although Putilov's rule only lasted 12 years, the plant retained his name well into the twentieth century. When the first revolution of 1905 broke out, sparked by a strike at the works, the banners carried by the workers were embroidered with the words 'In honour of Putilov'. The danger involved in striking or demonstrating under Tsarist rule is amply demonstrated by a poignant letter from a Putilov worker to his wife, written as he set off to join Father Gapon's tragic column en route for the Winter Palace on Bloody Sunday:

> Dearest Anya,
> If I don't come back alive please don't cry. I hope that you will be able to live without me and I hope that you will be able to go to the factory and find work to support the family. Take care of Vanya, and tell him, if I die, that I died as a victim, and for the happiness of the people. If I die, then I hope that in the end, this will bring you happiness.

In the years following Bloody Sunday the Putilov plant workers would strike on each anniversary of the infamous day, and troops would be sent to the site to keep order. There was a lull in political activity between 1905 and 1911, but by the time production rose to a peak in 1913–14, the workforce was as politically organized as ever. Conditions were no better; the hours were still long. There was no heating at the plant and workers often laboured in freezing conditions. In 1914 three shifts were introduced over a seven-day week to accommodate military production. As the First World War began the Putilov workers became some of the highest industrial earners in Russia. At this time a new government tactic sought to ward off any militancy – male strikers and activists were conscripted and sent to the front in exchange for war-weary soldiers, for whom a spell on the production line was infinitely preferable to life in the trenches. Unfortunately this probably caused more problems for the management as discontent on the shop floor began to rise as the death toll at the front increased. On 15 January 1917 the management posted an edict around the plant banning all meetings on the site. It had little effect.

Thus this huge, educated and skilled workforce would prove a major breeding ground for revolutionary activity. Many different movements and unions were founded here. The present museum's walls are covered with the portraits of men who would go on to be revolutionary commissars, military leaders and labour organizers. One of the first Marxist organizations was founded at Putilov, the Union for Freedom for the Working Class.

Anyone looking for those sometimes elusive, hands-on, blue-collar Bolsheviks and Mensheviks will find them here. It seems as if noone has been forgotten, no matter how detrimental their activity may have been to production. E.A. Klimanov, who led one of the plant's largest strikes in 1894, hangs alongside other revolutionary workers, such as Pola-tyev, who rose to be a deputy in the Third Duma from 1907 to 1912. Other faces look down, some fierce, others enigmatic: Gulbakin, Shulganov, Bodrov, Malinin and Grigori Zinoviev, a one-time Putilov union man. Many women worked at the plant, especially during the war years when male workers were sent to the front. One of their organizers, the beautiful A.K.

Kvanova, who lived through all of the USSR's hard times to the age of 75 before passing away in 1964, is commemorated. Mikhail Kalinin – a member of Lenin's cabinet in 1917, the man who had suggested freeing political prisoners from the Kresty prison in February 1917, and whose perspicacious behaviour towards Stalin after Lenin's death made him one of the few original Bolshevik survivors – worked at Putilov as a lathe operator. Not many lathe operators had a city named after them, as happened when Konigsberg became Kaliningrad following the Red Army's ousting of the Nazis there in 1945. His lathe still stands, polished to a fine shine, in a corner of the museum. Many other Bolsheviks, Mensheviks and Social Revolutionaries, whose contribution to the founding of the USSR looms large earned their humble living in these satanic mills. Their contribution to changing the world's political landscape for most of the twentieth century may have been eclipsed by the revolution's intellectual leadership, yet they are still remembered behind glass frames beneath the stark fluorescent lights. Anatoly Lunacharsky, destined to become the first Soviet Commissar for Education, devoted much of his skills as an orator in convincing the plant's workers to support the Bolsheviks' October Revolution.

The Putilov plant became a political barometer long before 1917. When the war broke out, none other than Nicholas II arrived in the works to spur on production. Lenin visited on three occasions. Putilov workers were some of the first to read *Pravda,* and among the first of Petrograd's workers to become Red Guard units. Many pictures of these men, armed to the teeth outside the Smolny Institute, are still on display.

So what was Lenin's attitude to these dedicated men?

Lenin enjoyed the company of workers, even more so when he returned to Petrograd. He may well have become the captain of the good ship 'Socialist Future', but he would broach no intransigence from even the most orderly trade union. Such was the case with the doyen of organized Russian labour, the Union of Railwaymen. Later in 1917, after the October Revolution this group had remained solidly opposed to a one-party state and had supported the remains of the Provisional Government, taking a stance against any violence threatened between socialists from the new government by taking over the railways. The Railmens' union, the *Vikzhel*, objected to orders from Lenin's 'usurper' government and threatened a national strike. Under pressure, with rumours of Kerensky marching on the city with an armed force bent on removing the Bolsheviks, Lenin compromised. But any amnesty he agreed to was soon forgotten once the Kerensky threat had been removed.

Some of the festivals enjoyed by Russian workers also irritated Lenin immensely. The summer festival celebrating the feast day of St Nicholas, known as the 'Nikola' festival, was accompanied usually by a day off work. Lenin's attitude to this seems brutal: 'We must get all the Chekas [Bolshevik police] up on their feet and shoot people who don't turn up for work because of the Nikola festival!'[7] As for celebrating the New Year and Christmas, if Lenin had had his way Santa's sleigh would have been downed in a hail of bullets and any strains of 'Auld Lang Syne' would have been accompanied by gunfire. It is a sad fact that this kind of bloodthirsty rhetoric coloured many of his outpourings in 1917.

Since Lenin's return his speeches concerning the war and his relentless onslaught against the Provisional Government had at best confused his close allies and at worse enraged a great number of soldiers and sailors. The sailors of the Second Baltic Fleet who had stood so smartly to attention at the Finland Station had, after hearing that Lenin's trip home was financed by Germany, issued a statement regretting their involvement in the auspicious occasion. Among the soldiers in the city a more drastic attitude prevailed. Regiments such as the Preobrazhensky, the Volinsky and the Moskovsky even considered arresting Lenin. Students demonstrated outside Ksheshinskaya's mansion, chanting for Lenin and his ilk to go back to Germany. With all this rumbling opposition, and a barrage of negative press attention, the Provisional Government became complacent. Lenin wasn't a threat after all. In the Petrograd Soviet, the soldiers declared all-out polemic war against the Leninists.

On 18 April Foreign Minister Pavel Milyukov confidently told the French Ambassador, Maurice Paleologue, that Lenin's speech to the Soviet the previous day was so extreme, clumsy and insolent that 'the hissing forced him to step down and leave. From this he will never recover.'[8] Lenin's delivery of his 'April Theses' both to the Soviet and in the pages of *Pravda* caused an uproar. Until these utterances, the grand debates at the Tauride Palace had been a series of diverse and lively dialogues between the Soviet, with all its radical factions, and the somewhat gentlemanly, upper-class, liberal leaders of the Provisional Government.

Lenin had no time for liberals, capitalists, bankers, businessmen or anyone else who claimed to aspire to revolution yet failed to grasp the nettle of his aims. To him, despite the February uprising and the blossoming spring of new freedoms in Russia, all that Messrs Kerensky, Lvov and the Mensheviks were doing was attempting to build their new society on the rotten foundations of the old. He told the meeting that the war could only be ended satisfactorily if capitalism itself could be eradicated. Under the call 'All Power To The Soviets' he demanded that the workers should control all the banks, and that all private estates should be confiscated and managed by peasant soviets. Land should be nationalized. Production and distribution should be taken over by the workers themselves. All this, he claimed, needed to take place on an international scale; there should be no conciliation or coalition with the Mensheviks. As for the Provisional Government, he vehemently dismissed it:

> The parliamentary-bourgeois republic restricts the independent political life of the masses, hinders their direct participation in the democratic upbuilding of the state from the bottom to the top. The Soviet of Workers' and Soldiers' Deputies does just the reverse.[9]

The wave of opposition to this political dynamite seemed to pose no problem for Lenin. Being shouted down in meetings, challenged in the press, these were all grist to his mill. When one of his oldest comrades, Kamenev, tackled him in the pages of *Pravda*, Lenin meticulously answered every one of Kamenev's concerns. He continued to defend his Theses against all comers. Slowly, the radical core of his ideas began to appeal. He had, as ever, shaken and stirred the body politic from its lethargy. Now it would be the job of the formidable Bolshevik propaganda machine to bring the errant workers, soldiers and sailors around to his way of thinking. It would not take long. Kerensky and Milyukov along with the rest of the Provisional Government had made the mistake made all too often by Lenin's opponents – they had underestimated his fighting capacity. For the time being, however, the political prizefighter would have several bloody bouts to face with a formidable and still popular opponent – Alexander Kerensky.

Prior to 1917, May Day had not been celebrated in Russia as it had in Europe. Nicholas, incarcerated at Tsarskoe Seloe, witnessed a new tradition springing to life as he wrote in his diary on 18 April:

> Abroad it's the 1st May today, so our blockheads decided to celebrate with street processions, musical choirs and red flags. Apparently they came right into the park and placed wreaths on the tomb. The weather changed for the worse during these celebrations, and thick wet snow started to fall! I went out for a walk at 3.45, when everything was over and the sun had come out. Worked for an hour and a half with Tatiana.[10] In the evening I started to read aloud to the children: *A Millionaire Girl.*[11]

If Nicholas had been in Petrograd he would have witnessed similar events on a much grander scale. A great symbolic occasion took place there when the population of the city turned out to bury the dead victims of the revolution. There was still slush on the pavements as a dramatic mass funeral took place of such dimension that many commentators had to agree that it outstripped any burial of a Tsar.

From six destinations throughout the city processions set out in the morning each bearing a number of red coffins, said to total 200 in all, and made their way to the Field of Mars by the Neva embankment. This wide open space had a long tradition of public gatherings, acting at one time as a kind of fairground where bear baiting, sports and other activities were popular attractions. At the end of the eighteenth century it had become popular as a place to drill troops – Tsar Paul I frequently paraded his Pavlovskiy Regiment there – but now the Field would take on a totally different aspect as a mass grave and the site of a memorial. Almost one million people filed past the graves during that grey, overcast day. Bands played the 'Marseillaise' repeatedly, and the chants for the dead, 'Eternal Memory', spontaneously rose from the crowd with great gravitas and dignity. Many regimental detachments paraded by, and the music which filled the day filtered through the corridors of the nearby British Embassy. At night the continuing spectacle was illuminated by searchlights. Maria Pavlova, the younger daughter of Nicholas's uncle the Grand Duke Pavel, saw the event from a different perspective through her drawing-room window:

> The ceremony was civil. For the first time the clergy did not participate in a Russian affair of state. And this parade of mourning served another purpose; it was a display of power on the part of the new government . . . The streets were carelessly cleaned. Crowds of idle, dissolute soldiers and sailors wandered continually about, while the well-dressed people who owned carriages and cars hid away in their homes. Police were not to be seen. Things ran themselves, and very badly.

This was not the way such witnesses as the correspondents of the western press saw it. Harold Williams summed up the occasion: 'The Stronghold of Old Russia has become the saluting battery of the New.' In line with her class, for Maria Pavlova the event was the source of more prosaic concern:

> Even those of our servants who had been in our service for many years, sometimes even for generations, were influenced by the new currents. They began to present demands, form committees. Few remained faithful to the masters who had in all times taken care of them, pensioned them in their old age, nursed them when they had been sick, and sent their children to school. Petrograd frightened me.[12]

She was right to be afraid. She would no longer be able to look out at the Field of Mars and see the Russia which her kind preferred. In subsequent years the site would contain the bodies of those killed in the October Revolution and the Civil War, and on the 40th anniversary of the revolution in 1957, the eternal flame was placed in the centre of the Field. It still burns there today.

On 24 April, the All-Russian Bolshevik Party Conference took place in Ksheshinskaya's mansion. In contrast to some of his earlier appearances, this time Lenin held court with confidence. His tireless repudiation of the Provisional Government and all its works, and his repeated hammering home of his 'April Theses' had taken effect. He had put paid to Stalin's transgressions regarding the war during his stewardship of *Pravda*. The majority of the Bolshevik delegates had now come around to Lenin's way of thinking, yet there remained some dissenting voices. Kalinin still raised Lenin's ire by continuing to push for a coalition with the Mensheviks, while Kamenev continued to lean bravely towards the idea of the bourgeois democratic state.

Lenin's cause was benefited significantly by the somewhat haughty self-assurance of the Provisional Government. Prior to the conference Foreign Minister Milyukov had issued a memorandum proclaiming on behalf of the Russian people that they would continue to support the Allies until Germany was defeated. He instructed all his Russian diplomats abroad to present this overconfident proclamation to their host governments, adding insult to injury by issuing the note on 18 April, May Day abroad, a day upon which thousands of Russian workers had demonstrated against the war. The workers and soldiers of the Petrograd Soviet were outraged. Despite a later amendment to the message which denied any notion that Russia wanted to annex territory or increase her world power, the damage had been done. Milyukov's behaviour confirmed Lenin's claims – that this old-style collection of landowners and capitalists were behaving as a separate government, bent on their own policy but with complete disregard for the Soviet. Confusion reigned at the front as soldiers learned of Milyukov's claim on their behalf. They were already suffering from low morale, and their government issuing such directives could only have one result – more anger and more disaffection. When Milyukov resigned as the Soviet's protest increased, Kerensky and the Premier, Prince Lvov, could see that the Soviet was the coming power, although as yet a power without authority. They made a pragmatic decision to ask the Soviet to join with the government as a coalition. But the vote went against the idea. On 1 May the War Minister, Guchkov, resigned.

At a meeting held by the Soviet on 4 May, many delegates noticed a new figure in the hall, although few knew who this intense, sharp-eyed, bearded character was. Yet Leon Trotsky wasted no time and was soon up on stage to speak. His message to the delegates echoed Lenin's: the workers should take their own power seriously; the ministers of the government could not be trusted.

Although the idea of coalition with the Provisional Government had been shelved, members of the Soviet outside the ranks of the Mensheviks and Bolsheviks agreed that they might at least take posts in the cabinet. The following day a new government, still headed by Prince Lvov as Premier, came into existence. It included some important changes:

Minister for War and the Admiralty: Alexander Kerensky (Social Revolutionary)
Foreign Minister: Mikhail Tereschenko (Cadet Party)
Justice Minister: Pavel Pereverzev (Socialist)

Minister for Posts & Telegraphs: Irakli Tsereteli (Menshevik)
Minister for Labour: Matvei Skobolev (Menshevik)
Minister for Food Supply: Alexei Peshekhonov (People's Socialist Party, *Trudoviks*)
Minister for Agriculture: Viktor Chernov (Social Revolutionary)

The most significant move in this reshuffle was that of Alexander Kerensky. To the non-Bolshevized sections of the military and the workers, and much of the peasantry in the countryside, Kerensky remained as the darling of the revolution. With his crew-cut hair and confident swagger, he seemed to embody the spirit of the uprising.

A British nurse who kept a diary, Florence Farmborough, was working with the Russian Army at the front when Kerensky came to prominence.

> I saw a picture of Kerensky this morning and was surprised to see how young he looked; clean-shaven, with an oval face, his appearance was striking in contrast with those heavily bewhiskered and bearded generals and politicians. One of our doctors, who had been a fellow undergraduate with him at St. Petersburg university at the beginning of the century, told us that he had a way with him which made even his tutors 'sit up and think'.[13]

Now he was about to fire a number of salvoes across the Bolshevik bows which would make the whole of Petrograd 'sit up and think'.

On 1 June 1,000 delegates arrived in the capital for the All-Russian Congress of Soviets, a gathering which would meet over three weeks to thrash out the future of the country. Of the 1,000 attending, only 105 were Bolsheviks. To many at the Congress, the figure of Lenin was still a mystery, although his legend went before him. As the first speaker, therefore, he was the focus of attention. He sparred with Kerensky over the suggestion that some capitalists should be locked up. Kerensky claimed that the idea of arresting people and imprisoning them simply for their economic position would liken the revolution to 'Asiatic despots'; Lenin's favourable comparison of Russia's revolution with that in France in 1792 brought the rejoinder from Kerensky that the French uprising ended 'in base imperialism'; and he went on to take a swing at Lenin's 'safe life in Switzerland'.

Over the weeks, the debates raged on, and despite the low percentage of Bolshevik delegates, more soldiers, sailors and workers began to follow their lead. Out in the countryside, the stark, no-nonsense appeal of Lenin's party was also having some effect. The Provisional Government's agricultural policy was all but stagnant and since April the peasants had taken to invading their masters' mansions, looting and pillaging; they had cut down timber, were grazing cattle on their former landlords' pastures and seizing farming equipment. There appeared to be no authority which could intervene.

Throughout this period the controversy of German assistance for Lenin and Trotsky's return had raged in Petrograd and beyond. Claims and counterclaims filled the newspapers. Whereas Lenin rode out the storm, Trotsky fought it tooth and nail. One right-wing paper, *Rech* (The Speech) ran a story that Trotsky had been given $10,000 by the Germans in New York to advance the revolution.[14] Trotsky issued a denunciation of this in Maxim Gorky's paper, *Novaya Zhizn* (The New Life) on 27 June, saying that he had never had even a tenth of that sum at his disposal at any time in his life, but that the émigrés in New York had collected a total of $310 of which $100 did come from German workers. The controversy over the 'German money' would run and run – and still does. The fact was, the exiles were back, and by the summer of 1917, compared to the political problems facing Russia, for Lenin and Trotsky this was but a flea bite.

The early summer inspired Kerensky to flex his muscles as War Minister. Ostentatiously he visited the western and south-western fronts, making sure that the newspapers back home reported his every move. He was pressing for a new offensive, a regrouping of the Russian forces, still believing that significant victories and advances could sway the workers to bring their support back behind the war. Aligning himself with General Alexeev, the Russian Chief of Staff, he used all his skills as an orator with the rank and file, and even donned a military uniform. But in many ways it was too late. Men were still deserting, still declaring 'Down with the War!' as they set out on their long march home. Kerensky and the generals had a hard task, yet for a while, he did seem to be having some effect. On 18 June General Brusilov pushed 31 Russian divisions forward on a 64km (40 mile) front with some success. General Kornilov, who had recently been in command of the Petrograd Garrison, led the Eighth Army, which attacked the Austrian Third Army, pushing it back some 32km (20 miles) with a renewed spirit. But by 6 July German reinforcements arrived, and within two weeks the whole Russian offensive had been pushed back even beyond its starting point.[15]

As Brusilov's offensive had pushed forward, the temperature of anti-war anger rose in Petrograd. A Bolshevik uprising was planned. The formidable sailors of the Baltic Fleet were summoned to the city. At the Putilov works the workers were printing leaflets demanding 'Down with the Government – All Power to the Soviets'. But the Provisional Government still had a residue of power. Rumours spread among the Bolshevik hierarchy on the night of 2 July that any planned insurrection would be put down by pro-government troops.

Lenin was exhausted. Despite all the political activity in the capital, he had gone on holiday with his friend Vladimir Bonch-Bruyevich in a Finnish village, Neivola. Given the news about the potential trouble brewing in Petrograd, Lenin knew he had to get back. His brief holiday was over.

As the talk of vigorous opposition by the government to any demonstration or insurrection spread throughout the city, the Bolsheviks pulled in their horns, and the proclamation announcing the uprising, to be printed in *Pravda* the following day, was withdrawn, the paper somewhat curiously being circulated the next morning with a blank front page. The Kronstadt sailors, however, 20,000 of them, had acted upon their orders and still arrived in Petrograd, assembling outside Bolshevik headquarters at Ksheshinskaya's house. Lenin was in attendance, angry at the way things had got out of hand in his absence. He had venomously castigated the comrades at headquarters, shouting, 'You ought to be given a good hiding for this!' The sailors were obviously ready for action, but the speech he gave to them from the balcony was not the expected fighting speech – instead he advocated a peaceful demonstration.

Anatoly Lunacharsky followed Lenin in addressing the sailors, and decided to lead them to the Tauride Palace. If nothing else, they would be a show of strength against the government. Yet despite the half-hearted attempt by the Bolsheviks to call off their planned demonstration, it was disregarded by many. As Red Kronstadt marched in columns through the city en route for the Tauride Palace, bent on 'saving the revolution', they were soon joined by throngs of demonstrators. Armed workers arrived at the Renault works where they confiscated new trucks which had just left the production line; minister's cars were commandeered. Once again, what looked like an armed uprising seemed to be running itself, with no organizational centre. Lenin knew it was too soon and too dangerous, yet it was still a demonstration of the spontaneous will of the proletariat.

The more demure and genteel citizenry of the city regarded all this with distaste and horror. On the banks of the Neva, at the British Embassy, close by the Troitskiy Bridge, the Ambassador's daughter, Meriel Buchanan, expressed the thoughts of the upper classes:

> Huge bands of workmen with rifles and fixed bayonets kept coming across the bridge. And a little after twelve three thousand of the Kronstadt sailors marched past the embassy, an endless stream of evil-looking men, armed with every kind of weapon, cheered by the soldiers in the Fortress, though the ordinary public in the streets shrank away at the sight of them. Looking at them, one wondered what the fate of Petrograd would be if these ruffians with their unshaven faces, their slouching walk, their utter brutality were to have the town at their mercy.[16]

Looting began, gunfire broke out. Someone along the Nevsky had taken a potshot at the sailors and within minutes they had replied with repeated volleys. 100 people died.

The bulk of the sailors arrived at the Tauride Palace late in the afternoon accompanied by a large crowd of workers and soldiers. When Viktor Chernov, the leader of the Socialist Revolutionaries, tried to address them a group of men from the mob abruptly arrested him and bundled him into a car. It seemed a random and unjustified act, but Chernov was a minister with the Provisional Government and deemed an enemy. The situation had turned ugly and Chernov may well have been killed had it not been for the intervention of Trotsky, who was unwittingly experiencing that same spontaneous mass action which had occurred during February whilst he was thousands of miles away. Apart from the slogan of the crowd, 'All Power to The Soviets', he did not like what he saw – Chernov had to be saved. Trotsky braved the mob, jumped onto the bonnet of the car and made a stirring conciliatory speech, ending with the words 'Those in favour of violence to Chernov raise their hands!' None were raised; the crowd was silent. Trotsky turned to Chernov: 'Citizen Chernov, you are free.'[17] Shaken, Chernov went back into the Palace with Trotsky. It had been a close-run thing.

Eventually the sailors, their fighting skills not entirely wanted after all, dispersed. Later in the evening, soldiers arrived from the 176th Reserve Regiment. Like the Kronstadt men, they too had come to defend the revolution and remained in the Palace grounds to guard the Soviet. During that night delegation after delegation entered the chamber demanding that the Soviet should take power. In the early hours of the morning, however, the beleaguered government ministers received news that the Volinsky Regiment, said to be loyal to the Provisional Government, had arrived from the front to protect them. The following day a disturbed Lenin confided in Trotsky that he thought they might both be shot.

In the right-wing press, the controversy over Lenin's German connections had reached a peak on 5 July. At the same time it seemed as if the Provisional Government had suddenly found a new strength and were closing in on the Bolsheviks – *Pravda*'s offices and the Ksheshinskaya mansion were both raided. When the following day, Prince Lvov threw in the in the towel as Prime Minister, warrants were immediately issued for the arrest of Lenin, Kamenev and Zinoviev. It was time for Lenin to disappear once again.

On 8 July Kerensky was given the ultimate power as he took his place. As Prime Minister he would waste no time – the riots and insurgency of the past few days were laid fairly and squarely at the Bolsheviks' door.

Lenin had considered surrendering himself to the authorities. He was no stranger to prison cells, and no doubt held such confidence in the turbulent political atmosphere that he might at least expect a shorter spell behind bars this time. In any case, if he was arrested and tried for all the perceived crimes the press were accusing him of, Lenin the lawyer, the brilliant master of polemics, might well be able to clear the air. But this time, giving himself up would play into Kerensky's hands. Time was of the essence – with the fiasco of his June offensive, the melodramatic Premier's ever-ascending star was suddenly falling.

Stalin's future father-in-law, Sergei Aliliuev, had just moved into a new flat with his wife Olga, a nurse. Stalin had been a lodger at their previous address and after preparing a new room for him, they were awaiting his arrival. It would be in this room that Lenin and Zinoviev would hide until they could escape from Petrograd. As an illustration of how unknown Lenin was visually, even after his much-publicized three months back in Russia, the military cadets sent to search for him at his previous address had no idea what he looked like and wrongly arrested a man who looked nothing like him.

But this visual anonymity could not easily be relied upon. Olga Aliliuev tried to disguise Lenin as a bandaged hospital patient, but he looked so ridiculous that the drastic step of shaving off his beard and moustache was the only answer. The razor-wielding barber who would lather up the father of communism was one Josef Stalin. He did a good job. Unless subsequent Soviet airbrushing has fooled us, the resulting passport photograph of the clean-shaven Lenin, complete with a youthful wig and a worker's cap, displays no evidence of any accidental razor nicks. With Lenin and Zinoviev was a metalworker, Nikolai Yemelyanov, who had a small house with a hayloft in the village of Razliv.

After a few days in the hayloft – not a moment of which was wasted, as Lenin wrote continuously – Yemelyanov suggested they move yet again, this time to a thatched hut alongside a hayfield. There was then a rare example of Lenin experiencing a little hands-on labour, as he and Zinoviev mucked in with Yemelyanov to mow the hay. This wasn't the only bit of physical work he would do on this trip. Zinoviev almost blew their cover whilst out hunting, having his gun confiscated by a gamekeeper, only extricating himself from the situation by pretending to be Finnish, and unable to understand Russian. Their time in the hut was depressing – the roof leaked and there were several downpours of rain; when it wasn't raining, they were all but eaten alive by mosquitoes.

It was time for another move. By August, kitted out with new toupees, new photographs and documents, their eventual destination would be Finland. Their journey, accompanied by Yemelyanov and two Finnish Bolsheviks, Alexander Shotman and Eino Rahja, was at times a fiasco. Lenin, the ultimate organizer, was disgusted with his hapless guides who, in the dead of night, managed to get the party lost in the woods, hadn't brought enough food for the journey, and even took them to the wrong village, but they eventually arrived, via various small hamlets, at the house of Emil Kaske, a Finnish factory worker. The following day Lenin donned the boiler suit of a locomotive fireman, and disguised as such, spent much of the trip across the border on the footplate, throwing wood into the firebox. It was a brilliant ruse. Once they had

boarded another train later in the day, Lenin, who had
adopted yet a different disguise, this time using a face mask
attached with theatrical spirit gum, suddenly discovered that
the adhesive was weakening, the premature removal of the
mask doing little to enhance his complexion. But the blotchy
Bolshevik leader's worries that his sore visage would attract
attention were unfounded.

His final hiding place would be just about as safe as a house
could be. Although there was a massive reward promised to
anyone who could bring Lenin in, he settled down in the
comfortable home of Helsinki's Chief of Police, Gustav Rovio,
another Bolshevik.

Trotsky had not been so lucky. He had, however, no qualms
about being arrested or imprisoned, even inviting it by writing
a letter to the Provisional Government supporting Lenin,
which finished with: 'You can have no grounds for exempting
me from the action of the decree by virtue of which Lenin,
Zinoviev and Kamenev are subject to arrest.'[18] He was soon
behind bars. Yet he was optimistic – as he told his sons, who
visited him in his cell, 'The real revolution is still to come.'

Kerensky's failed offensive had a number of unexpected
detrimental effects, widening the gulf between the Soviet and
the government, thereby playing right into Lenin's hand, and
spreading far greater demoralization among the troops and the
workers back home, the very opposite of his plans. Brusilov
had done his best, but despite his good reputation earned in the
early stages of the war, he was dismissed and substituted as
Commander-in-Chief by General Lavr Kornilov, a patrician
warrior characterized by the man he replaced as having 'the
heart of a lion and the brains of a lamb'. Kornilov demanded
the death penalty for all deserters. Kerensky agreed. This was
hardly going to improve morale. Although there had been a
decision in the German High Command not to attack the

Russians, this was now forgotten, and by before the end of August Russian morale would receive its final blow when General von Hutier's Eighth Army would storm into Riga on the Baltic coast.

Meantime, with Trotsky in jail and Lenin in Finland, feverishly completing yet another book, *State & Revolution,* Kerensky wrongly assumed that the danger from the left had been eradicated. *Pravda* and other seditious publications had been banned; all public demonstrations and marches were prohibited. From his cockpit in Finland, Lenin played yet another hand. If the slogan 'All Power To The Soviets' was such a sticking point, he would adjust his policies. Realizing that there could be no peaceful development of the revolution, he outlined the choices: on the one hand, a military dictatorship, on the other, 'the transfer of power into the hands of the proletariat supported by the poor peasantry to put into execution the programme of our party'. In Lenin's absence, the task of outlining this new form of words to the battered Bolsheviks fell to Josef Stalin.

For Kerensky, there was no choice at all, and now he suddenly faced another problem. The power he had given through promotion to Lavr Kornilov had gone to the stern General's head – he had requested 'all civil and military powers' to be placed in his hands. Kerensky, suspicious of the soldier's motives, refused, but when he told the General to give up his post, Kornilov also refused.

Everything which had happened since February, every new freedom, was suddenly under threat. With the ultra-reactionary Kornilov assembling his forces to march on Petrograd, the revolution was in danger, and only one force could save it – the Bolsheviks.

5

FROM CRISIS TO CONQUEST

Shock tactics were needed to grip the crowd
and force it to listen. Once, a bearded soldier in
an overcoat as stiff as tree-bark climbed the steps
of the Pushkin monument. Greeted by the usual
'Which division? Which unit?', he frowned angrily.
'What are you shouting about?' he yelled,
'I bet every third man of you has the Kaiser's photo in
his pocket – if anybody bothered to look. More than half
of you are spies! Who the hell are you anyway to
tell a Russian soldier to shut up?'
Konstantin Paustovksy (1892–1968), *In This Dawn*

Konstantin Paustovsky was 25 when the revolution came to
Moscow in 1917. The descendant of Ukranian Cossacks, he
was no stranger to hard work and had a variety of jobs before
he settled for the career of a journalist. Of the many descrip-

tions of Alexander Kerensky left by contemporary observers, Paustovsky's observations of the 'darling of the revolution' are sometimes overlooked. In August 1917 Kerensky's short career as Premier and War Minister was hanging by a taut thread – his offensive at the front had failed, and now General Kornilov was about to march on Petrograd. At this point Kerensky must have questioned his own powers of persuasion. Paustovsky leaves us in no doubt as to their nature:

> What he lacked in strength of ideas, he tried to make up for by pompous phrases, dramatic postures, grandiloquent but ill-timed gestures. Thus, standing on the parapets of trenches, he harangued the soldiers at the front, an incongruous figure but wholly unaware of it. One day, ripping off the epaulettes of an elderly, sick soldier, who refused to fight, he pointed imperiously to the east: 'Coward! Back to the rear! We will not shoot you – we leave that to your conscience!' he shouted in a tragic voice. He had tears in his eyes, the soldiers turned away, muttering and cursing . . . after a speech, he collapsed, sobbing, in his armchair and his ADC revived him with essence of valerian – he reeked of it like a nervous woman . . . in those days I believed that the smell of medicine was incompatible with the high calling of a popular tribune.[1]

He would need copious amounts of valerian to face the coming weeks. His options were stark. He could neither support Kornilov nor appeal to the Bolsheviks without surrendering his waning reputation and position. There was another possibility – he could bide his time and see if Kornilov could pull it off. If the aggressive General did bring order and stability back to Petrograd, then perhaps something of the revolution could be salvaged. Yet whatever might happen, any further attempts to keep elements of the more radical factions

in the government and the Soviet on his side would be doomed.
The Bolsheviks were still ostensibly banned from meeting,
although they held a conference in early August. The streets
were quieter not only because of the ban on demonstrations,
but because of the extremely warm August weather – it was
simply too hot to go out carrying banners.

The more rabid right-wingers in the Provisional Government had thrown their weight behind Kornilov, a fact which
verified all of Lenin's claims that this was an outdated rabble
of old-style gentry, capitalists and landowners. Kerensky had
been juggling too fast and too long; the balls were no longer in
the air; the workers could see the light.

Oleg Volokhov, 87, had some memories of the period. His
father was an engineer who had worked in Petrograd for a
British concern.

My father had been in the army but was working on the
machinery for the English company Thornton Mills. He had
always said that if Kornilov had succeeded and got to Petrograd without the Bolsheviks stopping him, then everyone
would have been in for a rough time. He would have strung
people up and tried to restore the old order. He would have
even arrested the men in the Duma – he disliked them as much
as the Bolsheviks. So in some ways, even if our family weren't
Bolshevik supporters at that time, it's easy to see why they
suddenly became much more popular in August and September
1917. They said the things my parents wanted to hear – that
they should have peace, run the factories for themselves, and do
away with the upper classes. The revolution caused a lot of
death and suffering, but if Kornilov had got his way, it would
have been far worse. I think that's what Lenin saw after
Kornilov's failure – an opportunity – that's why they pushed
ahead for what happened in October.[2]

Kornilov's plan was to disarm the regiments which had gone over to the revolution and destroy the Soviet. He ordered the Third Cavalry Corps back from the Rumanian front, with two Cossack divisions and the Caucasian Muslims of the Savage Division. Their orders were to assemble at the town of Velikie Luki, halfway between Moscow and Petrograd. It was hoped that, as Muslims, the Savage Division would have no qualms about shooting down Russians. The Petrograd Soviet had remained suspicious of Kornilov and for a short time, old differences were shelved as the Mensheviks, Bolsheviks, Social Revolutionaries and peasants joined together in a new grouping with the dramatic title 'The Committee for Struggle with Counter-Revolution'. The Soviet went about arming squads of Petrograd workers, while volunteers dug trenches and erected barricades. The armaments workers produced extra ammunition and arms in preparation for conflict. By now the angry sailors of Petrograd, who hadn't been paid for almost two months, were in a fighting mood.

But as Kornilov assembled his 'reliable' forces, the Bolsheviks were one step ahead – the railway workers went into action, blocking the lines which would bring the troops in.

The revolutionary role played by the ordinary Russian railwayman was crucial in 1917. In peace or war railways have always had a major strategic role. In Russia, especially after the failed revolution of 1905, they became an important conduit for the dissemination of revolutionary propaganda and literature. Between 1902 and 1911 6,600 more miles were built, with the state owning two-thirds of the infrastructure. Handbills, newspapers and other printed material produced in Petrograd and Moscow could easily be put onto trains, and distributed by politically active guards, drivers and porters at stations along the tracks. The Trans-Siberian railway, which extended 4,700 miles from the Sea of Japan to the Urals, employed over 7,000 workers along the route. Early in 1917, Alexander Kerensky had been involved in discussions with the Provisional Government to improve the running of the Trans-Siberian, which was crucial to the Allied war effort. The result was a request for foreign assistance. Just four days after the October Revolution, a party of 200 highly experienced American railroad men from St Paul in Minnesota were formed into the Russian Railway Service Corps (RRSC). Although they were in effect civilian employees, they were organized on a military basis and wore uniforms; they would spend the rest of the war and part of the Russian Civil War working on the Trans-Siberian. One of their senior officers was Benjamin Johnson, in whose extensive letters and diaries can be found an assessment of the Russian railwayman and his management:

> They are as fine a bunch of workmen as are found in the world. They are about 75% as efficient as our men, but are steady, good natured and very good workmen.

Johnson wasn't so keen on their management, however, finding them to be dishonest, incompetent and lazy:

> You have read stories and seen plays of comic opera South American armies with fifty generals and ten soldiers. The Russian way of running a railroad is along the same lines, and the comedy of the situation never appeals to the Russian railway officers. When it comes to morals for this office-holding class there is no such animal.[3]

Before 1763, the usual way of moving goods around Russia was by rivers and lakes, but even in the south of the country these were frozen for up to four months, and in the north for as long as six months. Russia's roads were inadequate, built with a layer of sand on top of earth, and with the thaw they turned into a morass of thick mud. The first hard-surfaced highway between St Petersburg and Moscow was not completed until 1834.

Russia's extensive railway system was built in the nineteenth century, like other national networks, by thousands of under-paid and underfed labourers. Prior to the abolition of serfdom in 1861, the workers building the Moscow–St Petersburg line, construction of which began in 1843, were little more than slaves. The 'contracting out' of 50,000 serfs by their masters as railway labourers is an example of how the peasant labouring classes were exploited by the landowners. It is true that some serfs managed to organize their own employment deal with the construction conglomerate, but their wages were totally in-adequate to sustain health and well-being.

The working day was set from sunrise to sunset, and this included all public holidays and Sundays. There was no leave and no reprieve from the Herculean task of moving mountains of earth, cutting through hills and laying rails. The one thing they could pray for was heavy rain – that at least stopped work. The conditions in which they were housed were often unfit for farm animals – malnutrition, epidemics of typhoid, scurvy and diarrhoea were common. Thousands never saw their home village again – the death toll was enormous – and those who complained or stepped out of line could be flogged. Yet those Tsarist engineers and officers in charge of this huge concern who harboured secret compassion for this pitiful army kept quiet. The main task was to impress the Tsar, and open the railway.

Russia's railway system was thus built on a grim, painful heritage. Whereas it had also relied heavily on the input of foreign expertise, investment and advice, the innovative nature of the Russian lower classes was often overlooked. The first two steam locomotives ever built in Russia were the work of two serf mechanics, E.A. Cherpanov and his son, M.E. Cherpanov, who worked in a factory at Perm province in the Urals. Unusually for serfs, their mechanical skill and ability earned them a trip to England where their mission was to study British steam road machines. Once back in Russia, this inventive, hard-working father-and-son team built two of their own locomotives between 1833 and 1835. The following year they designed and built a small railway connecting a mine to a factory, the 2-mile stretch being Russia's first steam railway.[4] Perversely the Cherpanovs' bosses at the factory chose to show disinterest in further locomotive building as they thought it unprofitable.

Because of Russia's industrial backwardness in the first half of the nineteenth century the only way to build a rail network was with foreign help. Charles Gascoine, the Scottish engineer who figures in the history of the Putilov works, helped to build a short tramway to transport industrial goods as early as 1788. When the main Russian lines such as the Moscow-St Petersburg were built, Britain supplied the rails, while the locomotives, staff and general advice all came from the USA.

By 1917 the All-Russian Union of Railroad Employees and Workers, known by its acronym as the *Vikzhel,* was one of Russia's most powerful labour organizations. Yet because of the far reaches of the track, unlike other such bodies in the factories of Petrograd and Moscow, the *Vikzhel's* membership was not concentrated in one area, so that their support for the Bolsheviks was not always unequivocal, as we shall see. They had, however, easily established their revolutionary credentials. Despite the extreme conditions they were working under, with hundreds of locomotives awaiting repair, fuel shortages and excessive military demands, they had nonetheless stood shoulder to shoulder and faced up to counter-revolution. To their credit, their less bloodthirsty attitude to violence seems to have differed to that of the language of some in the Soviets. For the Railwaymen, only a peaceful, multi-party socialist government would do.

As for the approach by rail of Kornilov's fearful Muslims, he had overlooked one salient fact: the Bolsheviks had Muslim workers of their own. A congress of Muslims had been meeting in Petrograd, and several brave delegates volunteered to go out to the Savage Division to expose the futility of Kornilov's mission. Twenty-seven miles from Petrograd, the train carrying Kornilov's Muslims was derailed by a bomb. Not far behind them in Luga, the men of the Third Cavalry Corps decided to call it a day. Bolshevik agitators and railway workers had blocked all the routes into Petrograd, with skilled mediators and speakers opening up long debates with the troops, telling them that rumours of riots in Petrograd were false, and that they were being duped into an unnecessary mission. The message to Kornilov's once-threatening horde was simple and direct: 'we're all comrades now'. It worked. The red flag was hoisted yet again.

As Russia's half-hearted war with the Kaiser lumbered on, the Germans could see ahead that their enemy's domestic plight offered great opportunities. By early September, they had captured the important harbour city of Riga on the Baltic coast. With the evacuation of the port by the Russian Army, the last shreds of morale in the ranks crumbled. It was a fearful situation for the people of Petrograd – the Germans were now less than a week's march away.

Meanwhile, Konstantin Paustovsky decided that autumn to visit his mother and sister on their dilapidated little farm near Chernobyl. He was wondering how the dramatic events in

Moscow and Petrograd were playing among the peasants. All through his journey the strength of the revolution seemed to remain undiminished. As he sailed along the River Dnieper in a scruffy little paddle steamer, the *Volodya,* he discovered it was:

> a conscientious little boat. Every now and then the Captain, a Ukranian with a grey moustache and a red ribbon on his chest, climbed onto the bridge, and grinning, shouted through to the engine room; 'Step on it, Volodya! Do your bit for the revolution!"

When he disembarked to catch a rickety horse-drawn cart to his mother's house, his suspicion that the uprising had fully embraced Russia's remote, hidden corners was confirmed.

> The driver, a little old man in a threadbare brown Ukranian cloak, kept asking me 'Begging your pardon, to be sure, isn't there any news from Moscow about when the general permit will come through?'
>
> 'What permit?'
>
> 'For us peasants to take the land and be the masters, and to stick it to all the big and little masters in the backside with our pitch-forks and send them to the devil's mother.'[5]

The old man must have been one of the more patient peasants, because in the countryside at large law and order had ceased to exist. Disturbances had broken out in Minsk, Mogilev and Pskov; cornfields, hay fields and forests were plundered; livestock roamed freely. It was not enough now for the peasants to evict their landlords from their mansions, their servants too being cruelly kicked out from the estates. Agricultural equipment was there for the taking, and buildings were being burned down. In the province of Ryasan it was reported that as many as five manor houses per day were being wilfully destroyed. Centuries of pent-up hatred and resentment were being unleashed in an orgy of uncontrolled violence.

Kerensky was out of his depth. He had lost control. Whatever the workers had gained during the euphoria of February now seemed to be under threat. It had been a hot summer, but as October loomed the winds off the Baltic became tinged with the dank promise of a hard winter. Clothing oneself adequately in the Russian winter can be a matter of life and death, yet now the clothing stores were empty. Those shops which were not damaged and still held window displays seemed totally incongruous, with nothing but wasp-waisted corsets, wigs, and collars for dogs, the customers for these, the rich, having long since given up the need for being fashionable or pampering pets. Another phenomenon, a result of the close proximity of the Germans, had developed on Petrograd's pavements, which was noted by an American occupant of the plush Astoria Hotel, the journalist Bessie Beatty, was that the middle classes were queuing for travel trunks. 'They feared to lose their peace, their comforts, and their lives. They feared to stay in Petrograd, and they feared equally to leave.'[6] They were clearly waiting for someone to come and sort the mess out, so that they could soon resume their pleasant lives – if the rabble could only be put back in their place. For working women, however, a tight corset would be no barrier to the freezing months ahead.

Ten English pounds would now buy you 280 rubles; cab fares had rocketed to 15 times their pre-war rate; trams still ran, but intermittently. So bad was the situation with food supplies that people were rising at three in the morning so that they could form queues just for bread and sugar. Those workers who relied on kerosene (paraffin) to heat their cramped apartments were also finding scant supplies. If one had enough money, there were still a few luxuries – some soldiers who had chocolate rations could sell these at a rate of 12 roubles to the pound.

Out in the country the harvest for 1917 had been a bad one so that grain was in short supply, making even the previously better-fed peasant life a bleak and rigorous struggle. Men desperate for tobacco were struggling to find supplies. From rural areas closer to the capital came daily reports of the looting of wine cellars and shops. Prisons were attacked. From the Provisional Government there was no response as food stocks dwindled.

At the front the soldiers had now given up fighting altogether. Hungry, dispirited and in many cases seriously ill, their only thoughts now were of peace and home. Riddled with lice, their uniforms falling apart, they faced the remnants of the officer corps with sullen anger, wondering if the wave of liberation they had felt after February was simply a dream. Agitators roamed the rank and file pressing for an immediate cessation of hostilities. Attempts were made to fraternize with the Germans. Soldiers were refusing to obey orders, whilst some exasperated officers who had dreamed of honour and glory committed suicide. Now the Bolsheviks seemed to make sense.

Kerensky was heading a third coalition government. Throughout the autumn various elections took place and in Moscow the Bolsheviks at last surged into a majority, followed by the Petrograd Soviet, whilst at the Kronstadt naval base the sailors gave the party massive support.

Trotsky, now a full-blooded Bolshevik with his Menshevik days well behind him, was released from prison, and on 25 September he was elected Chairman of the Petrograd Soviet. He wasted no time in organizing the Red Guards, a growing force of armed workers which had reached 20,000 members,[7] and forming the Committee for the defence of Petrograd.

The procrastination and inefficiency of the Provisional Government had brought Russia to a situation which, to many, seemed far worse than that which existed before the Tsar's abdication. Yet there seemed to be a growing inertia among the public. Turning out on the streets throughout the year had at first appeared to have achieved so much, yet many were now too tired, hungry or worried to bother. The danger of the old order creeping back seemed to be growing.

Lenin, still in hiding in Finland, desperately needed to get back, but his impatience for immediate and severe political action was still causing alarm in Petrograd. A request was made to the Central Committee to return but it was denied. Kerensky, in a last-minute move to salvage some kind of governmental order from the political wreckage, had formed a new five-man Directory. In addition, the Cadet Party, hated by the Bolsheviks for their right-wing leanings and parliamentary yearning, were still cohabiting with the Mensheviks and the Social Revolutionaries. With this situation, the Petrograd Soviet still faced a sizeable body of opposition, despite the Bolsheviks' growing success. Meanwhile Lenin's message to his party in Petrograd had been unequivocal and direct – the Bolsheviks should take power immediately. He would disregard the refusal to let him return, and go to Petrograd. By the first week of August the Petrograd Soviet of Soldiers and Workers Deputies had moved from the Tauride Palace to an equally grand location, the Smolny Institute. The Tauride, apparently, had suffered so much rough treatment from the unruly gatherings since February that it required redecorating.[8]

The revolution had dealt a fatal blow to the Smolny's original function as 'The Institute for Young Ladies of Noble Birth'. Completed in 1808 and designed by St Petersburg's legendary architect, Quarenghi, this sunshine-yellow ensemble graced by lofty white pillars was about to become the nerve centre of a new Russia.

In Finland, another of Lenin's farcical adventures in disguise began – this time it was a theatrical wig, a grey number which by all accounts added years to his appearance. In the company of the metalworker Eino Rahja, the staggered return journey across Finland via safe houses began. Eventually they caught a train with the coincidence that the locomotive driver was the same man for whom Lenin had acted as fireman during his escape from Petrograd.

He was soon in the city and in hiding at an apartment close to the Finland Station. As he was still officially persona non grata, he had to be vigilant. At the same time he set about devouring the city newspapers and every scrap of news he could glean from every political source. News was passed secretly to his closest comrades that he was back and needed urgently to address the Central Committee.

On 10 October in flat number 31 at 32 Naberezhnaya Street off the Karpovka Embankment,[9] just around the corner from the home of the great Russian bass singer, Fedor Ivanovich Chaliapin, members of the Bolshevik Central Committee finally faced their leader. With Lenin, they always expected something ground-breaking and dramatic. They would not be disappointed. But first there was a comic element to this gathering, for on his entry into the city Lenin had changed disguises once more, using yet another ridiculous hairpiece. This time his disguise was that of a Finnish Lutheran Minister.[10] As comrades Stalin, Trotsky, Kamenev, Zinoviev, Kollontai, Dzerzhinsky, Sverdlov, Uritzky, Bubnov, Lomov and Sokolnikov helped themselves to tea and biscuits, they found it hard to disguise their amusement as Lenin, in a suitably serious frame of mind, kept adjusting his wig which had come loose.[11]

He outlined the situation: the workers and soldiers were now squarely behind the Bolsheviks and the time for an armed take-over had arrived; a pan-European socialist revolution must surely follow; capitalism could be defeated. Zinoviev and Kamenev disagreed, urging caution, but Lenin's motion won the ballot by ten votes to two.[12]

The Committee met again at 13 Bolotnaya Street in the Vyborg district on 16 October, this time with representatives from Moscow, and a Military Revolutionary Committee was formed. Once again the cautious Kamenev and Zinoviev demonstrated how unsure they were that Lenin's plans could work, but again the vote went his way, with 4 members abstaining, 19 in favour and 2 against. All that remained now was the planning and the selection of the right moment.

There was no doubt that the workers had rushed to the Bolshevik cause – the party had steadfastly refused to sully itself by any collaboration with Kerensky's government. When Lenin had arrived back in Petrograd in April the Bolsheviks, with a membership of just 10,000, could not have hoped to control anything, but following the failure of Kornilov's plans, the party's membership had soared to 300,000. At the time of the February revolution, there were 300 Soviets – by October there were 900.[13]

It was three in the morning when Lenin set out to walk the darkened streets on the long trip back to his hiding place. A violent windswept rain had begun which blew his toupee off, plopping into the mud at the side of the road and needing a good wash when he arrived home.[14]

Lenin felt ill at ease. He knew that when the delegates from the meeting arrived back at the Smolny there was no guarantee that the rest of the party would see things his way. All his letters, notes and written instructions could not match the power of his persuasion in the flesh. He needed to be able to address the party. Once again, he had been away from the action for some time – many people hadn't seen him since early July. But although he remained frustrated at the lack of a summons to attend the Soviet's sessions, he need not have worried too much. The Military Revolutionary Committee, with Trotsky's steady hand at the helm, was indeed planning the uprising. Yet for Lenin, they still lacked urgency. He sent pleas and notes to the Smolny. They must act and soon.

The Provisional Government had been buzzing with rumours about an attempted coup, yet at the cabinet meeting of 16 October they displayed no alarm. The story had been luridly run in the newspapers over the preceding week so Kerensky imagined that the Bolsheviks, without the total secrecy needed to pull off such a move, had lost the element of surprise. Cockily, he told Sir George Buchanan, the British Ambassador, 'I only wish they would come out, then I will put them down.'

On Saturday, 22 October the staff in the British embassy in Petrograd had been surprised when a party of ten Russian military cadets arrived with the message that there was trouble brewing with the Bolsheviks and that they had been ordered to protect the embassy. The Ambassador didn't take this too seriously – but with typical British hospitality the ladies of the embassy found them beds. Within less than a week they would understand why they were there.

Then, on 24 October the disturbing news came in that Kerensky was already organizing resistance. At 5 a.m. that morning he had sent military cadets in to smash the typeset pages of the Bolshevik press and seal their offices. The bridges along the Neva had been raised, preventing workers from crossing. This concerned Lenin, but Trotsky, the wily strategist, saw it all as an exciting opportunity – it would give any uprising the nature of a defensive reaction rather than that of aggression. Every minute counted now and Lenin had no choice but to throw caution to the wind and risk going to the Smolny. Together with his worker companion Eino Rahja he set out (this time disguised as some kind of injury victim with a bandage wrapped around his head) by tram across the city. They sneaked into the Institute on forged passes and made for room number 71. At last he was face to face with his comrades. Trotsky and Stalin gave him a full update on the situation. Now he could push and cajole the Committee into accelerated action. A new Soviet Russia was but hours away.

By midday on 24 October Bolshevik forces had ripped off the government seals on the doors of Bolshevik newspapers and soon the presses were back in action. Armed squads of workers from the Putilov plant were making their way into town. Trotsky and the Military Revolutionary Committee (now known as 'Milvrekom') had taken up the gauntlet thrown down when Kerensky raised the Neva bridges and shut down the Bolshevik presses. The Red Guards were massing with special orders to take over the telephone exchange, power stations, railway stations and the State bank that night. Kerensky and his ministers had fled to the Winter Palace, he still vainly hoping for support from the front. After all his dealings with the soldiers of Russia, with his impassioned, histrionic pleas at the trenches and elsewhere, all he could muster now in defence of the remnants of the Provisional Government were a few war invalids, their unfortunate commander only had one leg. The force was completed by women soldiers, a mixed bunch of Cossacks, some cadets and military cyclists.[15] But Kerensky was confident enough, as were the upper classes.

All ears had been cocked for any further news of the planned insurrection, and during the afternoon of the 24th Trotsky was met at the Smolny by a deputation from Petrograd's City Hall.

On behalf of the Mayor, they wanted to know, was this rebellion about to happen or not? Trotsky pulled no punches and told them that it was, in fact, happening as they spoke, and was well under way. The mystified delegation left the Institute, probably imagining that Trotsky was bluffing. In the streets outside there seemed to be little sign that any kind of coup was going on.

Many other members of the bourgeoisie had come to the conclusion that all talk of an uprising was yet more hot Bolshevik air. It hadn't happened, and as far as they could see, it wasn't going to happen. That night they would confidently dress up and go out. At the Alexandrinskiy Theatre *The Death of Ivan The Terrible* by Tolstoy did good business. At the Marinskiy, Chaliapin packed them in with *Boris Godunov*. A number of bars, cinemas and clubs had crackled back into action. Those who did not have to get up in the early hours to queue for bread were now happily making their reservations for the Restaurant de Paris, oblivious to the fact that this was probably the last glimmer of privilege many of them would experience for years to come.

The opening of the Second Congress of Soviets at the Smolny was due to take place on 25 October. With the Bolsheviks now in the majority, Lenin and Trotsky felt assured that whatever they were going to achieve during the preceding night would go down well at the Congress. In any case, a successful coup would be presented as a fait accompli – there would be no turning back.

Considering all the subsequent glorification of 24–25 October 1917 by generations of Soviet spin doctors, the coup itself was hardly one of clockwork precision and planning. The one man who had his finger on the pulse was Trotsky, whose crucial involvement would, like the images of him in Soviet photographs, be carefully airbrushed out in later years. Lenin had been the argumentative instigator, but even on the eve of it he had little idea of what was happening, or how. An example of his comparative estrangement to events is a report that when he and Rahja caught their tram for the Smolny that night Lenin decided to talk to the conductress. She obviously thought this bandaged man with suspect grey hair and a worker's cap was well out of touch and seemed amazed by his questions, offering the retort, 'What kind of worker *are* you if you don't know there's going to be a revolution? We're going to kick the bosses out!'[16]

It all seemed to take place in a completely different manner to the February uprising, with all the main moves being made under cover of darkness. The large crowds of people of February weren't there, by this time many being content to simply observe rather than take part. Yet such events do not take place without drama. As darkness fell on 24 October, Kerensky's ministers settled down for an uneasy night in the Winter Palace. Soon it began. Armed workers stormed into the banks, the post office, the telephone exchange, railway stations and other government buildings. Taking control seemed almost effortless and there was little resistance. Sailors and Red Guards surrounded the Winter Palace. Kerensky had made it in the company of another minister to military headquarters, hoping that he would be present for the arrival of his reinforcements.

In the darkness on the River Neva another drama had taken place. By October 1917 the Russian Navy had reflected most aspects of the revolution ashore. Ships were no longer run by their captains unless they had the permission of the ship's committee. On the cruiser *Aurora*, Engineer Petty Officer Andrey Nicolaevich Zlatorgorskiy, Able Seaman Tomifei Ivanovitch Lipatov, Acting Commodore Evdokim Pavlovitch and the man who would be *Aurora's* first commissar, Alexander

Victorovich Belishev, had been forced into some hard bargaining with the ship's master, Captain Ericsson. As part of Milvrekom's strategy for the night, the *Aurora* had been ordered to sail up the Neva to a mooring by the Nicholas Bridge, opposite the Winter Palace. The harassed Captain told the men that he felt unsure of the soundings in that part of the river and feared that the ship would be grounded. His relationship with his Bolshevik crew was already hanging by a thread, but the sailors refused to accept his reticence to act, lowered boats and rowed up the Neva, taking soundings as they went. Once they had established that the cruiser could make it to the Nicholas Bridge, they informed Ericsson that if he wouldn't take the vessel there, then they would. It was the last major act in his naval career, for once the vessel was in position, he resigned from the Navy. In the Winter Palace the tension was growing. Staff and ministers looked out of the windows where they could see the *Aurora,* her guns trained in their direction. Outside in the Palace Square Bolshevik armoured cars, artillery and machine guns had been assembled. An ultimatum was sent to the Provisional Government telling them they had twenty minutes to surrender. The ministers ignored it.

Confusion has always surrounded which guns fired which shells across the Neva. One report states that at some time after 8 p.m. a loud retort was heard from across the river, followed by another – yet there seemed to be no explosions, no target hit. Everyone thought that the menacing cruiser had opened fire, but the shots were blanks, fired from the guns at the Peter & Paul Fortress. They were enough, however, to start an intense exchange of gunfire across the Palace Square between the besieged government defenders and the Red Guard detachments. What appears to be the case is that the *Aurora* had been instructed that, on the appearance of a red signal lamp from the Peter & Paul fortress, she should open fire. When the men at the fortress couldn't find a red lamp, a purple flare was fired instead. It was at sometime between 9.30 and 10 p.m. (this varies) that the legendary shot from the *Aurora* is said to have smashed into the corridor at the Palace. The fact is shells did hit the Winter Palace, although little damage was done. In some versions of events this is said to have happened at 11 p.m. and the culprits were at the Peter & Paul Fortress.

Soviet history and Sergei Eisenstein's superb cinematic storytelling in films like his 1927 epic, *October,* have for decades obscured what really happened, but the general view is that the *Aurora,* which was fresh out of dry dock, was only carrying blanks at the time.

Soon, Bolshevik workers had lowered the Troitskiy Bridge and traffic was flowing again. In the great hall of the Smolny the Second Congress was assembling – workers from Moscow, workers from Petrograd, peasants, soldiers, sailors – the air thick with smoke and the stale smell of heavy overcoats and muddy boots. There was an uneasy air of anticipation. Soon enough, when everyone eventually arrived, it would be time to break the dramatic news of the coup.

During the night, as events unfolded in the darkened city, Lenin and Trotsky attempted to snatch some much needed sleep in a room close to the meeting hall. Earlier in the day, Trotsky had asked Kamenev for a cigarette, but after three puffs he fainted – it had been 48 hours since he had eaten anything. The two men turned out the lights and settled down on a blanket spread on the floor, their heads resting on pillows, with an old carpet covering them. Sleep, with the culmination of their life's work taking place outside, would not come easy. No two toddlers on Christmas Eve could have struggled more to drift off. Lenin had surrendered any traits of romanticism in his life to his revolutionary cause. He couldn't listen to music –

not that he didn't love it, it was too much of a distraction – and had given up his hobby of reading Latin for the same reason. Yet this night, lying in the darkness, he allowed the iron curtain of his self-control to rise a little, and quizzed Trotsky about how he had organized the sailors and the workers. Dim flickers of light danced across the ceiling as cars came and went in the busy streets below. Something almost emotional came into his spoken thoughts. 'What a wonderful sight,' he murmured, 'a worker with a rifle, side by side with a soldier, standing before a street fire . . . at last we have brought the worker and the soldier together.'

At the Winter Palace, things were moving at a new pace, where N.I. Podvoysky[17] was one of the men in charge of the Bolshevik forces. As the guns roared over the Neva at the Peter & Paul Fortress, and a shell found its target, Podvoysky later recalled:

> Taking advantage of that, the sailors, Red Guards and soldiers rushed forward . . . the guns from the fortress fell silent, and the dry, unending rattle of machine guns was drowned out by the continuous triumphant shouts of 'Hurrah!'[18]

Already Milvrekom had handbills rolling off the presses, announcing that 'The Provisional Government is Deposed' and ending with 'LONG LIVE THE REVOLUTION OF WORKMEN, SOLDIERS AND PEASANTS!'

In the early hours of the 25th, the Bolshevik forces had entered the Winter Palace, led by a former Tsarist officer, Vladimir Antonov-Ovseenko, who had been under sentence of death since 1905 and whose military experience was supplemented by his journalistic work as editor of *Slovo* (Our Word).

An eager cadet approached one of the ministers, Kishkin, and asked him if they should 'fight to the last man'. Kishkin told him it was useless. 'Tell them that we want no bloodshed, that we yield to force, that we surrender.'

Soon, the captured ministers, now prisoners, were being marched across the bridge to occupy the cells at the Peter & Paul Fortress. Kerensky was not among them. He had planned to escape Petrograd and travel to Tosno, where he hoped to rally troops to march on Petrograd, still believing that the coup could be put down. He needed a vehicle, but the Bolsheviks had removed all the distributors from the cars in the government's motor pool. Unable to go himself, he sent out an envoy to look for a car. The first choice for this unusual request was the Provisional Government's cabinet secretary, Vladimir Nabokov, father of the novelist-to-be who would give the world *Lolita*. Nabokov had to leave his bath to tell Kerensky's desperate ensign that his car was unsuitable. He then tried the Italian embassy, but they refused. Eventually the Americans came to the rescue with a shiny new Pierce Arrow which belonged to the US embassy's Military Attaché, E. Francis Bigg. After several false starts as the driver lost his way, Kerensky was on his way out of Petrograd.

In somewhat premature speeches Trotsky and Lenin had announced to the delegates at the Smolny that the Provisional Government was overthrown and that the insurrection was a success. It was hardly so at that moment, but the sight of Lenin after all this time resulted in a long, loud ovation. Although Lenin had not been keen for the coup to take place at the same time as the Congress, the timing had been Trotsky's idea. He knew that with such a grand gathering of all the proletariat's representatives under one roof on the same night an armed uprising was taking place, that the seizure of power would look to all the world to be an act of the workers. Thus it would always be referred to as the 'proletarian' revolution, a revolution 'from below'. That had indeed been the case in February –

but what about October? The fact that a great number of the Congress delegates had little idea of what was going on did not matter to the Bolshevik leadership. Arguments and disbelief would rage throughout the next few hours. The SRs and the Democrats were appalled. An Army captain called Kharash rose to his feet, shouting indignantly, 'The political hypocrites who control this congress told us we were to settle the question of power – and it is being settled behind our backs, before the congress opens! Blows are being struck against the Winter Palace, and it is by such blows that the nails are being driven into the coffin of the political party which has risked such an adventure!'[19] Moderates, what few were there to oppose the Bolsheviks, left the hall in disgust as Trotsky roared after them 'Go to where you belong – in the dustbin of history!'

When the soldiers and Red Guards had entered the Winter Palace, many were amazed at witnessing first hand the sheer opulence in which their monarchy had lived. The entry of an ordinary worker into the throne room in any other circumstances would have been unimaginable. Yet there they all stood beneath the glittering chandeliers, in the halls, the palatial rooms, the corridors, aghast at the conspicuous wealth their rulers had possessed. Only the experience of Howard Carter, stumbling into the tomb of Tutankhamun five years later could match these revelations. And now, as many men imagined, all this was theirs. Thankfully for future generations, most of the more valuable works of art had been removed and hidden in a secret location a month earlier.

Tapestries were removed from the walls. John Reed recalled: 'one man went strutting around with a bronze clock perched on his shoulder; another found a plume of ostrich feathers, which he stuck in his hat.' Hadn't Lenin always said that the rich were thieves and that the people should 'steal back the stolen'? However, Bolshevik discipline snapped into action as the more responsible soldiers and Red Guard leaders suddenly realized their responsibility. Cries of 'Stop! Put everything back! Property of the People!' began to ring out. Squads of determined soldiers and workers formed into groups by the exits, checking every man who left, even ordering them to empty their pockets. The loot piled up on the tables and on the floor as the crestfallen looters filed past leaving bars of soap, bottles of ink, daggers, clothes, blankets and bed sheets.[20] Their pleas were disregarded. As for the boy soldiers, the *yunker* cadets who had willingly sought to defend the palace and the Provisional Government 'to the last man', they were made to surrender their arms with the question: 'Will you take up arms against the people any more?' With the answer 'No', they were set free.

Party discipline broke down, however, when a number of Red Guards and soldiers managed to find the Winter Palace's well-stocked wine cellar. The coming days would see many of them finishing off a rare vintage, straight from the bottle neck, as they sat around the Palace Square in groups. Alcohol was a growing problem which would not go unnoticed at the Smolny.

As for the Women's Battalion who had been involved in guarding the ministers, lurid reports were soon issued that some had been thrown from the Palace windows with the remainder being arrested and taken to the barracks of the Pavlovsky Regiment. There it was claimed that most of them had been raped, and many had committed suicide. A subsequent commission of enquiry visited the girl soldiers' headquarters at Levashovo to try and discover the truth. Dr Mandelbaum, a member of the commission reported to the City Duma that, following enquiries, it had been established that none of the women were thrown from the windows, three had in fact been violated, and one had committed suicide.[21]

In Moscow, the Bolshevik takeover was not to be such an easy ride. The Menshevik and SR leaders in the City Duma organized what came to be known as a 'White Guard'. Five days of bitter fighting would be the result, with many tragic deaths, compared to Trotsky's claim in Petrograd that the events in the capital resulted in 'only five casualties'.

Over on the Russian front, the news of the coup was met by some soldiers with further confusion. Writing in her diary, Red Cross nurse Florence Farmborough probably demonstrated the gulf of misunderstanding which still existed between the drama of Petrograd and the tragedy of the trenches:

> Friday, 27th October. There has been a big uprising of the *Bolsheviki* in Petrograd. A telegram has come containing the news that some members of the Provisional Government have been arrested by the rioters and that their so-called 'Socialist Organisation' intends to overthrow the Government and take power into its own hands. It seems that the man Lenin, who, with his accomplice, Trotsky, had been worsted in July by Kerensky's supporters, had reappeared and assumed complete control of the Organisation. Will Kerensky prove strong enough to withstand him? If not, a civil war will be inevitable!

Later that night Florence's unit was visited by the head doctor who told the assembled soldiers that he 'assured them of his complete faith in their loyalty'. The men felt that they should ask questions:

> One soldier, with a fine, open face, affirmed that he spoke on behalf of all his comrades. 'We are *malogramotnie* (half-educated),' he said, 'and they tell us that we are free men, but we do

not know what this freedom means or how we can use it. We are unable to decide what is best for us . . . But what we want is *peace*. They say that England and France can carry on the war for another ten or fifteen years; but we, in Russia, cannot. Russia must have peace.' *'Da! Da!'* assented the soldiers. *'Nam nuczno mir!* (We need peace).' '*Mir!* . . . *mir* . . . *preczde vsevo!* (Peace above all else!).'[22]

Peace, above all else, would be the first item on Lenin's agenda now that the coup was completed. This had been the people's slogan; 'Peace, Land and Bread'. The first two desires could flow from Lenin's busy pen. Bread, however, would be another problem, one of many the newly victorious Bolsheviks were about to face.

6

POWER AND DOMINION

Hell and damnation,
Life is such fun
With a ragged greatcoat
And a Jerry gun!

To smoke the nobs out of their holes,
We'll light a fire through all the world,
A bloody fire through all the world –
Lord, bless our souls!

Alexander Blok (1880–1921),
The Twelve

Lenin's first words to the Congress of Soviets on 26 October met with tumultuous applause: 'We shall now proceed to construct the Socialist order.'

Outside on the streets things seemed reasonably normal.

The trams were running. Shabby women, as usual, lined up outside the shops. Those who had work to do had slept through the night, risen early and gone to their workplaces. In the factories victorious meetings were held. At strategic points along the Nevsky and Liteiny, outside the railway stations, hotels and the banks, Red Guard squads stood around their braziers in groups, smoking and chewing sunflower seeds. News vendors were doing a brisk trade, and today the papers would have much to say – outrage, disgust, horror. As the news of the coup spread, the workers were now legitimately anticipating the final settlement of their cause – peace, land and bread.

One of Lenin's early critics had said to him, 'You can write the finest laws down on paper – but who will enforce them?' It was a valid question. Between February and October Russia had become a wild frontier, with no subordinate structure since the fall of the Tsar.

Vladimir Ivanovich Vryakov was born in Petrograd on 3 February 1920. In his teens, he had often discussed the aftermath of the revolution with his father, who worked as a bricklayer.

My father was a Bolshevik; not an important man, just an ordinary party member. He kept it secret from his boss. He said it took Lenin a long, long time to sort things out after October 1917. The country was like a chicken with its head chopped off. A lot of people, because there was no law, thought that they could do just what they liked. And they did. Robbery, looting, all kinds of things went on. It was because everyone was living just one day at a time. Even after October, when the country should have begun to settle down, no-one could get on with the job of running things properly, because there were so many threats from both inside Russia – Kerensky, Kornilov and that crowd, and from outside, including you, the British. That's the history I learned at school – that no-one wanted us to succeed. We always seemed to be under threat from somebody who wanted the 'old times' back. That's why we felt so committed in the Red Army. And you can tell how bad things were when Lenin came to power, because the bread ration during the blockade of Leningrad in the 40s was still double what they got in 1917.[1]

The administrative structure, which had run the Romanov Empire, had disintegrated, both in the border nationalities and the provinces. Replacing a functioning social system which had evolved over several centuries, no matter how loathsome it had been to the peasants and workers, with an efficient new infrastructure was going to be a mammoth task. All their lives Lenin and Trotsky had written, debated and theorized. They had studied Karl Marx, formulated plans of action. Yet Lenin's hopes for communism hinged on a further dimension to his dreams – that of Russia inspiring a pan-European socialist uprising. If this happened, then Russia would be the centre of a new, peaceful brotherhood, but many of the wise revolutionary elders, such as Plekhanov, held a more realistic view.

Contrary to what many people thought, the Bolsheviks at this time were not totally in favour of one-party rule. They favoured a Constituent Assembly, but whatever that body might comprise, it would not be allowed to oppose the power of the Soviets. The new urban working-class consciousness which had developed throughout 1917 had brought them to power, but across the vast expanse of Russia, beyond the cities, the party's influence was far from solid, for the Social Revolutionaries held sway with the peasants.

Armed with only his brain and his pen, Lenin at least made

Rasputin. The translation reads 'Nobody knows
what's going to happen to us in the morning.'

Vladimir Ilich Ulyanov, better known as Lenin.
1920s Communist propaganda poster.

Lenin's Office in
the Smolny Institute.

The ballerina Ksheshinskaya, whose Petrograd mansion was commandeered by the Bolsheviks as their headquarters.

Ksheshinskaya's house, commandeered as Bolshevik HQ in 1917. Lenin gave speeches to the crowds from the balcony.

Part of the revolutionary frieze on the old Putilov works in St Petersburg.

Putilov workers demonstrating, led by the factory band, 1917.

РАБОЧИЕ-ПУТИЛОВЦЫ ПЕРЕД ВЫХОДОМ НА ДЕМОНСТРАЦИЮ
18 ИЮНЯ 1917 г.

В этот день на улицы Петрограда вышло около
полумиллиона человек. Рабочие и солдаты, возмущенные
продолжавшейся империалистической политикой Временного
правительства, вышли на демонстрацию с требованием передачи
власти Советам. Путиловцы шли в первых рядах демонстрантов

Young workers at the Petrograd Putilov works with the first edition of *Pravda*.

Magazine cover, Petrograd 1917, showing Alexander Kerensky,
who reigned briefly as the 'darling of the revolution'.

Shopping in Petrograd, 1917.

Red Guards distributing bread in Petrograd, 1917.

The cruiser *Aurora*, star of the revolution.

Helena Matveievna Krapivina, born 1912; Vladimir Abromovich Katz, born 1910; Vavara Vassilievna, born 1913; Prince Andrey Gagarin; Maria Mikhailovna Alexandrovna, born 1915; Nina Petrovna Fedorova & Maria Timoferevna Schlegova. Veterans of the Siege of Leningrad: L–R Vladimir Ivanovich Vuryakov, Antonina Alexeyvna Jurina, Vladimir Fransevich Grunwald, Olga Ivanovna Balunova; Old Communists demonstrating on Victory Day, St Petersburg 2004.

an early start. He drafted the Decree on Peace, which invited all the powers in the war to declare an armistice and open peace talks. Hot on the heels of this came the Decree on Land, which proclaimed the end of private ownership of land except for smaller peasant and Cossack holdings. In this he had stolen a march on the Social Revolutionaries. Lenin had hijacked many of their ideas, the very campaigning concepts they had established throughout the years of struggle. Radical though they were, the cautious SRs had not sought to settle the land problem without the measure being sanctioned by a future Constituent Assembly. During the period in 1917 of the Provisional Government, the SR's leader, Viktor Chernov, had as Minister of Agriculture proposed no less than 12 bills on behalf of the peasants, but none of them had become law before Lenin's October coup. Therefore his move, taking the SRs' land policies word for word and issuing them under his party's banner, would have the effect in the countryside of uniting the peasants behind the Bolsheviks. What the decree advocated, however, had already been taking place in the countryside for some months. It also seemed possible that once the peasants on smaller holdings had finally settled who would get which parcel of land, human nature would dictate that they would become commercially competitive with one another. Any peasant entrepreneurship would in later years play into the state's hands and enable the Soviets to impose their will to stamp out any small-scale profiteering and introduce a state-run collective system.

Lenin's land decree split the SRs down the middle, with their left wing joining the Soviet Government.

Now they had the power to form a government, the question was – what to call it – and would there be 'ministers'?

Trotsky recalled the quick, off-the-cuff decision:

'What shall we call them?' asks Lenin, thinking aloud.

'Anything but ministers – that's such a vile, hackneyed word.'

'We might call them commissaries,' I suggest, 'but there are too many commissaries just now. Perhaps "supreme commissaries?" No . . . supreme commissaries does not sound well, either. What about "people's commissaries"?'

' "People's commissaries"? Well, that might do, I think,' Lenin agrees. 'And the government as a whole?'

'A Soviet, of course . . . the Soviet of People's Commissaries, eh?'

'The Soviet of People's Commissaries?' Lenin picks it up.

'That's splendid; smells terribly of revolution!'[2]

Thus in a few seconds the term 'commissar' would enter into political language, and eventually punctuate the literature of the cold war.

And so the first Soviet of People's Commissars (which quickly came to be known in its shortened Russian form as Sovnarkom), was established:

Chairman: V.I. Lenin
Commissar of the Interior: A. I. Rykov
Commissar of Agriculture: D.P. Milyutin
Commissar of Labour: A.R. Shliapnikov
War & Navy Committee: P. Dybenko, V. Antonov-Ovseenko, N.V. Krylenko
Commissar of Commerce & Industry: V.P. Nogin
Commissar of Education: A.V. Lunacharsky
Commissar of Finance: I.I. Skvortsov
Commissar of Foreign Affairs: L. Trotsky
Commissar of Justice: G.E. Oppokov
Commissar of Supply: I.F. Theodorovich

Post & Telegraph: N.P. Avilov
Commissar of Nationality Affairs: J. Stalin

For these hardened political veterans, to suddenly find themselves in such elevated positions, heading a revolutionary government after years of exile and covert struggle must have been breathtaking. Even Lenin had been conscious of the historical nature of events when he confided to Trotsky, 'You know, to pass so quickly from persecutions and clandestine existence to power . . .' He then broke into German: '*Es schwindelt*' (It makes you dizzy).

Support in the mills and factories for the coup was widespread. But a large number of workers in other industries remained solidly against this sudden storm of dictatorial activity. On 27 October almost all of Petrograd's civil servants were on strike, while over in the City Hall Mayor Schreider was presiding over a meeting of the struggling Committee for Salvation. How could these usurpers have stolen away the country and the city overnight? This had to be dealt with. He called Lenin's plans 'illegitimate government by bayonet', drawing support from his audience. When the Postmens' Union delegate stood up and declared that his members would not be delivering the mail to the Smolny Institute, someone from the Petrograd telephone exchange gave the welcome news that all the telephones at the Smolny had been cut off. What Bolsheviks there were in the crowd rose from their seats to leave in disgust as they were bombarded with accusations of being 'spies for the Kaiser', a political battering ram which was still in full swing.

But the most dangerous proclamation came from the delegate of the Railway Workers' Union, the *Vikzhel,* who announced that they would not allow access to the rail system for 'usurpers' and that his members were going to take the rail network into their own hands. The powerful and politically sophisticated railwaymen were important to all sides in the revolution, a highly organized body of working men who had a distinct desire to see a government in place which would include all shades of socialist opinion. They also threatened to call a general strike if Kerensky refused to enter into peaceful negotiations with the Bolsheviks. Without doubt, Lenin and Trotsky had a lot on their hands. Lev Kamenev was given the task of negotiating with the *Vikzhel*, the deal he came back with doing little to cheer Lenin up. The railwaymen were refusing to carry troops and had stated categorically their opposition to any inter-socialist fratricide. Travelling the length and breadth of the country as they did, they had seen the effects of both war and revolution first hand in dozens of cities and towns. Trains carried the wounded, the dead, the guns and the horses, often commandeered from poor families who could ill afford such sacrifice. Now they were telling Kamenev that their demands included full recognition of the Social Revolutionary Party as the country's largest political body, and the replacement of Lenin as the chairman of Sovnarkom with the SR leader, Viktor Chernov. To Lenin's anger, Kamenev had agreed to the railwaymens' demands. As usual, the Bolsheviks had managed to side-step this temporary disaster with a convincing show of political fakery which included what seemed like a temporary rapprochement with the SRs. It would prove to be an illusion, however, a play for time until the Bolsheviks had complete control. Eventually, faced with civil war and a 100 per cent Soviet administration, even the duped *Vikzhel* would have to come to its senses. Among their other disagreements, Kamenev and Zinoviev hated the idea of reneging on the railmens' demands, and resigned their posts as commissars.

In addition to the dormant Civil Service, one of the most

important cogs in the old machine, which had continued to function before the coup, was the banking and financial system. Bank employees now came out on strike, although they did not have to suffer the earlier privations of the mill and factory workers by withdrawing their labour. The new Soviet Government soon discovered that any bank worker who came out in opposition to the Bolsheviks was being paid a full salary whilst idle. A number of financial institutions, both Russian and international, had set up a strike fund. By the time the banking magnates reached the grim realization that the Bolshevik administration meant business and was there to stay, employees soon found that their wages were withdrawn.

The new government dealt with the Civil Service problem by appealing to the people. As he had with the peasants, Lenin maintained that the urban working class had to be convinced that they could be masters of their own destiny.[3] If the people were frustrated and angered by the deliberately short-staffed, slow, bureaucratic grind of local government institutions, then they should make themselves available and do the job themselves. The Bolsheviks printed posters and placards to this effect, posting them around the city, and soon had a stream of willing volunteers, so that the strikers, vilified as anti-social, were faced with embarrassment.

It was a clear-cut technique which would be adapted to deal with the problem of the Army. When the Decree for Peace had been announced, orders were given to the Commander-in-Chief, General Dukhonin, to open up negotiations with the Germans for an armistice. Dukhonin, who discussed his dilemma with representatives of the Allies, realized that to the French, British and Americans such a scenario was outrageous. Horrified, he refused to obey, no doubt expecting his dismissal as a matter of course, but his replacement, with the grand title of Commissar for War, Lieutenant Nikolai Kry-

lenko, held the lowest commissioned rank in the army. Dukhonin paid dearly for his disobedience, as his rank and file
soldiers strung him up. By now the Allies were further convinced that Lenin must surely be in the pay of Germany.

As administrative business was being carried out feverishly
around the clock in the Smolny Institute, 25 miles away in the
town of Gatchina, Alexander Kerensky, in the company of a
regiment of anti-Bolshevik Don Cossacks, had taken over the
old imperial palace. After his hasty flight he had settled down
and was feeling confident that within a few hours he might
march back into Petrograd and sort out the rabble. His orders
for loyal troops from the front, however, hadn't been too
successful, although there was good news from Moscow,
where the counter-revolutionary Cossacks and cadets had
successfully stormed the Kremlin. In Petrograd, leaflets appeared on the streets instructing the city's garrison to surrender
to Kerensky's advancing forces. Yet still there was no sign of
them. Threat or no threat, the Petrograd soldiers weren't
moving for anyone, including Lenin. He had sent the members
of the War & Navy Committee to the Volinsky barracks, but
the soldiers there appeared to be in a negative frame of mind.
Their attitude was that if Kerensky was marching on Petrograd, then there would be plenty of their comrades outside the
city to block his path. They were staying put for the time being,
which did not go down well with Lenin. On 29 October
Cossacks led by General Peter Krasnov entered Tsarskoe
Seloe. The counter-revolutionary enemy was at the gate. It
would be words, not bullets, which would defeat Krasnov.

The victorious Cossacks were surrounded by earnest agitators and bombarded with pleas. What made the Cossacks
more confused was the fact that the arguments ranged against
them were coming not only from the Bolshevik left wing, but
from many of the right-wingers in the Cadet Party, because the

Cossacks were there at Kerensky's behest. It had been his devious dithering which had resulted in the trouncing of their man Kornilov, making Kerensky yet another figure to hate. The arguments went on for some time. Did the 'brother Cossacks' want to turn their guns on workers, peasants and fellow Russian soldiers? Were they being duped into going back to Petrograd simply to re-establish an old order which would benefit no one? The arguments took their course and hit home. Krasnov compromised, and sent representatives to Petrograd with a proposal for an armistice which would grant amnesty to any forces who had opposed the Bolsheviks. A member of the War & Navy Committee, the huge, bearded sailor, Pavel Dybenko, arrived the next day, with an acceptance of the armistice. Humorously pushing his luck, Dybenko said, 'Give us Kerensky, and we'll turn over Lenin to you. Let's trade – an ear for an ear!' The sailor may well have been joking, but Krasnov, attracted by mental images of Lenin's corpse swinging on a gibbet outside the Tsar's nearby palace, took up the offer. The terrified Kerensky was upstairs awaiting the outcome when a soldier burst in and gave him the news. Ten minutes later, when the Cossacks came looking for him, he had gone, disguised as a sailor, escaping the Bolsheviks yet again.

The routing of Kerensky's forces at Tsarskoe Seloe reinvigorated the Bolshevik forces in Moscow and within two days they retook the Kremlin and accepted the surrender of the counter-revolutionaries.

Moscow's bitter, bloody struggle to duplicate Petrograd's success in the coup was a sad result of that city's support of a less daring schedule than that envisaged by Trotsky and Lenin. The Moscow Bolsheviks were in favour of the caution urged by Zinoviev and Kamenev, who, as members of the Central Committee, had both voted against Lenin's timetable for the uprising. Without a Trotsky on hand in Moscow to pull things together, the Bolsheviks were far from prepared, and for such a bold project, preparation was everything. The anti-Bolshevik forces in the city were more determined – and at the start they had the strategic upper hand. The small force of *yunkers* who sought to defend the Provisional Government, although in the main fresh-faced teenagers, were brave enough to throw in their lot with the hardened pro-Kerensky Cossacks. The Kremlin was defended by Cossacks and the 56th Infantry Regiment, like many regiments prone to agitation and Bolshevik influence. A great part of the Russian Army's urban garrisons could be considered as peasants in uniforms. With their distant comrades at the front no longer putting up a fight against the Germans, and the issue of Lenin's decree on land, the Bolsheviks had two powerful reasons behind any arguments needed to swing the vacillating soldiers in their direction. It was no surprise, then, that the 56th mutinied and went over to the Bolsheviks. But they were still in a hopeless situation. The outnumbered Cossacks held the Kremlin gate and the *yunker* cadets managed to get a field gun through. After a few threatening shells were fired, the trapped 56th had little choice other than to surrender. The streets in the city centre became a furious battleground and machine guns rattled around the clock. Despite the danger, many people had ventured onto the streets simply out of curiosity, many of these innocent bystanders paying with their lives, their bodies lying on the pavement for hours before any ambulance would dare pick them up. By Sunday, 29 October things had become quieter, with armed workers patrolling and firing sporadically at any threatening shadow or movement. The terrified population soon saw sense and stayed in their houses, doors firmly locked. One of them was Konstantin Paustovsky, who had returned to Moscow from visiting his mother in the country.

After the shelling of the Kremlin had died down, he described the view from his window.

A dead horse, its yellow teeth bared, lay across the tramlines. A thin trickle of blood led from our gate. The houses, riddled with machine-gun bullets, kept dropping sharp splinters of glass and we heard it tinkling all around us. Filling the street from pavement to pavement, columns of Red Guards, exhausted, silent, their red armbands twisted into string, were marching to Nikitsky Gate. Nearly all were smoking and the flashes of their cigarettes in the darkness were like silent crossfire. A white flag on a pole was tied to a lamp post near the Union Cinema. Near the flag, a row of *yunkers,* in crumpled forage caps and greatcoats grey with plaster, stood drawn up against the wall. Many looked half asleep as they leaned on their rifles . . . it was all over. From Tverskaya, through the chilly darkness, came the sound of singing and of several brass bands playing the *International.*[4]

For the moment, the crisis was over. Lenin had triumphed again.

It is hard to verify Trotsky's subsequent claim for a low casualty figure – five souls – in the defence of Petrograd during the Kerensky offensive. If one reads various accounts of the conflict the random mention of bodies and victims of stray bullets inevitably swells the figure. But the number of dead in Moscow was well in excess of 500.

As had happened on Petrograd's Field of Mars, the dead of Moscow would be ceremoniously buried without the age-old involvement of the Russian Orthodox Church. Marx's 'opium of the people', religion, had suffered since the rise of a politicized proletariat. It had not been forgotten in Petrograd that the autocratic Tsarist bishopric had allowed the unholy installation of police machine-gun nests on the roofs of churches, which proved a great vantage point from which to pick off striking workers. If this was a sample of Christ's mercy, then the workers were unimpressed. Land owned by the Church would be some of the first to be handed over to the people.

Enormous pits were dug facing the Kremlin wall in Moscow for the burial of the dead, to become known as the 'Brotherhood Grave'. The red-painted coffins of the fallen were made from rough, unplaned timber. The tragic entourage of mourners began at midday, and continued until sunset. As the coffins were lowered into the mass graves, the band of Lenin's praetorian guard, the Latvians, played a solemn funeral hymn. The bourgeoisie were wise enough to stay out of the way, yet they were horrified at this new secularity, this irreligious and irretrievable break with Russia's holy tradition.

In Petrograd, Lenin set about ruthlessly eliminating any adverse propaganda against his government by shutting down any newspaper which was giving the Bolsheviks trouble. Six popular newspapers covering a whole range of political opinion were shut down within days of the October coup. Bundles of critical newspapers were removed from news stands and burned in the streets. Any vendor selling critical news-sheets was liable to arrest and prosecution. All this played into the hands of the SRs and the Cadet party – those who had warned of Lenin's dictatorial capacity now had their caution validated. Sovnarkom explained to the public that shutting down the press was 'of a temporary nature and will be revoked when normal conditions of public life are re-established'.[5]

Of all the comic opera aspects of the revolution, such as Stalin's role as Lenin's barber, Lenin's penchant for ill-fitting hairpieces and his incompetence in disguising himself, and the casual distribution of tough ministerial portfolios to totally inexperienced candidates, the story of the foundation of the Soviet State's treasury takes some beating.

Stalin had been known to be involved in several bank robberies throughout Russia before the revolution to keep the Bolshevik funds afloat. The Bolsheviks had no moral misgivings about such events, which were seen as part of 'expropriating the expropriators', something about to be carried out on a grand scale. The haphazard process of throwing the first Soviet administration together resulted in more than a few novelty appointments. Confiscating private property too, as with the case of the ballerina Ksheshinskaya's house as the early Bolshevik headquarters, was in full swing by October 1917. Yet despite his decree to nationalize the Russian banks, Lenin was discovering soon after coming to power that getting the bankers to bow before Soviet authority and hand over their safe combinations was an uphill task.

One of Lenin's old-time sparring partners, Viacheslav Menzhinsky, (who would become one of Stalin's willing executioners) was a Bolshevik who, in exile in 1916, had even virulently criticized his leader in the pages of the French émigré journal, *Our Echo,* as considering Lenin to be 'the natural successor to the Russian throne . . . should he ever come to power, the mischief he would do would not be much less than that of Paul I'. Considering what a bloodthirsty, wretched career this one-time bank clerk, Menzhinsky, had ahead of him, his summing up of the Bolsheviks only a year before their rise to power really stands out. He called them 'a clan of party gypsies, who swing their whips so affectionately and hope to drown the voice of the proletariat with their screams.' This hypocrite would soon be swinging his own whip after Lenin's death, but in October 1917, he was there at Lenin's side in the Smolny, working away at any task put before him.

Lenin's close friend, Vladimir Bonch-Bruyevich, later told the tale of Menzhinsky's rise to fame as the man who attempted to make the first deposit in Sovnarkom's war chest.

Apparently Comrade Viacheslav, like all the members of Sovnarkom, had been burning the midnight oil and was exhausted when Lenin called him to his room in the Smolny. Lenin knew of his brief career in a bank, saying, 'You're not much of a financier, but you are a man of action, so you're appointed as Commissar for Finance.'

Having not slept for days, Menzhinsky reluctantly accepted the honour and wrote his new title down on a large piece of paper which he pinned to the wall over a sofa. He then lay down on the sofa and went into a deep, snoring sleep. The image greatly amused Lenin.

As it happened, the new appointee certainly wasn't 'much of a financier'. He was visited one afternoon by a keen young comrade called Pestkovsky, who told the new Commissar for Finance that he was looking for a job. Menzhinsky asked him what education he had, to his delight discovering that Pestkovsky had at one time, albeit briefly, studied finance at London University. The Commissar immediately informed his keen young visitor that he was therefore appointed as Director of the State Bank. Pestkovsky was horrified, feeling he was hardly qualified for such a lofty post. In any case, the State Bank had a director. But Menzhinsky explained that many of the State Bank workers were on strike, Sovnarkom needed money, and that the best way to get their hands on it was to kick out the legitimate director and install their own. Problem solved. Not long after, Menzhinsky presented Pestkovsky with a letter of appointment, signed by Lenin. But the ex-student was still completely reluctant. Within two days Menzhinsky had relented and Pestkovsky's short career as Director of the State Bank (which would be quite a plus on his CV) seemed over.

But not quite. The young comrade was sent to Stalin's Commissariat for Nationalities, where Stalin set the young man up with a desk – but he needed money. Stalin told him to go to Trotsky to borrow 3,000 roubles which Trotsky had 'found' in the former Provisional Government's foreign office. Menzhinsky, in the meantime, was still the Commissar for Finance but with no money at all. On paper, the Soviet Government was broke. A new Director of the State Bank, Piatakov, (another old Bolshevik with whom Lenin had had serious differences) was appointed. Lenin told him to go to the bank in his new role as Director and take out ten million roubles. 'And don't return without the money'. To make Piatakov's position to the bank clear, Lenin had the existing Director, Shipov, arrested and held him under guard in the Smolny.

As is the case with most robberies, things did not run smoothly at the bank. The senior bank staff regarded the request for funds illegal. Lenin's decree on banking was brought up, and the threat of the Red Guards introduced into the negotiations. The armed military guards at the bank began to look threatening. Eventually, fear overcame the cashiers, the vault was opened and huge piles of bundled notes were brought out. Some bags had to be borrowed to put all the money in, and eventually, Piatakov's party arrived back at the Smolny like a group of Santas with shouldered sacks. Lenin seemed disinterested when he was presented with the booty. (Accounts of the amount vary from 5 million to 10 million roubles.) It was taken to a Smolny bedroom and kept in a wardrobe, around which was placed a ring of chairs and a worker with a rifle. This then was the first treasury of the Soviet Union.

Needless to say, the bank workers were disturbed by this and the sudden disappearance from the vaults of large amounts of their customers' cash had to be explained. In the weeks following Lenin's first bold 'withdrawal', the following proclamation appeared on the streets of Petrograd:

> To The Attention of All Citizens
> The State Bank Is Closed!
> Why?
>
> Because the violence exercised by the Bolsheviki against the State bank has made it impossible for us to work. The first act of the People's Commissars was to DEMAND TEN MILLION ROUBLES, and on 27 November THEY DEMANDED TWENTY FIVE MILLIONS, without any indication of where the money was to go. We functionaries cannot take part in plundering the people's property. We stopped work. CITIZENS! The money in the State bank is yours, the people's money acquired by your labour, your sweat, your blood.
>
> CITIZENS! Save the people's property from robbery, and us from violence, and we shall immediately resume work.
>
> EMPLOYEES OF THE STATE BANK[6]

To many unskilled workers with no experience of banking the phrase 'money acquired by your labour, your sweat, your blood' would have met with some incomprehension. Somebody had obviously been banking the *profits* which had resulted from their toil, but it wasn't them. The one thing which wouldn't be deposited with the State Bank was proletarian sympathy. By early December 1917, all 28 banks had been taken over by 28 elite squads of Red Guards, their directors arrested and imprisoned at the Smolny. Those bank chiefs who were willing to work in their old positions for Sovnarkom were released.

Despite the Bolsheviks' desire to stifle any adverse opinion of their behaviour, they now pressed ahead with plans to hold elections for a Constituent Assembly. Herein was a dilemma: what would happen if the Bolsheviks, as Lenin hoped, did not get the majority of the votes? The industrial workers in the factories and mills were now awaiting a decree which would hand over in full the enterprises of their former employers to the proletariat, but it didn't seem to be forthcoming. Lenin was unsure that the working class had yet developed enough assertiveness to tackle such a huge undertaking. His attitude to the workers who visited him over this question seemed vague: take what you want, develop it, keep working and keep up production. The total nationalization of heavy industry was not one of his priorities.

On 3 November *Pravda* published Lenin's Draft Decree on Workers' Control. It would have made interesting reading for the eager class warriors in the Putilov works and the factories in the Vyborg district, and may well have been a source of slight relief for their employers. This provided for:

> the introduction of workers' control of the production, ware-housing, purchase and sale of all products and raw materials in all industrial, commercial and other enterprises employing a total of not less than five workers and employees – or with a turnover of not less than 10,000 roubles per annum.

It further stated that the workers' control be 'carried out by all the workers and employees in a given enterprise, either directly if the enterprise is small enough to permit it, or through delegates to be immediately elected at mass meetings'. Once elected, these delegates were to have access to the firm's books, warehouses and stocks of material, 'instruments and products, without exception'.[7]

All this seemed fine and bold on paper, yet the kind of workers' control the decree describes had already been in existence in the mills and factories, having been installed in some cases whilst Lenin was still looking for a way out of Switzerland. The sting in the tail was a clause which read: 'the decisions of the workers and employees are legally binding upon the owners of the enterprises but can be annulled by trade unions and congresses.'

Thus, despite the perceived extremity of many of the decrees pouring out of the Smolny, Lenin favoured the idea that the workers could control industry, but with the caveat of a final veto by 'the State'. Their effort would simply be part of a mixed economy which, surprisingly, would still have room for a few capitalists.[8] Also, if the factory committees stepped out of the Bolshevik line, their unions – and more importantly, a congress – could curtail their activity. In many ways the Decree on Workers' Control was a political conjuring trick, because in effect such control as the workers had achieved could now be subject to a higher authority. There were soon warnings being issued about any further strikes, that they would harm the new state, and that if the workers wanted socialism to succeed, they should get back to work, do their jobs and fulfil their duty to the people.

The glory days of February to October were well and truly over.

However, there were many new decrees which the ordinary Russian worker would find favourable. On 29 October the eight-hour day was finally fully proclaimed. The death penalty, which had been scrapped in the euphoria following February, yet reinstalled for soldiers at the front by Kerensky, was abolished yet again.

Housing conditions for the Russian working class were, compared to even some of the most industrialized cities in Britain, often appalling. A number had no homes at all. Many of these lived 'over the shop' in crude barracks provided by their employers. Others, often whole families, lived in cramped and unsanitary single rooms in dilapidated tenement blocks. The focal point of their domestic life in the winter was a wood-burning stove and the samovar; in the high summer there was little relief from the heat. However, there were other skilled workers, members of the Bolsheviks such as Lenin's companions on his escape to Finland, who were lucky enough, either by family connections or a legacy, to own that favourite Russian weekend escape, a country dacha. These were not always the grand structural affairs enjoyed by the bourgeoisie, but often simple wooden huts in pleasant rural surroundings which provided welcome escape from the city's grime. Perhaps the working-class equivalent in modern Britain would be the ownership of a permanently sited caravan at the seaside. But those with dachas were lucky. Unlike today, there was little concept of 'environmental health' for the Russian worker. One of the first acts of the People's Commissars was that of A.I. Rykov, Commissar of the Interior. Headed 'Concerning Dwelling Places', this boldly gave the Municipal Soviets 'the right to sequestrate all unoccupied dwelling places'. They could 'install in all available lodgings citizens who have no place to live, or who live in congested or unhealthy lodgings'. A service of inspection was established to look into the nature of living conditions, and housing tribunals would be established. The evidence is, however, that many prominent party activists would take advantage of this housing free-for-all, and snap up the best apartments for themselves.

Maria Mikhailovna Alexandrovna was not yet three years old at the time of the revolution, and lived in Petrograd with her aunt, patiently awaiting the return of her parents who had been sent to work in Omsk.

I would be five years old before I met my parents. Because my uncle, Pavel Ivanovich Ivanov, was a Bolshevik party member he and my aunt got a big apartment in Petrograd. As a child the place fascinated me because I remember there were many things there, including a selection of toys. You can imagine my mother and father's disappointment when they returned to Petrograd as, unlike favoured party members, they had to live apart and had to live in cramped, tiny, individual flats.[9]

Many previously better off Russians would therefore be appalled when they came to visit one of their houses in Petrograd or Moscow to discover several families occupying what had once been their property. Yet by this time they had no avenue of redress and to complain too assertively was often a grave mistake. The Soviets had decided, yet the allocation of accommodation certainly seemed a long way from the egalitarian share-out they might have expected.

The People's Commissar of Labour, Alexander Schliapnikov, also issued a proclamation on social insurance, a national insurance scheme which encompassed old age, childbirth, sickness benefits, widowhood and unemployment. The workers would have self-government of all insurance institutions, and the cost of the scheme? 'All the costs of insurance to be charged to employers.'

On education, Anatoly Lunacharsky really got down to work. In his lengthy proclamation he sought to improve the status of teachers, especially elementary school teachers.[10] There are echoes of every subsequent western politician's fascination with this well-worn vote-winner:

However needful it may be to curtail other articles of the people's budget, the expenses on education must stand high.

> A large educational budget is the pride and glory of a nation.
> The free and enfranchised peoples of Russia will not forget this.

Lunacharsky was also very keen that adults should have schools, too, as 'they will be anxious to save themselves from the debasing position of a man who cannot read and write.'

One of the less savoury aspects of almost nine months of rebellion and civil unrest had been the constant plundering of wine cellars which had come to a head after the raid on the Winter Palace. The drunken antics of Red Guards, soldiers, sailors and workers in the streets once they had stumbled upon Nicholas and Alexandra's substantial stash of rare vintages had filled many citizens with disgust. There had even been reports that when the snow was on the ground, where the contents of wine cellars had been looted and bottles broken in the streets, some people had scooped up the crimson, wine impregnated snow and had eaten it.[11] More responsible party members and some foreigners realized the dangers which could result from an already enraged group of workers or soldiers, suddenly faced with the spoils of revolution in the form of a cellar full of thousands of bottles which had previously been a luxury only the rich could afford. Sovnarkom's response to this growing problem was brisk and all embracing by November 1917:

> Order Issued by the Military Revolutionary Committee:
> 1. Until further order the production of alcohol and alcoholic drinks is prohibited.
> 2. It is ordered to all producers of alcohol and alcoholic drinks to inform not later than on the twenty-seventh inst. of the exact site of their stores.
> 3. All culprits against this order will be tried by a Military Revolutionary Court.
> THE MILITARY REVOLUTIONARY COMMITTEE.

The problem of food shortages had become even more acute and would require drastic action to remedy. On 7 November heavy snow began to fall and soon the additional constraints of surviving in winter were added to the population's problems. The persistent snow and ice had an immediate effect on public transport. The Petrograd tram service, which was already struggling to function due to breakdowns and a lack of spares, was now hit hard, with some tramcars being left where they had stopped, iced up on the rails. Whole trains were having to be abandoned in sidings when their locomotives ceased to work. The age-old challenge to keep warm was back with a vengeance as people began searching for fuel and wood again. The previous winter of 1916–17 had seen all kinds of desperate measures with fences, trees and anything which would burn being removed. Furniture had been readily chopped up so that some apartments even lacked chairs or tables. Now the poorer people began to attack the very fabric of their living quarters, breaking into loft spaces and removing roof and ceiling joists. In many cases the result was tragic – as more snow piled up on the roof, the tiles would cave in from the weight, and often the ceiling of the top floor would crack asunder under the weight of snow. Whole families in tenements without central heating would die, frozen to death in their unheated apartments.

To tackle the food problem, large detachments of sailors, soldiers and Red Guards were established to go out far and wide across Russia in the search for grain, vegetables, eggs, dairy products, anything edible, often finding mountains of grain which had been hoarded in churches or barns. Those responsible were arrested or shot. Throughout Russia the Bolsheviks issued their food requisition notices, which would be pinned in advance to farm gates or village halls, warning that the sailors were coming and that they would not expect to be leaving empty handed. On the Trans-Siberian Railway, wagons were loaded with all kinds of goods – bolts of cloth, household items, anything which could be used to barter for food in the remote peasant communities of Siberia. Peaceful hamlets, thousands of miles away from any ocean, which had seemed untouched by the drama which had taken place in the cities, were suddenly confronted with incongruously large parties of rapacious Baltic sailors, far from any ocean, hell bent on taking anything from a chicken to a cow.

Yet still the people went hungry.

Throughout 1917 the Bolsheviks had promised to call an elected Constituent Assembly. The idea of a body encompassing all shades of political opinion which could ratify bills and decrees democratically had been a dream with a long history. In 1903, however, Plekhanov had warned that if a good assembly was elected, it would be kept; if it was a bad one, it would be dissolved. The Provisional Government had scheduled the election for a Constituent Assembly for 12 November, and the Bolsheviks had complained during the year when the Provisional Government had delayed the election. Now Lenin wanted to do the same. He sought to expand suffrage to 18 year olds and take some kind of action against the Cadets and those who had supported Kornilov. Trotsky argued the case that they could not further delay the election, because this would look bad for the Bolsheviks. Trotsky won the argument, but no matter which option they might have taken, the results would not please Lenin, and were even worse than he had anticipated. In the large urban areas the Bolsheviks did poll well, with the Cadets coming a close second. But in the countryside, the Social Revolutionaries won enough votes to give them an overall majority in the election. The results[12] were a shock:

Social Revolutionaries (SRs)	
(including Ukranian SRs)	48%
Bolsheviks	24%
Kadets	4.7%
Mensheviks	
(including Georgia Mensheviks)	4.1%
Unaccounted	10.3%
Others	8.9%

Out of 703 deputies, only 168 would be Bolsheviks, with 380 SRs. In percentage terms, however, the soldiers at the front and the Baltic sailors displayed a 60 per cent majority for the Bolsheviks. The confusion and the failure of Kerensky's June offensive had pushed the armed forces into a new wave of support for the left.

Freedom to campaign during the election was curtailed, especially for the right-wing Cadet Party. Also, the peasants had been confused by the split in the Social Revolutionaries – they had difficulty in establishing which SRs were Bolshevik allies and which had retained their former orthodoxy against Lenin. But for Lenin, the statistics proved nothing. As far as he was concerned, the people had had their election and that was that. He would commence to render the Assembly impotent by any means possible. If there was to be a government it would be a Soviet one, a point he made clear in *Pravda,* saying that this would be the only way the Constituent Assembly could survive. It was a doomed body from the start. Some deputies were arrested; others went into hiding. The Cadet Party was outlawed, with two of its leaders, Fyodor Kokoshkin and Andrey Shingarev, murdered a few weeks later in a hospital.

The New Year of 1918 was hardly a week old when the Assembly held its first – and last – meeting. When the SR's Viktor Chernov was elected as president of the assembly over

Maria Spiridonova from the left wing of the SRs (which was a front for the Bolsheviks) the vote went 244 to 153 in Chernov's favour. Three measures were debated, on land, peace and, controversially, a decree proclaiming Russia to be a democratic federal republic. The session lumbered on throughout the night and the early hours under the baleful gaze of sneering sailors and workers in the public galleries. Some sailors even raised their rifles to take imaginary potshots at the speakers. At 5 a.m. a sailor interrupted Chernov to tell him that the 'guard is tired – time you dispersed'. The sailors then began turning the lights off. When the assembly attempted to reconvene at midday, their way was barred by armed Bolsheviks. Those demonstrators in the street who protested came under fire from pro-Bolshevik soldiers. The last legitimate forces opposed to Bolshevism had been ostracized.

On 20 November a delegation had gone to Brest-Litovsk to enter into negotiations with the Germans for an armistice. Headed by Krylenko, the deputation must have looked odd to the autocratic, upper-class German military staff. To begin with, Nikolai Krylenko had until recently been just a lowly Lieutenant. Also, the deputation included an elderly peasant, a woman, a factory worker and a sailor. It was hoped that their presence would have some propaganda effect among the German working class, whose uprising Lenin still counted on to prove his theories. Although the fighting did stop for a while, the terms brought back from the Germans were shocking. They made a demand for 215,000 square kilometres of Russian territory – wherein lived over 20 million Russians – and 3,000 million roubles in gold.

Elsewhere in Russia the forces bent on destroying the Bolsheviks now realized that only a full-scale civil war could return the country to what they regarded as its former glory. In the south on the Don, after swallowing the humiliation of his defeat in July, General Lavr Kornilov was busy assisting the Tsar's former Commander-in-Chief, General M.V. Alexeev, in assembling a volunteer White army.[13] Other powerful military figures from the old regime were amassing their forces. Admiral Alexander Kolchak had, until the summer of 1917, commanded the Black Sea Fleet. When faced with the mutiny of his men after the visit on board his flagship of a committee of sailors and workers, he had sternly lectured his crew. He completed his harangue with the symbolic removal of a very valuable golden sword, which he tossed into the sea with the words: 'The Japanese left me this sword when we evacuated Port Arthur – and I will *not* give it over to *you!*' after which he resigned his position. Now Kolchak, after spending some time in America, was back, assembling a White force of his own.

Whatever troubles the Bolsheviks had faced during 1917, they were nothing compared to those which stood on the threshold of the New Year.

7

SWEPT AWAY

Where are the wealthy, the fashionable ladies,
the expensive restaurants and private mansions,
the beautiful entrances, the lying newspapers,
all the corrupted 'golden life'? All swept away.
                              Pravda, 1 January 1919

If for any reason you had been away from the action in
Petrograd during 1917 and were about to return, then a bleak
surprise would lie in wait. Now in her 90s, retired Professor of
English Grammar Vavara Vassilievna was four years old and
had longed for her father to come home from the war. Yet he
would never be the same man again. He would have to change
to survive.

I think the fact that my mother was a doctor saved us in some
way. When my father came back he had to keep it a secret that

he had been an officer in the Tsarist army. He would simply tell people that he was an engineer. He managed to live as an engineer for a few years after the revolution, but he earned such little wages. All his life he was under a threat of being arrested, exiled or shot. Informers were everywhere. Honest people vanished, although among them were several people who managed to stay out of prison. I don't know how, but this for us didn't change the climate of the country. It was those I call 'traitors' who remained free. But those poor, sad workers. How much they were fooled they never knew.

The February revolution was better than the October, but not much. The ordinary working people astonished us. They were so naïve. They actually believed it when they were told that they had the power, that they were the 'best' people. There were poorly dressed working people everywhere who suddenly thought they were the best, but really they didn't understand the situation. They were still underpaid, and still exploited. Yet they imagined that they were the rulers of the country. My parents didn't like Lenin or Trotsky at all. They knew at an early stage that they were dictators, cruel persons, always giving orders for people to be shot. And then before long there was Stalin – he shot everybody. All my younger years were very difficult. We had very little money and lived hand-to-mouth. What can I tell you, what can I say about how desperate things were? 50 grammes of bread per day, one egg per week if we were lucky, and little or no sugar in our tea. What kind of a new life was that? Our previous lives were turned on their heads. There was no more comfort. Of course, I was too young to realise all this. I was a child, and to me my parents were nothing but loving kindness. They devoted themselves to me and my sister. It was what lay ahead of us which was so much of a worry.[1]

The Bolsheviks had the power now. The disbanded, longed-for Constituent Assembly would become a sick joke, a discarded fag-end of democratic liberalism. The touching naivety of the elected delegates at their one and only session, who fondly thought that they could carry on debating, passing resolutions, planning a future; the very memory of it was celebrated by Russia's new masters with hollow laughter.

But Lenin and Trotsky stood at the foot of a mountain of troubles. To begin with, there was still the problem of the railwaymen. They knew they had been duped by Lenin's subterfuge, his pretence at 'cosying-up' to their favoured party, the Social Revolutionaries. News was coming in daily of the formation of counter-revolutionary forces. And where was Kerensky? What wild adventure might he be planning? He was still nursing his wounded pride hidden away in a secret location provided by more sympathetic SR members, less than two hours away from Petrograd. He could not resist issuing a statement to anyone in the capital who would listen, telling them what many already knew – that 'your simplicity has been abused' and that he had been democracy's champion all along.

With Lev Kamenev's resignation, Lenin had appointed Yakov Sverdlov as the Chairman of Sovnarkom's central executive committee, seemingly no longer bothered by resignations. Critics of the regime were many, but in rebuffing their constant complaints a new and sinister attitude was creeping into Bolshevik reaction. Even the much respected writer and editor Maxim Gorky, a reliable champion of the lower classes, had been branded an 'enemy of the people', a term everyone would soon dread. It had the same connotations as it would have had in the bad old Tsarist days, and with similar, or even worse, punishment.

Meanwhile, apart from the Red Guards and some ad-hoc

militia, the country had not reconstituted its police force. This would soon be remedied.

The dismissal of the Constituent Assembly would come as a shock to many of those more committed civil servants and government workers who had stood by the regime through its various shifts in power and composition. The Assembly had been a dream close to the heart of most Socialists, something they hardly expected to be trampled into the dust. The various commissars suddenly had to face a new wave of opposition as the staff they so much needed to push through their plans decided that the Bolsheviks were now beyond the legal pale. Many members of management in smaller companies essential to the government had been outraged at Sovnarkom's illicit behaviour, and had stopped work. Lenin raged against them as 'bourgeois scum' and 'parliamentary obstructionists'. Even at the mighty Putilov plant, clerical workers and management staff staged a walkout, inevitably resulting in mass lay-offs of workers. It seemed as if the bad old days would never end. Foreign investors in oil companies, gold mines and Russian heavy industry were demanding 'stable government'.

In an attempt to get people working again any notion of proletarian fraternity seemed to be abandoned as Milvrekom began sending armed Red Guards into offices, banks and other institutions. People with years of service were dismissed on the spot. Managers who refused to toe the line were marched off to prison. But still the sullen wall of opposition failed to break.

Those who seemed to be enjoying a better life, holed up in the plush international hotels such as the Europe and the Astoria – the rich who still had some control over stocks and shares, Russian speculators who had not yet quite grasped the seismic social shift the Bolsheviks had set in motion – soon exchanged cocktail bars for the iron bars of the Kresty jail in the Vyborg district.

To bring together all the corrective forces Lenin required to deal with anything which smacked of counter-revolution, some kind of organizational body was needed. In Tsarist times the police had worked hand in hand with the secretive Okhrana. Everyone of any influence in the Smolny Institute by early December 1917 had at one time in their revolutionary careers fallen foul of Tsardom's well-oiled repressive police force. Exile, imprisonment, torture, execution, blackmail, hard labour, these were the sharpened swords of the old regime which the public fondly imagined had been sheathed for good. Now came the biggest paradox of all – the Bolsheviks decided to have an Okhrana of their own.

At the age of 40, Felix Dzerzhinsky, despite being a descendant of Poland's nobility, had, like most of his comrades, paid his dues as a revolutionary. He'd experienced arrest, imprisonment and spent over a decade of his life performing hard labour in exile. He was a slender, angular and demonic-looking man, an image completed by his aquiline nose and neat, pointed goatee. To many at this stage the quiet-spoken Pole was an unknown quantity. His task until early December had been a comparatively minor one for the new regime. As commandant of the Smolny forces he was in charge of the security in the building, and made sure that the machine guns which stood on the rooftops were always well maintained. No one got past his interrogative welcome to the building. Name, address, position, party membership and status, political reliability – these were all hurdles anyone in the Smolny faced when Dzerzhinsky appeared. His efficiency impressed Lenin. On 7 December the quiet commandant was summoned to Lenin's office and asked to form the Extraordinary Commission for Combating Counter-Revolution and Speculation. The new organization would be known by its Russian acronym as the Cheka. As part of his decree on nationalizing the banks,

Lenin had stipulated that universal labour duty should be brought in for the propertied classes – that they should do manual work when ordered to do so, otherwise they would be classed as enemies of the people. Few Bolsheviks displayed class hatred with as much venom as Felix Dzerzhinsky. He would be the man to get the 'bourgeois scum' working. The Cheka's foundation was not something the party wished to trumpet too loudly – it only warranted a couple of lines in *Pravda*. Many would also be taken aback by the fact that the organization's new headquarters would be the very same building which had housed the dreaded Okhrana, at number two, Ghorokhovaya Street.[2] The Cheka would go through many hideous transformations in subsequent decades – the OGPU, NKVD, MVD, and eventually, the KGB. Dzerzhinsky had no regard for any real concept of legality, as his first speech to his newly-assembled Chekists proved:

> Do not think that I am on the look-out for forms of revolutionary justice. We have no need for justice now. Now we have need of a battle to the death! I propose, I demand the initiation of the revolutionary sword which will put an end to all counter-revolutionists. We must act not tomorrow, but today, at once![3]

He saw his task as a 'new front' every bit as real as the trenches, saying that 'we must send to this front the most stern, energetic, hearty and loyal comrades'. Within days a long dark age of purges had begun. Cheka agents moved by night. Every scrap of information, every overheard word, every suspected plot against the Bolsheviks which landed on Dzerzhinsky's desk triggered a new raid. At each grey, cold dawn the 'hearty comrades' would bring in their prisoners. The old Okhrana cells were back in action with a vengeance. Soon he earned a new title – he became 'Iron Felix', the man who would not bend. Felix had no time for the liberal notion that counter-revolutionaries might repent, perhaps be re-educated and see the light. He believed merely in extermination. His attitude to torture swept away all the euphoria the workers had experienced in February when the Okhrana had ceased to exist. Maxim Gorky, who by December 1917 had achieved a state of high anxiety about the direction in which Russia was heading, wrote bitterly of the Cheka: 'It seems as if these people brought up on torture have now been given the right to torture one another freely.'[4]

As the strains of *Auld Lang Syne* were ushering in the final year of the First World War in Britain, Petrograd's pinnacle of revolution was celebrated by Sovnarkom with the establishment of new labour battalions, formed of all kinds of former 'possessing' classes. Bank clerks, suspect ex-army officers, priests, stockbrokers, lawyers, fashion designers, shopkeepers, anyone who even vaguely smelled of 'old' Russia now found themselves with a shovel and a pick in their hands. Their job was to dig trenches. Resistance was futile; Red Guards had their instructions – shoot anyone who refuses to work.

Thus the 'terror' began. Lenin, for all his passion to change the world and turn it over to the working man, had never had any qualms about the use of terror in his class war. Those who had left it a little too late to flee Moscow or Petrograd to take up their lot with the growing White forces of Denikin, Alexeev and Kolchak would receive a bullet should they be caught in flight. Anyone caught distributing unauthorized leaflets or posters would be shot on sight. Soon the Cheka grew, extending its long tentacles across Russia like a rapidly growing octopus. The ending of capital punishment had been forgotten. New kinds of regional variations on the death penalty appeared. Drowning became popular in the south, preferably with a large stone around the neck. Some thieves were drowned in the Neva. South of Moscow in Brjansk the non-Bolshevik behaviour of having one too many vodkas could get you shot on the spot. An 8 p.m. curfew was set up in many regions. Failure to observe this meant death by shooting. Eventually anything which displeased the Cheka could be punished this way.

Within a short time Iron Felix had become a dreaded spectre in the corridors of the Smolny, even among hardened Bolsheviks. In many ways his sinister, mechanical persona would only be matched a couple of decades later by a failed chicken farmer in Bavaria, one Heinrich Himmler. Lenin was unperturbed by all this. With his terror machine in full action, he at last had an organ which would encompass the role of secret police, civil police and militia – a body of men who had taken 'justice' into their own hands to interpret it on the spot, with a gun. Death became a casual, daily occurrence.

A grim example of all this was outlined in the unpublished memoirs of a young Bolshevik, Alexander Naglosky.[5] Like many party members, Naglosky had fallen out with Lenin on his arrival back from Switzerland, but by October the keen young comrade had hopped back onto the Bolshevik bandwagon.

It transpires that after Sovnarkom sessions, Lenin and Dzerzhinsky would often get together to discuss proceedings, on one occasion Lenin casually asked Felix how many 'vicious counter-revolutionaries' he had in his prisons. The Cheka chief replied, 'About fifteen hundred'. Lenin made a note of this on a slip of paper and handed it to Dzerzhinsky, who noticed that Lenin had made a cross by the figure of 1,500. The following morning, all 1,500 prisoners had been shot. Lenin's secretary, Lidia Fotieva, later explained that Dzerzhinsky's night of blood was the result of a 'misunderstanding', as Lenin always put a cross alongside various points of memoranda.

Yet such terror was not declared official government policy until the Cheka was almost a year old, when in August 1918 Lenin was almost killed in the attempted assassination carried out in Moscow by a young Social Revolutionary, Fanya Kaplan. By this time Dzerzhinsky, along with the rest of the Soviet Government, had fled from Petrograd in the fear of a German advance and declared Moscow to be Russia's new capital, which it remains today. Dzerzhinsky's new Cheka HQ at number 22 Lubianka Street would be destined to enter history as one of the most fearful places on the Moscow street map. On the same day Fanya Kaplan's two bullets smashed into Lenin's chest and neck, the man who had taken over as Cheka head from Iron Felix in Petrograd, Mosei Uritsky, was assassinated by a young student.

Pravda symbolically took off the gloves, demanding: 'For the blood of Lenin . . . let there be floods of blood of the bourgeoisie – more blood, as much as possible.' As if the red river wasn't flowing deep enough, it was about to burst its banks.

As 1917, the year of revolution, drew to a close, the problem of the war was still not entirely solved. The peace negotiations which had begun before Christmas in Brest Litovsk proved to all those adherents of a continuation of the war that the Germans could be as brutal at the negotiating table as they were on the front line. For many Russians, too many fine young men had died for them to accede to the cruel demands the Kaiser's men were making. Trotsky's wild dream of an achievable situation which would result in the vague notion of 'neither peace nor war' now looked as crazy as it sounded. Apart from the massive sums of money the Germans wanted, they also stipulated independence for Ukraine, Poland, Finland and the Baltic States. Nonetheless, Trotsky declared hostilities to be over whilst simultaneously turning down the German terms. Lenin played for time. The Germans used the situation as everyone expected they would, and continued to advance into Russian territory. Ukraine signed a separate deal with the Germans, who soon took over the running of the territory with the aid of collaborators.

A White army was massing in Manchuria; the Japanese were threatening Vladivostok. By 3 March 1918, there was no other option but to sign the Treaty, which would be ratified on the 16th, a disastrous decision for the new Soviet Russia – 60 million Russians would now become subject to German puppet regimes; 32 per cent of her arable land would be surrendered; 75 per cent of her coal and iron-ore production; valuable oil fields; 33 per cent of Russia's factories; and 26 per cent of the railway network. Bolshevik prestige had never suffered such an immense body blow. By the end of March the left Social Revolutionaries resigned from Sovnarkom. Even within this hideously expensive peace, Lenin had a strategy, correctly predicting that the German war effort would flounder. Now the only thing which could save his party and his government was the very thing which the Bolsheviks had so violently campaigned against – war. But worse than a war with a foreign enemy, this would be a civil war, the death toll of which would pile tragedy upon tragedy. The cost would be as many as 1,250,000 Bolshevik deaths, equally as many Whites, and 2 million deaths from dysentery, typhoid and smallpox. A further 6 million would perish between 1921 and 1922 in the Volga region and Ukraine from disease and famine.[6]

It is amazing, given the massive forces – both internal, and those of Allied intervention ranged against them – that the Soviets managed to ride out such compressed storms of horror to emerge victorious. Perhaps the reason capitalism did not wipe out this bold new enemy lay in the fact that after 1918 the fight had gone out of society. The First World War had produced a weariness like no other in history. The families of fighting men in Britain, America and Europe had lost their jingoistic gung-ho feel for battle. Millions were in deep mourning. Let the Russians fight it out – everyone else had had enough. Yet one could argue that the whole machinery of Bolshevism, soon to become known as communism, was flawed after October 1917. All the hopes and innocence of February had been flushed down Russia's drains in a torrent of blood – a bad foundation upon which to build a new society.

The aftermath of 1917 provided little consolation for those dedicated Bolsheviks who had thrown in their lot with the party. Their effort and sacrifice, their years of exile and imprisonment, and their loyalty to their leader's cause would rarely be rewarded.

By the summer of 1922, for Vladimir Illych Lenin, now 52, the strain of five years of solid work was beginning to show. He confided in his doctor, Darkevich, that his headaches, insomnia and a general feeling of depression were wearing him down. After suffering a series of strokes, he died on 21 January 1924. His final months had seen him disabled, at times unable to speak. In the meantime, in the political vacuum created by Lenin's enforced absence during the last two years of his life, Stalin had been elevated to become General Secretary of the party. He had built around him a devious fortress of support behind a suspect façade of being one of Lenin's strongest supporters. One of Lenin's saving graces is the fact that he knew instinctively that Stalin was the wrong man for the job, regarding him as 'too rude', and doubting his ability to 'yield power with sufficient caution'. He felt that Stalin should be replaced by someone 'more patient, more loyal, more polite, and more attentive to comrades.' Sadly, whoever was listening did nothing, and the eventual result would be Russian communism's tombstone.

Vladimir Ignatiev was only four when Lenin died. His father had been a sailor in the Baltic Fleet, a Soviet Navy career his son would eagerly take up in the 1930s to provide some hair-raising submarine adventures in the Second World War.

My father had mixed feelings about Lenin, although I can't deny that he was very sad when he died. My father had lost many of his comrades when the communists sent troops to Kronstadt in 1921 when the sailors there began to vote for a return to things like freedom of speech. Father survived because he was at sea on his ship when the trouble started, but what made him so angry was that those sailors didn't want to overthrow the Soviet government. They weren't Whites like Kolchak. They were ordinary men who had supported the revolution and they wanted some of the freedoms given back which they thought they'd won in 1917. I think that as many as 2,000 sailors were shot, and another 6,000 sent to jail. It was a terrible thing to happen, but of course nothing compared to the mess when Stalin took over. Kronstadt was like a wound to my father, and I don't think he ever got over it, but he did once say to me that no matter how much we criticised him, Lenin was still a great man. The day Lenin died all the shops closed, the trams stopped, trains were halted. There was national grief. My father said that every ship could be measured by the self discipline of her captain, and I think that's probably the way he thought about Lenin – like a captain of a ship. When I joined the navy, I learned by then that the best thing to do was your duty – just keep quiet. You couldn't do much else in the 30s and 40s.

In the three decades which led up to the drama of 1917 thousands of well-read political alchemists carried on their clandestine struggle to turn the cold steel of feudal autocracy into the warm gold of socialism.

Many were workers, some were poets, professors, intellectuals. In the interim period of the Provisional Government the soft underbelly of old Russia, as typified by Prince Lvov, Kerensky and others acted as temporary caretakers of the workers' wishes, to be replaced by the bold firebrands who had patiently waited for the liberal gentry to fail. The majority who ended up at the helm after the fall of the Romanovs were the strained, hardcore survivors who knew, after all that exile, struggle, debate and organization, that their chance had come. We know how Lenin died. We know that Stalin's vindictive fist, clutching an ice pick, stretched as far as Trotsky's study in Mexico in 1940. But what of the others? In most cases, even Shakespeare could not match the reality of their tragic fate.

'Iron' Felix Dzerzhinsky swung his whip for a mere nine years, dying of a heart attack in 1926. Yakov Sverdlov, Lenin's appointee as Chairman of Sovnarkom's Central Committee, succumbed to influenza aged 33 in 1919. Vladimir Nabokov, the novelist's father and Cabinet Secretary, who had refused Kerensky the loan of his car, was beaten to death by White supporters in Berlin in 1922. Grigory Zinoviev and Lev Kamenev both experienced Stalin's implacable spite in a show trial in 1936. They were both shot. In the same year the ailing Maxim Gorky died, some saying that Stalin had 'influenced' his doctors. Lenin's entertaining and ebullient fellow passenger on that famous 'sealed' train, Karl Radek, eventually became a Stalinist, but somehow managed to be accused of treason and was shot in 1939. Julius Martov died in Germany in 1923 from tuberculosis. He remained a Menshevik to the last. Nikolai Chkeidze, who had greeted Lenin on his return at the Finland Station, died in France in 1926. Prince Georgy Lvov also died in France in 1924. Alexander Kerensky carried on his anti-Bolshevik struggles for two decades to reappear in Paris in 1940. His skills as an escapologist were still intact as he dodged the approaching Germans and made his way to America, living to the ripe old age of 90 despite his missing kidney, finally passing away in 1970. You can see his grave in Putney Vale cemetery in London. One time Lieutenant, Nikolai Krylenko, the member of Sovnarkom's Navy and War committee who replaced General Dukhonin in 1917 became a much-detested Commissar for Justice under Stalin. Like many of his victims, Krylenko was himself browbeaten into a forced confession at another show trial and was shot in 1938. His comrade in the Sovnarkom triumvirate, the bewhiskered sailor Pavel Dybenko, married the lefter-than-left Bolshevik Alexandra Kollontai. Somehow she managed to avoid Stalin's paranoia and live to the age of 80, passing away in 1952. Dybenko did not fare so well – he was accused, quite wrongly, of being an anti-Soviet spy and was shot in 1938. The third member of the War and Navy committee, one of the stars of the storming of the Winter Palace, Vladimir Antonov-Ovseenko, managed to struggle through Stalin's early years to become a political adviser in 1938 to Spanish Republicans. But not for long – called back to Moscow accused of spying, he flatly refused to sign a confession and was shot. The list of names of murdered men and women whose revolutionary determination had helped to elevate Stalin to the post of Russia's high executioner would fill a far longer book than this.

The prima ballerina Ksheshinskaya, whose mansion became the first Bolshevik HQ, fared better. Although she was not entirely penniless after the revolution (she had a house in the South of France), she did have all her Russian property confiscated. After marrying a Russian duke, she went to Paris to run a successful ballet school and was still dancing in 1936, one of her pupils being Dame Margot Fonteyn.

The Romanovs' fate is well known. Few members of the family escaped the long arm of the Bolsheviks. Nicholas, his wife and children died in bloody squalor in a cellar in Ekaterinburg on the night of 16 July 1918. The man who murdered Grigori Rasputin, Prince Felix Yusupov, survived until 1967. His punishment by the Romanovs was far from severe, being banished to one of his many distant estates. After leaving Russia he had a comfortable life living in places such as Italy and Corsica. Always extremely wary of any media mention of his involvement with Rasputin's death, at a time when his funds were running low, he took Hollywood's MGM to court after their 1932 film *Rasputin And The Empress* was released. Directed by Irving Thalberg, it starred the three Barrymores, John, Ethel and Lionel. To avoid trouble, the name Yusupov was changed in the film to Chegodieff, with the plot requiring this character's wife to be raped. Despite not being mentioned by name in the script, Yusupov, who claimed his wife had not been raped, sued MGM for a million dollars, of which he received an estimated $375,000, a fortune in the 1930s.[7]

When Lenin died on 21 January 1924 his coffin was taken to Moscow and placed in the House of Trade Unions. His funeral on Sunday, 27 January took place in sub-zero temperatures. Trotsky had been recuperating from illness and exhaustion – conditions which were exacerbated by the campaign of defamation against him which was being orchestrated by Stalin in the Kremlin – far away from Moscow at Sukhum on the Black Sea coast. The telegram from the Kremlin informed him that the funeral would be on Saturday the 26th, and that as he would be unable to get back in time for Lenin's funeral, he should stay put and continue his treatment. Had Trotsky been given the correct date for the funeral, Sunday, he could indeed have arrived back in Moscow in time. But the thought of Stalin sharing pall-bearing duties with the loathed Trotsky could not be faced. Thus Lenin's coffin was shouldered by eight of the new Stalin clique, including Stalin himself, Kamenev, Zinoviev and Dzerzhinsky. Although Lenin was lowered into his grave officially in front of the Kremlin Wall in Red Square at 4 p.m. on that bitter day, the Politburo had other plans for his body, despite objections by Nadya, his wife. He would be embalmed and put on permanent display.

Trotsky seemed to be Lenin's natural successor, but as Stalin's formidable rival, who argued for a policy of permanent worldwide revolution, as opposed to Stalin's plans for 'socialism in one country', he clashed with Stalin on all fronts. Stalin had worked hard at the Kremlin to build a power base around him. Kamenev and Zinoviev also disliked Trotsky, and this drew them into Stalin's camp. It would do them little good. In 1924 Trotsky was defeated at the thirteenth Congress of the Communist Party. Two years later he was expelled from the Politburo, and the following year from the Communist Party itself. By 1929 none of this was enough for Stalin and Trotsky had to leave Russia. Both Kamenev and Zinoviev were expelled after disagreements with Stalin, but soon recanted their sins and crept back into the party.

One night in December 1927, film director Sergei Eisenstein was busy in his editing suite working on another cut of his epic on the revolution, *October*. Unknown to him, Stalin had entered the studios to see a version of the film, which had been made to celebrate the revolution's tenth anniversary. Having watched the film he immediately demanded that every scene which included Trotsky should be removed. He also wanted those scenes which included Lenin edited, saying that he didn't want him shown 'in an unsatisfactory light . . . Lenin's liberalism is no longer valid today.'[8]

Soon, a generation would grow up who would have little or

no knowledge that a man called Trotsky built the Red Army and forcefully drove Russia to victory in the Civil War.

Before his cranium was punctured by a GPU ice pick [9] on 20 August 1940, Leon Trotsky's family had played cat and mouse with Stalin's agents for 15 years, sometimes with tragic results.

Stalin's accusations against Trotsky were, in the main, the concocted fantasies of a paranoid demagogue. He had always loathed Trotsky, calling him 'an operetta commander, a chatterbox'.[10] In building the Red Army, the pragmatic Trotsky had often relied on the available military expertise of those ex-Tsarist officers who had come over to the revolution. Stalin's hatred of their class was implacable – to him, anyone who even associated with the old guard, no matter how re-educated they had become, was worthy of suspicion, and Lenin's second-in-command headed the list. At one point he accused Trotsky, a Jew, of being an 'agent of fascism' – this, from the man who would sign a pact with Ribbentrop within a few short years. Perhaps there was an element of deep-seated jealousy, too.

Unlike Lenin, Trotsky was a man who possessed a degree of physical bravery which complemented his superb organizational skills. He was, after all, the hands-on Bolshevik who had organized the October Revolution.

Stalin, the tough peasant, possessed courage and intelligence, yet his rough-hewn sophistication, which sometimes surfaced in a penchant for poetry and literature, was obliterated by his natural cunning, and his devious and untrustworthy character. Stalin carried the deep-seated prejudices of his youth forward into his days of power. The Jews, the Church, the Kulaks, the press, all would fall victim to his paranoia and intolerance. The sheer severity of what it takes to be a true revolutionary, where political expediency subjugates notions of friendship, family love and magnanimity were all greatly magnified in Josef Stalin.

Most western observers today tend to measure their view of the Bolsheviks' main players not so much on their achievements as revolutionaries but on a scale of dislike and distaste. If such a scale were laid down from one to ten, perhaps Lenin would come in at five, Trotsky at seven. Stalin would justifiably score the full ten.

In character Trotsky and Stalin were poles apart.

Despite being stripped of his Soviet citizenship in February 1932, Trotsky would remain the international conscience, albeit sullied, of the revolution and a constant thorn in Stalin's side. He continued to organize conferences in continuance of what he saw as Lenin's work. He published the Russian *Bulletin of Opposition* and formed the International Left Opposition in an attempt to exert external pressure on Russia to return to Lenin's principles. Shunted around the world as an exile, each country which accepted him felt the heat from the Kremlin – Turkey from 1929 to 1933, France until 1935. In January 1933, his daughter, Zina, committed suicide in Berlin. The closest Trotsky got to his beloved Russia was a spell in Norway from 1935 to 1937, too close for Stalin. In August 1936 Trotsky's Norwegian home was raided by fascists headed by Major Vidkun Quisling, the man who would come to head Norway's pro-Nazi government. Stalin had no qualms about accepting favours from fascists. They stole documents which were bound to see Trotsky ejected and by December he was forcibly placed on an oil tanker bound for Mexico, where he arrived on January 9th 1937. Within three years he would be murdered.

During these exiles he had to suffer the knowledge that one of the defendants with Zinoviev and Kamenev at the show trials held in Moscow in August 1936 was his own son, Leon

Sedov. Although not meeting the same fate as the other defendants, he became a victim of the GPU in a Paris hospital where he died, somewhat mysteriously, in February 1938. In January 1937 another son, Sergei, was sent to a Soviet concentration camp to die. In July 1938 Trotsky's former secretary, Rudolf Klement, who was making preparations for the Fourth Socialist International Conference in Paris, was kidnapped and murdered by Stalin's agents. On 24 May in Mexico, Stalin's GPU agent, the artist David Alfaro Siqueiros, broke into the Trotsky compound with a machine gun and attempted to murder the family. He failed, but managed to kill one of Trotsky's guards, the American Robert Shelton Harte.

Throughout his final years of exile Trotsky worked tirelessly to expose Stalin's staggering immorality, publishing countless articles exposing the falsehoods which propped up the show trials of his old comrades. Sadly, when he died on 21 August 1940, he left behind an unfinished manuscript, the title of which was 'Stalin – An Appraisal of The Man and His Influence'.

After the historical evidence, it comes as a shock sometimes to know that Stalin is still revered by many older Russians today.

'Stalin held us together in the worst times' were the words of an unrepentant communist, Leonid Vasavski, 68, one of a half dozen who had assembled on Victory Day 2004, still Russia's most important national holiday on 9 May. Holding his photocopied A4 picture of Uncle Joe, Leonid continued to make his point.

Every great nation needs a man of steel. If we had a Stalin today there wouldn't have been any of this problem with the Chechens. Stalin would have obliterated them. He fulfilled his duty to Lenin. Yes, I agree; many people had to suffer, but they often had only themselves to blame. It was Stalin who made the Soviet Union a powerful country. We could take on the world and people in the west feared us. Look at Russia today. We have become a joke. We didn't have *mafioso* and criminals in Russia when I was a boy. You wouldn't have dared to step out of line, because the police then served the people and the state – not themselves, like they do now. We had work, we had pensions. We had culture. You people from abroad like to praise Mikhail Gorbachev as if he was some kind of a saint. To communists he was just a traitor. He couldn't be bothered to hang on to socialism's achievements. He listened to the capitalists and the imperialists like Reagan and that Margaret Thatcher – and what did he learn from them? We only have to look around to see. Rising prices, shrinking pensions and benefits, profiteering, crime. Well, there are many people today in my country who think that we are like dinosaurs – that communists should be treated as mental patients. We have the same status as a beggar or a lunatic. No-one takes us seriously. But I would rather be a mad beggar than serve capitalism. But until people in this country come to their senses, that's what I will have to be. It is very sad what a poor memory Russia has.[11]

Not, perhaps, such a poor memory but a highly selective one. Sergei Kirov was the head of the Leningrad Communist Party from 1926 until his assassination on 1 December 1934. During that time this favourite Stalinist worked hard for the party, the city and the state to achieve a popularity with the people to match even that of Stalin himself. But such popularity was a dangerous gift. Stalin was eagerly looking for a suitable crime with which to charge two of Lenin's closest old comrades, Gregory Zinoviev and Lev Kamenev, as punishment for their tendency to wander off-message. What Stalin really wanted to do was put Trotsky on trial (simply because he hated him), but he was in exile. The easy solution was a trial-by-proxy of Trotsky through people who could be claimed to be part of a 'Trotskyite plot'. The massive show trial of Kamenev and Zinoviev was played out to a script written – in every sense of the word – by Stalin himself. They were implicated in the murder of Kirov as being members of a fictitious 'Leningrad opposition centre'. Like drugged sheep the two men confessed to every imagined crime that emanated from the vicious mouth of Procurator-General Vyshinsky, who referred to these devoted old Bolshevik fighters as 'mad dogs of capitalism'. Yet even as their sentences were announced, they exclaimed from the dock, 'Go forward . . . follow Stalin' and 'Long live the cause of Marx, Engels, Lenin and Stalin!'[12] There would be no brave gallows speeches in the mode of such martyrs to freedom as Thomas More or William Wallace. The party line, no matter how distasteful, was adhered to even in the face of their own murders.

Some did find a little defiant dignity at the end. The doomed young officer who had stormed the Winter Palace, Vladimir Antonov-Ovseenko, on his way from his cell to be shot outside Moscow's Butyrka prison, distributed his clothes and his boots to fellow victims and asked them that, should they ever be free again, to tell their comrades that he had remained a Bolshevik 'until his final day'.

Latter-day socialists do not associate anti-Semitism with their creed. It must be remembered, however, that even within the revolutionary ranks of Petrograd in 1917, there were many who referred to the Bolsheviks as 'the Yid party'. Pogroms against the Jews had been a part of Russian life. The Tsar Nicholas I passed a law which conscripted Jewish boys into the Army at the age of 12 for a period of 25 years, the idea being that by the time they re-entered public life, well into their 30s, they would have been forcibly turned into Christians. Jewish

children, even immediately after 1917, were the victims of a
quota system for entry into primary and secondary schools.
The early marauding mobs who stormed the countryside in the
first half of 1917 often proclaimed that 'the Jews are next'.
Stalin was not a rabid Jew-hater in the way that Hitler was, but
he often formed his paranoid opinions of his opponents more
rapidly if, like Zinoviev, Trotsky and Kamenev, they happened
to be Jewish. But in 1917 anti-Semitism, as is evidenced by the
memoirs and diaries of many of the foreign diplomats in
Russia, was rife. Meriel Buchanan, the British Ambassador's
daughter, when writing in disgust of a group of Bolsheviks,
makes the sweeping statement 'obviously Jews, every one of
them.' One American diplomat, upon being asked about
Trotsky's character, exclaimed, 'He's the greatest goddamn
Jew since Jesus!', a comment which would no doubt have
appealed to Trotsky's mild vanity.

The story of Russia in 1917 ends not on a note of bright
hope but on a promise of dark struggle, war, privation and
death. There would be some good things ahead. Education
would flourish. Great strides would be made in industry,
medicine, and the arts – even within their monolithic shackles.
Russia would have a formidable army, navy and air force.
They would even be the first nation to enter the space race.
Within 20 years of Lenin's death the people would have a
society vaguely recognizable as the one they had hoped for in
February 1917, albeit a long way from Lenin and Trotsky's
vision. It would not be permeated with that glorious sense of
joy and liberation which had swept through Russia between
February and October in 1917. Lenin's dream of a worldwide
socialist uprising did not happen, but the massive population
of China plunged into their own socialist experiment, as did
other assorted states around the globe. Yet as it is with
Christianity, there are as many ways of interpreting the Lord's

word, in this case Lenin's. Sects and factions among communists have fractured any combined front the movement would have needed for global success. The result of this political infighting was demonstrated in the Spanish Civil War, when rather than form a united front against Franco, many communists resorted to fighting each other.

The Bolshevik revolution remains, therefore, a broken dream. Like most wars, it was violent and bloody. Yet it had a flickering core of hope and a degree of romance which continues to inspire. The American John Reed decided to return to Russia in 1920 after writing his classic *Ten Days That Shook The World* to join the Communist International, only to die of typhoid in a Moscow hospital. He is buried near the Kremlin Wall, and even the Red Cossacks used to sing a song about him – 'John Reed Walks In Petrograd'. Reed was no blue-collar worker. He was a Harvard-educated communist, but an observer who could translate the spirit of the revolution into fine words; here he is on the battle between the *yunkers* and Red Guards to take control of the Petrograd Telephone Exchange in 1917:

> Tired, bloody, triumphant, the sailors and workers stormed into the switchboard room, and finding so many pretty girls, fell back in an embarrassed way and fumbled with awkward feet. Not a girl was injured, not one insulted. Frightened, they huddled in the corners, and then, finding themselves safe, gave vent to their spite. 'Ugh! The dirty, ignorant people! The fools!'. . . Romantic had been their experience passing up cartridges and dressing the wounds of their dashing young defenders, the *yunkers*, many of them members of noble families, fighting to restore their beloved Tsar! These were just common workmen, peasants, 'Dark People'.[13]

Common workmen. Dark People. In Russia and around the world, they still exist. They labour for long hours making trainers and sportswear in the sweat shops of the Far East. They work beneath the earth as children in the mines of South America. They beg in the streets and railway stations of India. Closer to the epicentre of the revolution, what was once the 'proletariat', visibly at least, has ceased to exist. We're the ones with the tattoos, the mobile phones, the credit cards, laptops, I-Pods and wide-screen TVs.

What on earth Lenin and Trotsky would have made of us is anyone's guess.

8
CHILDREN OF THE REVOLUTION

In those days there were only two factions of the population in Russia. One was 'The Father of The People' – Stalin. Everyone else was the enemy. There was no margin in which to think.

Vavara Vassilievna, 91.

Maria Mikhailovna Alexandrovna was born in Petrograd in 1915. Her ancestry forms a direct link to the February revolution of 1917. Unlike many Russians of her age, her living conditions, in a smart, comfortable apartment off Nachilnaya Street on Vasilievksiy Island, have benefited from the success of her children who have made a new life in America. She is a vivacious and generous woman, making us welcome with a fine spread of food including caviar, salmon and *blini*. She likes nothing better than to share a glass of

vodka and talk of her family's history and the revolutionary
years.

I am a descendent of the Lvov family. My father was Mikhail
Mitreievich Lvov. My grandfather's family lived in Moscow
and they were very involved in state affairs. When Peter the
Great left Russia to go to Holland, he left a Lvov in charge in
Moscow. This is the same family of Prince Georgi Evgenievich
Lvov, the liberal politician who headed the Provisional Gov-
ernment after the February revolution in 1917. Before the
revolution our family had a large estate and many servants,
close to Tolstoy's estate. They would dine on occasions with
Prince Lvov. He was a gentleman.

My father was the main engineer of the government's construction bureau for machinery and was invited to St. Petersburg to work at the Putilov plant, first in 1911 and again in
1913. He came here without his first wife Alexandra Alexan-
dronov because although they had been together for fifteen
years, she was very ill and unable to travel. His second wife, my
mother, Maria Ivanovna was only 18 when she met my father
and he was 40. She was a very talented person, a fashion
designer who specialised in hats. Although my mother and my
sister were connected to the noble classes and worked mainly
for them, they had to be very careful. They dressed as neutrally
as possible and wore red armbands so as not to give their class
away. They couldn't be recognised as being nobles. They didn't
want the ordinary people to know what they were. But my
mother and grandmother had simple backgrounds; they were
from peasant families. My grandmother had worked in the
laundry at the Winter Palace where she washed clothes for the
Emperor.

When I was born my mother and my father were not married
yet.

My father baptised me to give me my second name.

The revolution had a bad effect on the life of my family. My mother and father were not communists, but my mother's brother (my uncle) and his wife were active Bolsheviks. I suppose you could say that there was an element of conflict in our family over this. But my father continued his work despite this. The revolutionary government of Petrograd decided to send out groups of 5 or 6 skilled Putilov workers to cities and small towns in Siberia and the Urals. There they could fight and help to set up small centres of industry. They could live better there and develop working communities. This decision was very important because it would contribute to new industry in the country. My father was sent far away to Omsk to help in this campaign. Eventually my father sent for my mother to come from Petrograd to Omsk. She was not allowed to take much luggage. But this was a dangerous time as Admiral Kolchak's White army was approaching. My mother and father helped to erect barricades in the city. Kolchak came to Omsk and there was a terrible massacre. The fighting continued for two years. Kolchak's army would not be allowed to march on Moscow, and eventually he was beaten back. I remained in Petrograd with my grandmother and my aunt. We only survived the revolutionary years by accident and chance. We had no contact with father and mother or letters for two years. Our daily rations were just 100 grams of bread. We ate horsemeat. I once saw a horse fall dead on the street in Petrograd and the people came and butchered it right there on the pavement. My grandmother took great risks in going out alone looking for food. By this time the occupation of the women in my family, that of fashion designers, meant nothing any more. There was no need for fashion as it had been known. The working people raided the old houses and apartments of the rich and took what they needed – and that often meant clothes, so whatever they found they just put it on and wore it.

Maria had to wait five years before meeting her father. The family would experience an element of socialist hypocrisy when he returned, forced as he was to live in separation from them in a very small flat, whilst Maria's Uncle Pavel, the Bolshevik, lived in the spacious luxury of an ex-bourgeois apartment, courtesy of the party.

But when I was re-united with my parents I was so happy. As we grew up we enjoyed life the best way we could. I was taken to Omsk whilst I was still young. I remember going to concerts, two in particular. Once was when my father took me to see the pianist Serota, and the other was a performance on a new electronic instrument called the Theramin, which was the invention of a Russian after whom it was named.

Looking back I think that if Lenin and Trotsky hadn't returned to Russia then we might have had some kind of western democracy. Although my father continued to work for the state, the majority of our family remained anti-Bolshevik. My father thought certain aspect of the Soviet government were stupid, especially when people like Bukharin and Lunacharsky, who was then Commissar of Education, were sold to us as heroes. Before the revolution, my parents said that Tsar Nicholas should have stopped the war. He could have done it. And there was the tragedy of Bloody Sunday in 1905 – all those innocent people killed. They were peaceful, carrying icons. He should have understood the situation in the city. He should have punished the men responsible, but he didn't. We didn't talk about Stalin in the family. Too many people disappeared.

What people should do now is look back at events more objectively. The economic situation in the country when I was a child made the revolution inevitable, but that doesn't stop me thinking that the Bolsheviks were all liars. Their slogan of

'Peace, Land and Bread' was never really fulfilled. They stood in the way of any private initiative. But Lenin was a very clever person, because his NEP (New Economic Policy) meant that many new products appeared and for a while life improved. If Lenin hadn't died and had developed his policies further I think that he could have changed things for the better. But he didn't and we got Stalin. When I was in Omsk every one of the ten families who were our neighbours lost people during the purges. It was terrible. The most precious thing the Russian people have right now is the freedom to speak as we feel without fear of arrest.[1]

Like many ageing Russians, Dimitri Naryshkin, 86, Ex-Soviet airman and forestry worker,[2] had much to say about his country, most of it, naturally, about his own formative years under Stalin.

What I have to say now is no different to what I had to say fifty years ago. Lenin was a great man but tried to do too much in too short a time. It was other people who ruined the revolution – and war. It changed Lenin into a cruel man, and Stalin always had to go one better – and the result was that everybody in 1917 and the generations who followed had to suffer.

If one stopped an elderly pensioner on the streets of Britain and started asking what memories they had of Lloyd George or Stanley Baldwin, detailed responses would not be too forthcoming. It would seem equally unfeasible to stop their Russian counterparts in St Petersburg or Moscow and ask questions about Lenin and the Bolshevik Revolution. However, the randomly selected cross section of Russian senior citizens whose memories, or in most cases those of their parents, have contributed to this story proved remarkably articulate. Having spent most of their lives in fear of expressing an opinion to anyone, the one thing they enjoy most today is open conversation, especially with foreigners.

The more extended interviews had been pre-arranged before I arrived in Russia. Andrey Gagarin is approaching 70, and knew a number of people in the city much older than himself who had stories to tell. Others we met simply by chance. Many openly wanted to berate the government of Vladimir Putin or complain about the current state of Russia, but I have managed to extract whatever short passages of our conversations seemed relevant to 1917. Of the six pre-arranged interviews, one candidate was too ill to speak, and another decided at the last moment that he had nothing to say. This was a pity, because his name was Alexei Mikhailovich Bonch-Breuvich, a descendant of Lenin's close friend, Vladimir Bonch-Breuvich. His appearance on the list was quite exciting, but an hour before we were due to meet, he called, saying, 'I have nothing to say about 1917. I am only a distant relative of Vladimir and I do not wish to speak about the revolution.' Other contributions came via the kind permission of the excellent English-language newspaper, the *St Petersburg Times*. There was, however, still a residue of reticence which represented the 'bad old days' with some contributions. The sight of a tape recorder and a photographer often curtailed what might have been more revealing exchanges, but what relevant responses could be salvaged from these truncated encounters have been kept.

On 9 May each year the population of St Petersburg turn out en masse to witness celebrations for the anniversary of the 900-day siege of Leningrad. Victory Day is still one of Russia's most important public holidays. Massive military parades pound the cobbles of the huge square at the front of the Winter Palace. Later in the day many more thousands of

fresh-faced conscripts march the length of the Nevsky Prospekt
– soldiers, sailors, airmen, the massed military might of Russia
with hearty choirs, regimental bands blaring, flags and red
banners fluttering in the warm spring sunshine. And at the
head of each regiment stride the aged veterans of the one-time
Red Army, Navy and Air Force. Thousands of elderly people
mix with the throngs of eager young Russians who frequently
run out into the parades and present the heavily medalled
veterans with red roses or carnations, with an accompanying
pat on the shoulder and the often repeated words 'Thank you
for what you did'. It is remarkable to see Russian teenagers
acting in this way – something which could well be regarded a
phenomenon in Britain should it ever happen on Remem-
brance Sunday in the vicinity of the Cenotaph.

The opportunity to spend a long day talking to older
ordinary Russians, many of whom were born whilst Lenin
was still alive, was too good to waste. Was there still an echo of
October 1917?

Ivan Pavlovich Zaitsev was born in 1921, and spent almost
40 years of his life in the Soviet Navy. Wounded in the
blockade, he still likes to visit the hospital which cared for
him in those dark Leningrad days.

There are those in Russia today who say we should forget
Lenin and the October revolution and put all that behind us.
That may be alright for younger people since 1990, but people
like me grew up with communism. What Lenin planned, we
lived through. He believed in the workers and a workers' state.
It was a good thing. Today, things like gas, electricity and
water no longer belong to the people. They have become items
of profit once again. Can this be right? Take my pension for
instance. I gave my life to the Soviet Navy and I live on a
pittance of a few hundred roubles. Because we now have

capitalism again, I have to rely on members of my family to get by and will people like Vladimir Putin pay attention to our plight? I think not. So no, Lenin should not be forgotten. He was part of our history. We should have some respect and remember.

Like many old Russians, in contrast to the general view of their western counterparts, Ivan has a great respect for Russia's youth, who he believes could equal the effort his generation made in defeating an enemy. This he puts down to patriotism and conscription. At the age of 17, most Russians can expect a spell in the military. There are growing exemptions, but national conscription explains the predominance on the country's city streets of fresh-faced young sailors, soldiers, airmen and militia.

Nina Petrovna Fedorova was born in 1921. Together with her friend, Maria Timoferivna Schlegova, born in 1929, she struggled through the blockade of Leningrad as members of the Red Army. Among their many tasks they helped to clear rubble, retrieve bodies from the streets and shelled buildings, and assist with the transportation of supplies across the frozen Lake Ladoga.

Nina's respect for Lenin is obvious:

He was a dedicated man. Yes, he was tough and could be very ruthless, but what else could you be in those times? Lenin ran the country after the October revolution and he did it on a worker's wage.[3] Can you imagine that today? The country needed changing and the Tsar was a very weak man. Russians have always been prepared for sacrifice but in 1917 they had sacrificed enough. Life after Lenin wasn't always what he'd planned it to be and at times it was very hard for us, especially in the 1930s and during the Great Patriotic War. But we made the best of it and I prefer that Russia to the one we have today.

Maria agrees.

> No country should forget its history. The revolution and Lenin
> will always be important. What the Bolsheviks did was change
> Russia for ever. Perhaps it could have turned out better, but we
> still enjoyed our childhood and even when times were hard we
> all stuck together. And look at the young people today – they
> might not be interested so much in Lenin now, but they still
> respect us old folk, so whatever we did under communism must
> have had some effect. Do I prefer today's Russia? Well, we can
> say what we like these days, which is good, but on the other
> hand there were a lot of good things in the Soviet times.

Yuri Stephanovich Grusian was an artilleryman who had
fought the Japanese. He had been a sportsman, proud of the
fact that in 1944 he won the annual ski race in Novosibirsk.

> I can't say a lot about Lenin. We learned all about him at school
> and what I recall is that he seemed to be a good man. He
> represented something in the end that pulled us through the
> Great Patriotic War – in the Soviet times there was a spiritual
> reach, a strength of love between us all. That is fading.
> However, I still believe that, faced with the kind of challenges
> we had from the fascists in the 40s, our young people today
> could still rise up and defeat the enemy. Russians are very
> patriotic. They would fight hard for their homeland, because
> that's all part of the Russian character.

Not everyone has a good word for Lenin. Among the post-
perestroika generation of young Russians, eagerly coming to
terms with the wheeler-dealer atmosphere of a free-market
economy, the very iconography of the Soviet era seems to be
one big joke. On Rubinsteyn Street in St Petersburg there is

even a themed restaurant ironically named 'Lenin's Mating Call', which serves an odd menu under such headings as 'Soviet food' and 'Pre-Soviet food'.

Our generous hosts in Russia, Edward and Svetlana Emdin, today run one of St Petersburg's top modern art galleries, The Sol. Edward is totally puzzled that anyone should want to be studying the revolution. Now aged 34, for him, the market economy can't develop fast enough.

All I can tell you about having 'glorious October' and Lenin force fed us at school in the 70s is that I think that Lenin, Trotsky and the whole Bolshevik clan were a bunch of very evil men. The Bolsheviks were criminals. I remember visiting England ten years ago and walking along the street in Islington where I saw posters for British political organizations called the Revolutionary Workers' Party and the Socialist Workers. These posters had pictures of Lenin and Trotsky on them, and I was appalled. It was as if you people in the west hadn't learned *anything*. And you can be thankful that when you were at school over there, you didn't have regular Kalashnikov practice like I did – stripping down the gun and putting it back together again in 30 seconds.

So there was no further opening for discussion there.

The discussions went on all day, on the Winter Palace parade ground, along the Nevsky Prospekt, and at the Piskaryovskoye Memorial Cemetery. The general impression at the end of it all was that when the current generation of Russian senior citizens finally fades away, Lenin will probably fade with them. In 50 years' time he may well be a historical figure in Russia in the same way that Keir Hardie, Churchill or Clement Atlee in Britain – someone who oversaw a massive social change at a momentous time.

Many contacts with Russian veterans were fleeting; one such was a brief conversation with the pragmatic ex-Soviet Air Force General Nikolai Petrovich Rashensev. Proud of the hundreds of parachute jumps he had made in his career, his attitude to the British and the Americans was careful: 'Their economic and military assistance during the Patriotic War was very important.' He had a high regard for his country's Soviet past.

> The revolution had to happen and meant significant change in society and the country at large, but these things do not happen instantly. That is what people must realise about the changes Russians have had to face since *perestroika* – economic change of any kind is a long process. As for the current generation of young Russians then I have every confidence in them, even though they behave differently to the way we did in Soviet times. But they could cope with a war, of that I have no doubt. They *are* Russians, after all.

Prince Andrey Gagarin's family of Russian nobility pre-dates the Romanov dynasty by 500 years. As he approaches 70, he still works as a science professor specializing in laser technology. His off-duty time is spent at his computer screen, gathering together all the many international émigré strands of the Gagarin dynasty. They were – and still are – an artistic family, friends of writers, poets and painters. Among his noted predecessors, Grigory Gagarin (1810–1893) stands out. One of Russia's great nineteenth-century artists, his paintings hang in St Petersburg's Russian Museum. He illustrated books for Pushkin and Lermontov and made his name whilst a student with Turgenev as a translator of the works of Jean Jacques Rousseau.

When we experienced Andrey's frequent generosity at dinner in his 6th floor apartment in St Petersburg, the artistic connection remained unbroken – one of the guests was Andrey's fellow academic, the author Mikhail Mikhailovich Glinka, a descendant of the famous composer of the opera *Russlan and Ludmilla.*

In 1917, the Gagarins had to think on their feet as the Bolshevik storm broke.

> The Gagarin mansion at Pskov was called Holomki. The people were taking the land and houses over everywhere. Our family was known to have many friends in the artistic community; poets, writers, painters. We had to find a way of holding on to Holomki whilst at the same time pleasing the Bolsheviks. Other members of the family joined the White Armies, but at Pskov they stayed behind and turned the mansion into a kind of sanatorium for those artists and poets who had been sympathetic to the revolution. It didn't last. Eventually we lost Holomki. But I still have one privilege left from the old times. Each year we can go back to the estate and collect the honey.

The subsequent fate of the dispossessed Gagarins after 1917 was outlined in grim detail when we were invited to spend an afternoon with Andrey's mother. We travelled across St Petersburg to arrive at yet another somewhat gloomy apartment block and were ushered in to a spacious study, overflowing with thousands of books from floor to ceiling. Once again we experienced that Russian generosity – a meal had been prepared for us in advance.

Vavara Vassilievna is 91 and was born on 16 December 1913.

> I was four years old at the time of the revolution. We lived in Finland at a place then called Orgelvu. I don't know what it is

called today. My mother was a doctor. She was one of the first women doctors who graduated in the second year after the opening of the first medical institute for women. My father was a military man. He was an artillery officer for the Tsar's army in the fortress. Although he served the Tsar, my parents had a low opinion of the Romanovs. They blamed his weakness for the revolution. Had he been different it wouldn't have happened. And his wife – she was of German origin. This didn't help. Nicholas was a kind man, but no good as a leader, and so the country was ruined by the Bolsheviks. As a child I was very happy because my parents were wonderful people. No one could have done more for their children than they did. I had a sister who was seven years older than me. She died ten years ago. All my life she helped me, and my parents dedicated their lives to their children.

After the revolution broke out we moved to Ukraine, to a small town which was eventually to be known as Kirovograd. My father decided to go and join the army of General Denikin in the Crimea. He wanted to save Russia from the communists. But he fell ill with typhus and went into a hospital, where he remained for over a month. The illness was very severe. When he left the hospital, he had nowhere to go because Denikin's army had been defeated. It was no more.

He was a long, long way from home and had no idea where his family was, so he set out to find us. My mother, although she worked as a doctor, found it very hard to earn enough to care for her two daughters. She didn't know anything about her husband. She had no idea where he was or even if he was still alive. Then one day, suddenly, out of nowhere, he appeared. I remember that when we lived in Ukraine my mother would go to her office and my sister would go to her school and they would be locked in their rooms. In the apartment we lived in there were patches of blood on the walls, because people had

been killed there before we moved in. But we were at least
happy to have somewhere to live at all.

Vavara is convinced that her mother's medical qualifications,
still a precious commodity in Bolshevik times, helped to save at
least one strand of the family. She and her parents thought that
the working class had been duped by the Bolsheviks. They had
low opinions of Trotsky and Lenin, and an abiding hatred of
Stalin, whose influence would bring repeated tragedy into her
life.

I had three husbands. They all died. My first was Prince
Gagarin. He was nine years older than me. And that's why
he was taken away and shot. Simply because he was a Prince,
from a very old family, although they insisted he was an
English spy. Before he married me he had been approached
by the police who wanted him to act as an informer. They told
him he had two possibilities; one that he could become an
informer and then he would be left in peace. The other was
that, if he refused, he must sign a statement admitting that he
was a counter-revolutionary. They warned him – 'if you sign
this, then you'll see what will follow' but he signed it. When he
proposed to me, he said that he wasn't sure if he had the right to
ask me. I said of course he did – why should we pay attention to
what they say? So we married in church.

But life had to go on, and as we grew up under the new
regime and moved to Leningrad we never the less learned to
enjoy ourselves as best we could. My husband and I had season
tickets to the Philharmonic Society. We would go twice a week.
We admired Shostakovich – he was the best. And Prokofiev,
another great composer. We enjoyed going to piano concerts,
especially those given by Sviatoslav Richter.

They took him away along with my father. We never went to

bed until two in the morning in those days. We would sit up and wait for the bell to ring, or the knock on the door. Eventually, it came. At first some professors campaigned for my husband's release and he was released for a while, but re-arrested.

I never saw them again. They just allowed me to send my husband one little parcel; a little food, a small cushion, some linen. I don't know if he ever got it. I had become a teacher of English but it was decided that as the wife of an 'enemy of the people' I should be banned from teaching. I was sent into exile at the age of 23 and had to learn to become a typist. But you know, there were always changing waves of political decision. When I was 26 I was allowed to return and looked for work as a teacher. I went to my old professor at the Institute of Languages. He was a Jew, Boris Alexandrovich Ilyish, the institute's director, a very brave man. I told him that I had returned from exile and had no place to work. He risked his entire career by giving me a job, but said, 'I don't know anything about your exile. I don't want to know.' But he gave me a full time job. At last I could earn enough money to feed my son properly. Boris Alexandrovich became a life-long friend. He was a good, honest man. When Stalin concocted one of his conspiracy fantasies, this time that the Jews were plotting against the regime, Boris was prosecuted and dismissed from his post as director. We always tried to help and support him. He was often here, in this same room. He was a very worried man. In those days there were only two factions of the popula-tion in Russia. One was 'The Father of The People' – Stalin. Everyone else was the enemy. There was no margin in which to think.

When they arrested my husband I was told that he had no rights to contact me in any way for a period of ten years. I did try and find out about him, but nine years passed and when I spoke to the authorities they said, 'You should get married'. I said 'But I am already married. My husband is Gagarin.' They said 'Well, perhaps you should get married again, because we shot him nine years ago.'

And then they asked me if I would be an informer. I refused.

My next husband was a shipbuilding designer. We would have liked to travel, but they wouldn't let us travel. They were scared we might defect. Throughout the years we have seen so many difficult times. In many ways a lot of the time it was a complete nightmare. Today I regret not being able to travel widely, and now I am too infirm at my age to start. I have never been out of the Soviet Union. Today I still read my books and give lessons to children whose parents have no money. Has Russia improved? Well, they don't lock people up as much as they used to, and even speaking to you as I have done today takes my breath away when I look back. Gorbachov was a great talker, but he didn't change things all that much. He just talked about it. But the best thing about now is that we can speak and not be afraid. As for the Bolsheviks and what the revolution achieved, well – I will let you decide – you've heard my story.

There are epic stories hidden behind the locked doors of dusty entrance halls off the back streets of St Petersburg which can plunge Pasternak's *Dr Zhivago* into the shade. On a rainy, cold, Sunday afternoon we made our way up numerous dark staircases to the tiny, cramped, single-room apartment of one of the sweetest and most creative old ladies anyone could wish to meet.

Helena Matveievna Krapivina was born in Petrograd on 16 November 1912. At 93, she lives quietly in this small room, looking out onto a blank concrete wall. Around her hang the mementoes of a long creative life: tapestries, paintings, sepia photographs of long-departed friends and family. Although Helena was only five when the revolution occurred, she does have memories of the time. Her father was a Petrograd lawyer. Her mother had a noble background in Siberia, and links to the White Admiral Kolchak. One of her ancestors fought with Napoleon. She recalled the darkness in Petrograd when they returned from their dacha to the city in 1917, the broken glass, the looted shops. They lived on horsemeat and huddled around the gas stove. Their privileged lives had been obliterated, and her father, like many of his class, at first found it difficult to adjust.

But eventually he found work as a lawyer for a Latvian company. Father's salary improved and some new shops began to open where you could buy food for foreign currency. We exchanged some of our family's silver and gold items for foreign currency. But we were lucky. The members of the working class hadn't any gold or silver to exchange and for them life remained very hard. Many people began to appear on the streets selling small pastries but it was dangerous to buy some of these things – no-one knew what was in these pies and pastries. Nobody knew how they were made. But there were sunflower seeds to buy – they were cheap and quite nutritious. Everybody in the streets ate sunflower seeds and the husks were all over the pavements and under your feet in the cinemas and theatres. All over the city in 1917 I remember the queues. Everywhere, outside every shop, there was a long line of people. And what I remember is that these queues were black; everyone seemed to wear black in those days.

Our servants did not leave us. They stayed with us until the end. As a family, including my brother and our servants, we had nothing to do with politics. We didn't even discuss the subject. The most incredible thing is that we actually managed to hold on to our apartment when everyone else seemed to be losing theirs. It was quite large, and the Bolsheviks insisted on turfing the better off people out of their homes and putting workers from more underprivileged areas in their place. But somehow, we escaped this. One of our servants was illiterate but after the revolution she began attending school and learned to read and write. In 1925 I began work as a school teacher. I can't recall what my parents thought of the Romanovs. I was only five at the time of the revolution. Even in the early 20s I didn't even realise that the Emperor had been killed. Nobody knew about it at that time in Russia.

My mother told me that when I was one year old we had a dacha in Strelna and Tsar Nicholas had a palace there. The Tsar's family visited Strelna and my mother had taken me out for a walk in my pram in Orlov Park. She was approached by three princesses, all dressed in white, and they were fascinated, they said 'by the beauty of your child'. They asked my mother if they could take me for a walk and she let them. She said the princesses spoke English or French, and not Russian. Of course, I don't remember it!

As for Lenin and Trotsky, I can't imagine what the government would have been like if they hadn't returned. However, I do think that Trotsky was a very clever man. But in those days I didn't understand politics. I was a child. We never visited Lenin's mausoleum in Moscow. When I grew up I enjoyed many things. I liked great singers, particularly the Russian tenor Sobinov – he was a very handsome man. And my parents took me to see the ballet, which I loved, especially the ballerina Ulanova. I never got to see Ksheshinskaya dance. The Bosheviks commandeered her house as a headquarters in 1917. She left Russia in the 1920s and never returned, but her son stayed behind and became a very good teacher. When I was at school I was quite a lazy girl but after school I did manage to graduate and did many things. I began writing poetry. My poems were successful at the time and eventually I had a book of poems published – but only when I was 88! In the 1930s I went back to college to study art and then came the war. I got a job in Leningrad at the Marinskiy Theatre as a theatre artist, and I also designed theatrical costumes. I designed the costumes for operas such as *Rigoletto* and many other productions. Whilst working at the Marinskiy I met my husband. He was making sets and scenery. We worked together for eleven years, but sadly we divorced and I left the theatre. I also worked for the Theatre of Musical Comedy and even at one time worked in the circus. After my theatrical work I became a fashion designer. I retired at 65 and began painting. I had four exhibitions in Leningrad. When I was 82 I met a young girl who was a journalist. I had been putting my memoirs together and she helped to get some of my stories published in magazines. My memoirs have since been published in small books. The latest volume is called *Forgive Me and Accept My Regards*. These books haven't sold too well because they were small print runs, but one of my works is being published in Germany. I live on my pension today which is fortunately better than that of many people of my age. This is because I remained in Leningrad throughout the siege in the war, therefore I get a military pension, and it helps that I have written about the siege in some of my works.

Looking back across the years to 1917 and the two decades which followed my only reaction is to try and forget. What the Bolsheviks gave us was a climate of fear. My opinion of Stalin is that he was much worse than Hitler. Hitler murdered people who, in the main, he didn't know; he murdered strangers and races who were alien to the Nazis. This in itself was unforgivable – but Stalin murdered us, the Russian population, the people who had brought about the revolution. He made us all into potential 'traitors' if we spoke out of turn. Can you imagine what it was like in the 1930s if you went to a cafe for the evening with four or five friends and you said the wrong thing? You never knew which of them might have been compromised into being an informer, and that was the case in families, too.

As for Russia today then I am not too impressed with what is going on. The good thing is freedom of speech. That is precious. But many people are still in poverty. Of course there are rich people now, but not many. I can't say whether or not Vladimir Putin is a good president or not, but the people he has around him aren't up to the job and I can't see any improvement in the country.

By a chance meeting with an English-speaking Russian photographer, Andrey Samatuga and his partner, Sasha, a doctor specializing in chest and respiratory diseases, we were introduced to one of St Petersburg's rising TV stars and jazz aficionados, Sergei Polatovsky. When Sergei discovered that we were looking for Russians who might recall 1917, he invited us to his apartment off Mayakovsky Street where he lives with his grandfather, Vladimir Abromovich Katz. Vladimir was the oldest Russian we met, born on 18 January 1910.

I was born in Odessa in the Crimea. We lived close by to the ancestral home of the legendary Prince Potemkin. This was in the state of Gubernia, in the vicinity of the River Dneiper. Leon Trotsky came from the same town. We lived on Volokhinskay street. In Odessa the export of agricultural goods was important because we were connected to the Black Sea. The Potemkins lived next door. We lived at number 4, they lived at number 5. My father was in the timber trade. Just before the

First World War he went away on business and never came back. Near to our house there was a sweet factory making candy. All of us, big or small, found work there. I had two brothers and one sister. In Odessa, discussion about the nature of the Romanovs didn't involve us. We had no connection with what was happening so far away. The revolution came late to us. Our employer at the sweet factory was prosperous. We wrapped the sweets. We were the exploited ones. But after the revolution sweets with wrappers weren't so important.

We were not really fully aware of the nature of the revolution or of what had happened in Moscow or Petrograd. It was a long way from Odessa, and we had a much smaller population than those cities. As to whether the February revolution or the October was the 'real' revolution I have no idea. I do remember, however, that there were new banners on the streets with new slogans, and a couple of the parks in the city soon had new names – Lenin and Trotsky. And the year after the revolution, one thing I do recall very well, was the arrival of warships in the port. They must have been part of the intervention forces who were supporting the Whites. Hundreds of soldiers disembarked from these ships. They were Greeks. It was horrific; they rounded up hundreds of people, men, women and children, and locked them in barns or warehouses, then set fire to them. People had to go to the ruins of these places days later to see if they could find the remains of their families. The Greeks shot lots of people.

I don't know where he got it from, but there was a man aged about 30 in our apartment block who had got hold of a machine gun and some ammunition. Eventually the Greeks arrived in our street and they got a surprise as our neighbour opened up with the machine gun and raked the street. I saw several Greeks killed in front of me. But it did the trick – they left and didn't bother us after that!

But that period after the revolution was tough. The port, which had been so busy before, became quiet, and the harbour was completely inactive. Businesses closed, schools closed. But I did get an education for 8 years when they set up the labour schools. In 1925 when I was fifteen I got a job in Petrovsk as an apprentice to a film projectionist. This led to a job as an electrician in a factory. I combined my work in the factory with study, and in 1929 there was a special call by the government for 30,000 young working men to go into higher education. I was one of the chosen ones. At this time I had a romance with the daughter of a sculptor. But the sculptor had been a White and the romance was soon over.

Of the workers chosen for the higher education, every one of us failed the exams. So I attended a workers' educational institute in Odessa. There, as an electrician, I wanted to study national electrical power, strong currents and high voltage. But this line of study was unavailable so I studied communications, such as telephony and radio. I was transferred to the Institute of Communication to study. After my first year the Commisar for Education, Anatoly Lunacharsky came to Odessa and ordered that all our education should be carried out in Ukranian. It was a time of great hunger and we seemed to live on nothing but soya beans. Boiled soya. Soya soup. It was soya everything. Sick of soya, I filed a petition to leave Odessa as I couldn't speak Ukranian and I had grounds to leave because my mother was in Leningrad. Because of the huge unemployment she and my brothers and sisters had left to find work.

It didn't help either at the Institute; I remember the mathematics tutor who taught us was 80 years old. He spoke in such a slow, faltering way, and had a habit of breaking into French when running through his calculations. It was very frustrating for us as students, but the poor old man was too set in his ways at that age to change. I agreed to go to Leningrad and lead a seminar for worker students there. My job was to talk to factory directors and find them places and locate dormitories. The pay wasn't much but it was OK. I was happy; I had a scholarship and a job.

In 1935 I went to work in a research institute in the afternoons. I was in a good team. We were carrying out research work in radio location. In 1939 I was sent to the Far East to study this project further. I stayed there until 1941. When the war broke out at first I was exempted from military service. I received four exemption cards in a row rather than draft cards and then suddenly, the fifth card was delivered at five o'clock one morning – this time I was drafted – and the man from the army said 'Be there at seven.' By this time Leningrad was surrounded by the Nazis. Suddenly I was a Captain in the army. At first I was in charge of a squad, then a platoon, and soon I was promoted to company level as a Lieutenant. One of my tasks in Leningrad during the blockade was to locate and arrest agent provocateurs who were deliberately showing the Luftwaffe where to drop their bombs. These pro-German people did exist and they had to be dealt with. I also had to organise the collection of bodies in the city. Later in 1941 I left to join the anti-aircraft units. I was in the transmission and telecoms centre. By the end of the war I was the army's head engineer in anti-aircraft telecommunications. I was promoted to Major, then sub-Colonel. I met my wife, Rita Zuckerman in 1937 in Leningrad. You know, in 1913 in the telephone directory for Petrograd, there was only one Zuckerman – Tobias Zuckerman, my future father-in-law. We had a daughter in 1946. In 1967 we built our own dacha, which we have enjoyed ever since. I worked for 20 years after the war in the Leningrad area. I left the army in 1961 and worked until 1980 as controller of Leningrad City telephone network. In 1968 I designed the first radio communications mast which stands next to the Mosque in St. Petersburg. It was the first of its kind and I was the engineer in charge. I was running a construction company around the city to install telephone systems. I was also an inventor of items in the field of TV amplifiers and transformers, and modulators and transmitters, some of which were patented in the USSR.

In 1995, following the 50th anniversary of the blockade all of us who were sub-colonels in the Red Army were promoted to full-colonel. So today I'm a retired colonel. Two years ago our pensions were doubled. Unlike some from the army, I'm doing alright. As for the country today . . . well. Putin is OK – it's just the people around him who are no good. Yeltsin made attempts to win the people's hearts and he succeeded. As for my attitude to the Bolsheviks taking power, well I have no complaints. I worked hard and the system worked for me.

There is a very sad side to the revolution's descent into Stalinism and 'socialism in one country'. For eight decades, with the exception of a brief window we in the West had into Russia when they defeated the Germans in 1944–45, the insularity of communism has kept the lives of ordinary Russians separate from the rest of the world. Their day-to-day existence, their culture, their views on the rest of the world were made a mystery. They became the ultimate aliens.

Those who favoured their cause in the West were also alienated.

What the Bolsheviks did in 1917 was bold, ruthless and new. Lenin's vision of a one-dimensional society was vastly different to that of the liberated working class who took to the streets in February that year. Until 1989 the jury was still out on communism. It seems such a paradox that, in the end, the verdict was decided by the Russians themselves. I asked one old soldier if he thought anything like 1917 could ever happen again. He threw his head back and laughed.

I very much doubt it. Lenin never had colour TV, radio and hamburgers to contend with. Today the working class are more keen to buy a car or a cellphone than they would ever be to attend a political meeting. The media now is too strong. Lenin's message was strong – it lasted a long time. But fighting in the streets and taking over the government? I don't think the people of today would know where to start.

APPENDIX I

A CHRONOLOGY OF EVENTS

Dates here correspond to the Julian Calendar which was used in Russia until 1918.
This was 13 days behind the western (Gregorian) calendar.

> *The young here tonight may have the good fortune of witnessing the coming proletarian uprising. However, we – the old ones – may not live to see the decisive battles of this coming revolution.*
>
> Lenin (then aged 46) in a lecture to
young workers in Zurich, January 1917

12 January Britain's Ambassador, Sir George Buchanan, meets Tsar Nicholas and warns him that he has '*come to the parting of the ways, and that it rested with him either to lead Russia to victory and a permanent peace, or to revolution and disaster*'.

January to February Hunger, the intense cold, military defeats by the Germans and governmental chaos all fuel the growing strike movement in Petrograd.

23–28 February Celebrating International Womens' Day, thousands of women leave the breadlines and join the strikers from the Putilov arms works, taking to the streets with banners declaring 'Down With The Autocracy'. They are dispersed but reassemble later in the day as a massive, 200,000 strong crowd. Yet more workers join the demonstrations. Cossacks at first harass and attack demonstrators all along the Nevsky Prospekt, then refuse to intervene.

Ordered out to fire on the demonstrators, the Vohlnia, Preobrazhensky and Latvian Regiments mutiny and join the strikers.

Even larger crowds assemble and the Tsar orders his troops under General Khabalov to fire on the demonstrators. The troops refuse. Khabalov wires the Tsar: 'I cannot fulfil the command to re-establish order in the capital.'

28 February Rodzianko, the Duma President, writes to the Tsar suggesting he makes reforms to prevent a national disaster. Nicholas ignores him. The Tsar dissolves the Duma; it continues to sit.

1 March More and more regiments have gone over to the discontented masses. Workers break into arsenals unopposed and take 40,000 rifles. The Petrograd Soviet of Workers' Deputies is formed, along with the Committee of the State Duma, which declares itself to be 'The Provisional Government'.

The Petrograd Soviet issues Order No. 1 to the troops, ending saluting off duty, banning harsh treatment by officers and calling for the election of Army Committees in all units. Prince Lvov becomes leader of the Provisional Government. The death penalty is abolished.

2 March Nicholas II abdicates. His brother Michael takes over.

3 March Michael abdicates. Josef Stalin returns from a three-year exile in Siberia to resume his old post as editor of the Bolshevik newspaper, *Pravda.*

14 March The Petrograd Soviet issues a manifesto which calls on all belligerents to bring an end to the war. In New York, Leon Trotsky and his family board the Norwegian ship *Christianafjord* in the hope of eventually reaching Russia via Norway and Sweden.

22 March The Trotskys are taken for interrogation from the *Christianafjord* at Halifax, Nova Scotia, by the British naval detectives Machen and Westwood. Trotsky's wife and children are left in Halifax whilst Leon is taken to a concentration camp for German prisoners at Amherst.

27 March Lenin, his wife Krupskaya and 20 leading Bolsheviks board the train in Zurich which will take them across Germany on the first leg of their return journey to Russia.

3 April After travelling via Sweden and Finland, Lenin arrives at the Finland Station in Petrograd where he makes his speech to the waiting crowds from the turret of an armoured car.

7 April Lenin publishes his 'April Theses' which embodied the following ideas:

To end the war. All power to the Soviets. All land and property to the people. World revolution.

18 April The Provisional Government's Foreign Minister, Milyukov, issues a note to Allied embassies stating Russia's continuing support and involvement in the war. British Prime Minister Lloyd George sends the Provisional Government his support.

20 April Massive anti-Milyukov demonstrations.

27 April Petrograd Soviet joins the Provisional Government.

2 May Both Milyukov and Guchkov, the War Minister, resign from the Provisional Government.

4 May After ten years in exile, Leon Trotsky and his family finally arrive in Russia. At the Finland Station in Petrograd they are given a hearty welcome. Trotsky is not yet a Bolshevik, but is elected onto the Executive Committee of the Party in an advisory capacity.

5 May Prince Lvov forms a Coalition Provisional Government which will include some Bolsheviks, Social Revolutionaries and Mensheviks. The energetic young lawyer, Alexander Kerensky, becomes Minister for War.

7 May Trotsky and his family, who have been living in one room in Petrograd's run-down Kiev Hostelry, are offered a sumptuous apartment by an old comrade from the 1905 revolution, the one-time blacksmith-turned-successful engineer Serebrovsky. Unfortunately, their politics are at serious odds and the Trotskys are forced to return to their room at the Kiev.

17 May Since April the peasants have embarked on a continuing campaign of looting manor houses, seizing goods and allowing their animals to graze on the landowners' pasture. Social disorder in rural areas now spirals out of control with no intervention from the authorities.

3–24 June The First All-Russian Congress of Soviets is held in Petrograd. Lenin speaks openly about the possibilities of seizing power from the government. However, with the majority of delegates at this time being Mensheviks and Social Revolutionaries, his views are not taken all that seriously.

7 June The entire Machine Gun regiment of the Russian Army mutinies and 20,000 sailors arrive in Petrograd with the demand that the Bolsheviks take over the Provisional Government.

18 June Despite being faced with massive public opposition to the war, Alexander Kerensky orders a new war offensive against the Germans and Austrians on the Russian, western and south-western fronts. The result is huge anti-war demonstrations in Pétrograd.

20 June Under cover of a massive artillery barrage, the Russian offensive begins. For a few days it appears that Russia is gaining superiority as a few localized successes are celebrated. Kerensky reports from the front that 'the Russian Revolutionary Army with colossal enthusiasm assumed the offensive.' Within two weeks this grinds to a halt as whole regiments surrender and an atmosphere of mutiny and disobedience grows in the ranks.

2 July The Constitutional Democrats (Cadets) resign from the Provisional Government.

3–5 July Kerensky manages to put down Bolshevik-led demonstrations which descends upon the Tauride Palace of Petrograd with the aid of troops. He takes measures against Bolshevik leaders causing Lenin, Zinoviev and others to go into hiding in Finland.

8 July Kerensky is made Prime Minister.

19 July Kerensky appoints General Kornilov as Commander-in-Chief of Russian Armies. However, Kerensky has replaced left-wing intimidation with an even greater threat from the extremely right-wing and power-hungry Kornilov.

24 July Kerensky forms the Second Coalition Provisional Government which this time includes the Constitutional Democrats (Cadets).

Trotsky and Lunacharsky (eventually to become Soviet Commissar for Education) are arrested.

26 July–3 August Sixth Bolshevik Congress. In his absence, Trotsky's group join the Bolsheviks.

12–14 August Kerensky's Provisional Government holds a

State Conference in Moscow. Meanwhile, Kerensky's fears grow as he receives disturbing intelligence that his appointed C-in-C, General Kornilov, who sought 'all civil and military powers' was assembling a counter-revolutionary force to march on Petrograd. The Petrograd Soviet springs into action and a broad mix of Mensheviks, Bolsheviks, peasants and social revolutionaries form 'The Committee for Struggle with Counter-Revolution'. Trenches are dug, sailors arrive from Kronstadt ready to fight, railwaymen divert trains. Committee members ride out to debate with Kornilov's cavalry; their arguments convince the soldiers not to attack.

28 August Kornilov's move on Petrograd collapses in disarray. He is arrested along with his closest Cossack officers.

31 August–6 September A Bolshevik Resolution is passed in the Petrograd Soviet. In the absence of a cabinet, Kerensky organizes a 'Directory' as an alternative. As he dissolves the anti-Kornilov committees, he releases Trotsky from prison. The Bolsheviks gain a majority in the Moscow Soviet.

23 September Trotsky is elected Chairman of the Petrograd Soviet.

25 September Yet another new Coalition Provisional Government is formed with discussions under way for a proposed Parliament.

10–12 October The 'Pre-Parliament' holds a meeting. Meanwhile, Lenin has returned from his Finnish exile, still in disguise as a Lutheran vicar. He attends a meeting in Petrograd of the Bolshevik Central Committee, where it is decided to plan and organize an armed insurrection. Kamenev and Zinoviev vote against this plan. The Military Revolutionary Committee is established by the Petrograd Soviet. Trotsky sends commissars to all the Petrograd regiments and authorizes the city arsenals to arm the workers.

24 October Kerensky suspects an imminent uprising and

orders the Army to take precautions. These involve cutting the phone wires to Bolshevik HQ at the Smolny Institute and raising the bridges on the Neva to prevent crowds from entering the city centre. To 'protect' the Winter Palace Kerensky sends three detachments of student soldiers, a bicycle unit, the 'Women's Death Battalion' comprising 140 volunteers, 40 war invalids led by a one-legged officer, and a few light artillery pieces. Kerensky closes down the Bolshevik press.

25 October Trotsky and Lenin complete the preparations for the armed rising as the Second Congress of Soviets, with the Bolsheviks forming the majority, gathers to meet at the Smolny Institute, now the Bolshevik HQ.

25–26 October During the night Lenin and Trotsky's plans are put into action. It was Trotsky's idea to use the Congress at the Smolny as a cover whilst the insurrection took place. The rest of the insurrection progresses smoothly. One by one, the railway stations, the telephone exchanges, banks, bridges and the military HQ at the Engineers' Palace are occupied.

Following the Provisional Government's failure to respond to an ultimatum to surrender, shots are fired at the Winter Palace from the cruiser *Aurora*, and from the Peter & Paul Fortress.

Kerensky escapes in a car borrowed from the American Embassy.

26 October The new Soviet Government sets out Decrees on Peace and Land, but angry controversy rages among the delegates of the Second Congress of Soviets which had met whilst the insurrection was being carried out. The Central Committee considered that the

> 'Congress did not take place . . . We regard it as a private gathering of Bolshevik delegates'.

The following statement is released to the press:

TO THE CITIZENS OF RUSSIA!

The Provisional Government has been deposed. Government authority has passed into the hands of the organ of the Petrograd Soviet of Workers and Soldiers' Deputies, the Military Revolutionary Committee.

The Council of Peoples' Commissars is Established (Sovnarkom).

27 October Krasnov's Cossacks begin move towards Petrograd under direction from Kerensky intending to put down the uprising.

28 October Successful action at Krasnoye Selo and Gatchina by Red Guards against Cossacks.

29 October A revolt by *yunkers* (military cadets) is put down by Bolshevik forces in Petrograd.

30–31 October Soviet victory against Krasnov's Cossacks at Tsasrkoe Selo.

1 November Battles in Moscow between Red Guards and Cossacks to control the Kremlin. Krasnov captured at Gatchina.

2 November Red Guards achieve victory in Moscow, but with heavy casualties.

7 November Acting C-in-C of the Army, General Dukhonin is instructed to open peace negotiations with the Germans.

9 November Dukhonin disobeys order to discuss armistice with Germany. He is replaced as C-in-C by low-ranked Lieutenant N.V. Krylenko. Dukhonin is subsequently murdered by his troops.

14 November Krylenko approaches Germans to negotiate an armistice. The German Eastern Front Command agrees.

20 November First peace delegation meets the Germans.

22 November Agreement at Brest-Litovsk signed with the

Germans ensures no hostilities between 24 November and 4 December.

25–28 November Counter-revolutionary forces under Generals Kornilov and Kaledin signify the start of civil war with battles against Red Guards and Bolshevik troops.

2 December Kaledin beats Red forces on the Don at Rostov.

11–18 December Battles rage in the south between White forces and Bolsheviks. Decree issued by Sovnarkom abolishing all ranks and titles in the Army (16 December).

20 December The All-Russia Board for Organizing the Red Army is formed.

24 December Red forces establish a headquarters at Kharkov commanded by Commissar Antonov with General Muravyov as Chief of Staff.

27 December Negotiations at Brest-Litovsk resume.

31 December Krylenko outlines to Sovnarkom the need to establish a regular, Socialist Revolutionary people's army.

APPENDIX 2

AN A–Z OF POLITICAL PARTIES, PROMINENT PEOPLE AND ORGANIZATIONS

This is not intended as an encyclopaedic listing of the dozens of organizations and personalities associated with the revolution, but a basic sampling of the more prominent ones as they apply to this work.

Prominent Parties

Anarchists

Not really a 'party' at all. By their very nature, the Anarchists (derived from the Greek *Anarchia,* non-rule), despite their general support of communism, failed to gain much overall influence in Russia in 1917 due to their policy of not forming political parties. Therefore they possessed little in the way of connected organization across the country. They did, however, form a powerful cutting edge among the various parties, frequently dislodged the upper classes from their property and established themselves as communes in various houses, a pattern which the Bolsheviks would develop further when coming to power. The anarchist creed 'every man should be his own law, his own government and his own church' meant that they were not only against property, but any form of state control. They were, however, believers in direct action by the workers. Prominent Russian anarchists were Mikhail Bakunin (1814–1876) and Peter Kropotkin (1842–1921).

Bolsheviks

(From the Russian for 'member of the majority'.) The Bolsheviks, or in Russian, *Bolsheviki*, were a group formed following the 1903 split within the Russian Social Democratic Party. As a radical faction Lenin led them on a more forceful path to that of the other bloc resulting from the split, led by Julius Martov, the Mensheviks. The Bolsheviks opposed the Mensheviks' more moderate policies, were adverse to parliamentary government, and sought immediate action led by the proletariat to control and own the land, industry and the banks. Their support was stronger among the urban workers, although during 1917 they had increased rural support among the peasantry.

Cadets

(Also known as *Kadets* from the Russian *Konstitutsionnye Demokraty*, or Constitutional Democrats.) Their original name was 'The Party of the People's Freedom'. Although they were a revolutionary party, and critical of the Tsar, their support came mainly from the academic and liberal professional strata of society. They were heartily loathed by Lenin and Trotsky, and after the October coup in 1917, the Cadets pressed for a democratic Russian republic, a move which the Bolsheviks dealt with in January 1918 by outlawing the Cadets as 'enemies of the people'. Their leader was Pavel Milyukov.

Communist Party of the Soviet Union

In 1918 (as Lenin had sought to do earlier in the previous year), the Bolsheviks changed their name to the Communist Party, a term more fitting Lenin's adherence to Karl Marx's communist philosophy and his *Communist Manifesto*. The term 'Soviet Union' would come later, but at the same time as the Bolsheviks changed their name, they formed the Russian Soviet Federal Socialist Republic (RSFSR). Following the Russian Civil War, when the communists re-took parts of the old Tsarist empire which had declared independence, by 1922 many new soviets were absorbed into the RSFSR, which warranted a new name-change to the Union of Soviet Socialist Republics (USSR), which became known as the Soviet Union.

Left Socialist Revolutionaries

Like the Bolsheviks, the Left Social Revolutionaries believed in the dictatorship of the proletariat, but had many reservations about Lenin and Trotsky's more extreme attitudes to gaining power. They did, however, work with Sovnarkom, (the early Soviet government) holding a portfolio on Agriculture. The party gained many peasant members from the slightly less radical Social Revolutionaries (SRs) which increased their power base as they supported the confiscation of land without compensation to the landowners. Among the Left Socialist

Revolutionary leaders, the left-wing terrorist Maria Spirido-nova was prominent.

Mensheviks

(*Menshevik*, Russian for 'member of the minority'.) With their left faction led by Julius Martov, this was the more moderate faction resulting from the 1903 split in the Russian Social Democratic Labour Party. Their belief was that there should be a slower path towards the goal of socialism during which the working class would have to achieve political power. There were many socialist intellectuals in the Menshevik ranks, a large proportion of whom tended to lean to the right in support of the more liberal propertied classes. Trotsky was their most radical member and left to become a Bolshevik in the summer of 1917. After 1922 the party was formally suppressed.

Novaya Zhizn (New Life)

This grouping also went under the more cumbersome title United Social Democratic Internationalists. 'New Life' was the shorter name taken from their widely-read newspaper, which was edited by Maxim Gorky. Their support among the proletariat was limited, and their aims roughly matched those of the Mensheviks.

Octobrists

Taking their name from the 1905 October manifesto, this was the right-wing faction of the Cadet Party. They had no opposition to co-operation with the government in the Duma, and had strong support among the business community. Closely associated with the Monarchists, led by Mikhail Rodzianko, by 1917 they had fallen foul of most of the other parties and led a clandestine existence. Their leader was Alexander Guchkov.

Social Revolutionaries

Usually known in shorthand by their initials, the 'SRs' drew the greater part of their support from the peasants. Until February 1917 their central policy, the confiscation of land from the rich landowners, differed inasmuch as the SRs sought to compensate the dispossessed landlords. They were in favour of a republic. Their attitude to the war was that it should continue to be fought to defend Russia, an attitude which brought them into conflict with the Bolsheviks, who wanted an immediate end to hostilities at any price. Among their leaders were Alexander Kerensky and Viktor Chernov. They too had an internal split into two factions – the Left Socialist Revolutionaries, whose radicalism drifted towards the Bolsheviks, and the Right Social Revolutionaries, who attracted a more educated intellectual membership along with some of the better-off peasants. Fanya Kaplan, the young woman who almost succeeded in assassinating Lenin in August 1918, was a member of the SRs.

Trudoviks

Also known as the Populist Socialists or Labour Group, this small group represented some of the lower middle classes, or petit bourgeoisie, such as small businessmen and white collar workers. Because of their tendency to compromise when faced with more traditional forms of government, their existence was limited after February 1917, at which time Alexander Kerensky was among their leaders, a fact which Lenin and Trotsky would not forget.

Yedinstvo

The brainchild of socialist theoretician George Plekhanov. In the last two decades of the nineteenth century, for a time Plekhanov had Lenin among his admirers. Following the October coup in 1917, the elderly Plekhanov's innate patriotism and conservatism ensured that Yedinstvo, by this time a very small party, was destined to vanish from the political scene.

Prominent People

Armand, Inessa (1874–1920)

Born Inessa Stephane in Paris, this woman's involvement with the Bolsheviks is not always featured too prominently in histories of the revolution. Inessa Armand does, however, tend to throw some light on an area of Lenin's life – his seemingly suppressed 'romantic' side. Inessa was an impressive all-rounder; good-looking, she was also an accomplished pianist who would often play Chopin and Beethoven to Lenin, whose wife Krupskaya simply had to weather the presence of this young woman in their marriage. Speculation around her relationship with Lenin was rife throughout their lives. Inessa married a Russian industrialist, Alexander Armand, in 1892, when she was 18. Her father was an opera singer and in Russia she was raised by her aunt after his death. Alexander Armand was far from being a revolutionary and Inessa eventually left him. The marriage produced five children yet despite the split Alexander continued financial support for his wife and offspring. Her interest in feminist politics led her to join the Moscow Society for Improving the Lot of Women, where she became involved as a welfare worker amongst the city's prostitutes.

Drawn towards socialism, she joined the Bolsheviks in 1905. She worked in Moscow on party propaganda, and in the face of the sexism which existed at the time, won over many male workers due to her skills as a communicator. After being arrested and exiled to the Russian Arctic, she escaped to France and met Lenin in Paris in 1909. She was a good orator, organizer and party fund-raiser, and despite Lenin's obvious affection for her, became such a part of the Lenins' childless life that, with her five children, she accompanied them on their holidays, when Lenin and Kruspkaya would treat the children as their own. It is thought that the affair became a physical one between 1910 and 1913, but this aspect came to a halt before the outbreak of the war. Inessa, however, continued to work as Lenin's assistant and after 1917 worked on the executive committee of the Moscow Soviet as an economic administrator. Long hours and the tuberculosis she had contracted in exile had ruined her health, but it was cholera which led to her death in 1920. At her funeral all the rumours about her relationship with Lenin seemed confirmed by his intense grief at her graveside, and Krupskaya mourned her loss as a friend and comrade.

Chernov, Viktor (1876–1952)

Viktor Chernov had been one of the founder members of the Socialist Revolutionary Party. Following the abdication of Tsar Nicholas II in March 1917, Chernov became a member of Kerensky's Provisional Government. Although he worked hard to bring about the transfer of the land to the peasants, issuing ten draft bills during 1917, he had relied on these becoming law through the government or the proposed Constituent Assembly. Thus his thunder was stolen by Lenin in October that year, whose Decree on Land following the

Bolshevik coup incorporated the SRs' policy. In January 1918 Chernov became President of the Constituent Assembly, but following its dissolution by the Bolsheviks, he decided to fight against the party and fled to Samara, on the Volga in southern Russia, where he set up an anti-Bolshevik government. By 1921, after the successful advance of the Red Army, he was forced to flee Russia. He died in New York aged 76 in 1952.

Chkheidze, Nikolai (1864–1926)

Chkheidze hailed from Georgia. He had been a member of Russia's Third (1907–12) and Fourth (1912–17) Dumas, and was a prominent member of the Menshevik Party. He became a member of the Provisional Government and was among the various revolutionaries who were at the Finland Station to welcome Lenin on his return to Petrograd in April 1917. Following the Bolshevik takeover in October, he was appointed Chairman of the All-Russian Soviets, and in 1918 of the Constituent Assembly in Georgia. With the overthrow of the Mensheviks in Georgia by the Red Army in 1921, Chkheidze abandoned his political career, and in 1926 committed suicide.

Dzerzhinsky, Felix Edmundovich (1877–1926)

Known eventually as 'Iron' Felix for his merciless resilience in tracking down 'enemies of the people', Dzerzhinsky, a prominent Bolshevik, was descended from a noble Polish dynasty. Whilst employed as the commandant at the Smolny Institute after the October coup, he was given the task by Lenin of setting up a counter-revolutionary militia force, the All-Russian Extraordinary Commission for Combating

Counter-Revolution and Sabotage, which became known under its Russian acronym, the Cheka, whose methods were as grimly efficient as its Tsarist predecessor, the Okhrana, which existed from 1881 to 1917. Dzerzhinsky's reign of terror against anyone who spoke out against the Bolsheviks reached its zenith in 1918. He went on to head other sinister organizations such as the GPU, the State Political Directorate. The GPU was incorporated into the NKVD (People's Commissariat of State Security) in 1922. The OGPU (Unified State Political Directorate) was the Soviet State's security service from 1923 to 1924. These and other organizations eventually led, in 1954, to the founding of the KGB (Committee of State Security).

Dzerzhinsky died from a heart attack in 1926.

Kamenev, Lev Borisovich (1883–1936)

(Original name Rosenfeld.) After the 1903 split in the Russian Social Democrat Party, Kamenev (who happened to be Trotsky's brother-in-law) supported Lenin's Bolshevik faction. Like many revolutionaries, Kamenev was no stranger to exile and after his arrest for his political activities in 1915 he was banished to Siberia. Like Lenin, he returned to Petrograd not long after the 1917 February uprising. As was the case with Zinoviev, Kamenev often disagreed with Lenin's ideas, especially during the planning of the October coup. However, when the first Communist Party Politburo was formed, Kamenev became a member.

After Lenin died in 1924, Zinoviev, Kamenev and Stalin formed a triumvirate to take over the party, a move which saw the exclusion of Trotsky. By 1925, Stalin had gathered all the authority he needed by surrounding himself with supporters, and with his majority managed this time to exclude both

Zinoviev and Kamenev from his new power base. They turned to Trotsky's opposing faction, which led to Kamenev's expulsion from the party in 1927. Kamenev recanted his 'sins' and was re-admitted, to serve in several minor posts. In 1934, following the murder of Leningrad's communist leader, Sergei Kirov (which appears to have been the work of Stalin, who resented Kirov's immense popularity), a 'Trotsky plot' was invented in which Kamenev was implicated. He was arrested, and along with Zinoviev, was executed in 1936.

Kerensky, Alexander Feodorovich (1881–1970)

In 1912 this ebullient young lawyer, famed for his role in defending strikers and revolutionaries, was elected to the Fourth Duma as a member of the Trudoviks (a moderate Labour group). Following the 1917 February revolution, he changed his affiliation and joined the Social Revolutionaries, becoming Minister for Justice in Prince Lvov's Provisional Government. He moved on to become Minister for War, and following Lvov's resignation in July 1917, Kerensky became Prime Minister. As a 'defencist', he supported the continuance of the war in the belief that the revolution could not be a success unless Russia defeated Germany. This put him at odds with many in the Provisional Government and especially in the Petrograd Soviet. He failed to deal with other serious problems as Premier, such as the distribution of land. After the fiasco of the Kornilov affair and Kerensky's failed June offensive against the Germans, he became a hate figure to the rising Bolsheviks. After Lenin's successful coup in 1917 he fled to France, setting up an anti-Bolshevik group with which he would continue to oppose the Soviet regime. In 1940 he left for America, and died there in 1970.

Kollontai, Alexandra Mikhailovna (1872–1952)

(Maiden name Domontovich.) Kollontai was a proponent of free love, a subject which occupied her frequently in her writings (she wrote novels) throughout her life. Her background seemed unusual for such a dedicated left-wing communist. Her father was a Tsarist general and she married an officer in the Tsar's army. In 1908, to avoid arrest and exile, she escaped abroad, and in 1916 worked with Nikolai Bukharin in New York City where she edited the communist daily *Novy Mir* (New World). The following year saw her return to Russia to take part in the revolution, and in 1920 she took up the post of People's Commissar for Social Welfare. She opposed Lenin's plan to exert governmental control over Russian trade unions by becoming the leader of an organization called 'Worker's Opposition', but was roundly defeated in this by Lenin in 1921. Considering the fate of many of the early Bolsheviks under Stalin, Kollontai appears as a remarkable survivor. She took up important diplomatic posts in Norway (1923) – one of the first women diplomats – and in Sweden from 1930 to 1945, reaching the rank of Soviet Ambassador in 1943. The following year she was prominent in the armistice negotiations between the USSR and Finland. She died a peaceful death aged 80 in 1952.

Lenin, Vladimir Ilich (1870–1924)

(Original name Ulyanov.) Lenin's father, Ilya Nikolaevich Ulyanov, worked as a civil servant. Like Lenin's mother, Maria Alexandrovna Blank, he was a liberal thinker who sought free education and democracy in Russia. Lenin's maternal grandfather was a Jew who had converted to Christianity. Vladimir was born at Simbirsk on the River Volga on 10 April (old style) 1870. In 1887 Vladimir's eldest brother,

Alexander Ulyanov, was hanged after being arrested due to his implication in a plot to assassinate the Tsar, Alexander III. Lenin is reported as having said, 'I will make them pay for this,' and his brother's death appears to have been the catalyst for his career as a dedicated revolutionary. Although a brilliant and hard-working student at Kazan University, Lenin was expelled for his revolutionary activities but continued in his private studies to become a lawyer. By 1895 he had absorbed the teachings of Marx and Engels and, following his arrest, spent the next year in prison. This was followed with exile to Siberia, a period which he made full use of with intensive reading and writing. In 1898 he married another socialist, Nadezhda (Nadya) Krupskaya. In 1900, his exile over, he published several books and whilst travelling in Europe founded a left-wing newspaper, *Iskra* (The Spark). He wrote many pamphlets and tracts on revolutionary socialism, and his pamphlet *What Is To Be Done* contributed to the split in the Russian Social Democratic Labour Party in 1903. This resulted in the creation of the Bolshevik and Menshevik factions, with Lenin leading the former and Julius Martov the latter. After exile in Finland and Europe he returned to Petrograd in April 1917 to take full control of the Bolshevik Party, which he had nurtured from afar for so long. Together with Leon Trotsky he planned the successful October coup which brought into existence the first Soviet government.

His iron will and self-discipline in his political mission served to subdue many aspects of his personality. His love of reading Latin, an early passion for music, and skill as an artist were all buried by the sheer volume of the political tasks he set himself. He possessed a brutal hatred for his opponents which was taken up eagerly by his commissars after the revolution. On 30 August 1918, a young Social Revolutionary, Fanya Kaplan, attempted to assassinate Lenin. She was furious after he had shut down the promised Constituent Assembly and had begun the persecution of groups opposed to the Bolsheviks. The result was a reign of terror during which hundreds would die, with thousands more deaths to follow in subsequent years at the hands of the Cheka.

In May 1922 Lenin suffered a stroke which left him paralysed down his right side. Another stroke followed in December, and a third and fourth stroke meant that by January 1924, bedridden and unable to speak, he died. Legend has it that he took his revolutionary pseudonym 'Lenin' from the River Lena – George Plekhanov using another river name as a pseudonym, 'Volgin'. (The Lena runs in the opposite direction to the Volga and is longer.)

A man who detested iconography and overt celebration (he once commented on statues 'They only attract pigeons', and refused to attend his own birthday parties), he was nevertheless turned into a cult by his devious successor, Josef Stalin. Petrograd was renamed Leningrad, statues of Lenin soon proliferated, and ignoring the protestations of Lenin's wife, Nadya, Stalin had Lenin's body embalmed and put on permanent display in a mausoleum in Moscow's Red Square, where it remains today.

Lunacharsky, Anatoly Vasilyevich (1875–1933)

Lunacharsky was a member of the Bolsheviks from the beginning. However, at one time he was a member of a group within the party which opposed Lenin; this had been formed with Alexander Bogdanov (Lunacharsky's future brother-in-law) and Maxim Gorky.

Lunacharsky set out on his revolutionary career at the age of 17 in 1892. He was always involved in the arts, both as a dramatist and a critic, and one of his driving passions was the education of the proletariat. With his opposition to Lenin a thing of the past by the summer of 1917, he supported Lenin's efforts in the overthrow of Alexander Kerensky. Following the successful Bolshevik coup of October, Lunacharsky became a member of the Soviet Government as Commissar for Education, a post which he held with some success for 12 years. He was appointed Ambassador to Spain in 1933, but before taking up the post, he died, aged 58.

Lvov, Prince Georgi Yevgenyevich (1861–1925).

In the foundation of the Russian system of local self-government known as the *Zemstvos*, Prince Lvov played an important role during the First World War. Lvov, who became the first head of the new Provisional Government in Petrograd after the February revolution in 1917, was a liberal-minded member of the landed gentry who hated violence, a 'weakness' which unfortunately made him quite unsuited for the turbulent times ahead. As a prominent member of the Cadet Party in the Duma, he had fervently hoped that some form of democratic, constitutional government could be salvaged from the political storms of 1917. However, the Soviets had little time for Lvov and his stance on the war. When his War Minister, Alexander Guchkov resigned, along with Pavel Milyukov, the Foreign Minister, and with the suppression of yet another uprising by the workers in July 1917, Lvov decided to resign, and was replaced by Alexander Kerensky. He left Russia to live in Paris, where he passed away, aged 64, in 1925.

Martov, Julius (1873–1923)

(Real name Zederbaum.) Martov, a member of the Mensheviks, was born in Constantinople to a middle-class Jewish family. Along with George Plekhanov, Fedor Dan and Irakli

Tsreteli, Martov became an important Menshevik leader who, at the start of his career, had worked closely with Lenin before the 1903 split in the Social Democratic Party. Despite this he was an ardent left-wing Menshevik and supported the idea of reuniting with the Bolsheviks in 1905; but by 1907 the split re-emerged and would not be repaired again. Martov opposed the First World War as an 'imperialist' conflict, a view shared by both Trotsky and Lenin. He became marginalized after the October coup and was on the receiving end of Trotsky's vitriolic admonition: 'Go to where you belong – the dustbin of history!' Although the Mensheviks were banned (with all other parties) after 1917, Martov continued to support the Red Army in the civil war, but his campaign of denunciation against the suppression of a free press forced him into exile in Germany in 1923. He died there, in Schömberg, the same year, having set up his own paper, the *Socialist Messenger,* which was read avidly by exiled Mensheviks around the world. Oddly enough, it is rumoured that Lenin, probably displaying a rare nostalgic regard for his old partner, helped to fund Martov's paper.

Milyukov, Pavel Nikolayevich (1859–1943)

An implacable anti-Bolshevik, Milyukov, a member of the Cadet Party, became Foreign Minister in the Provisional Government following the abdication of the Tsar. Fully committed to working with Russia's allies, he sought to carry on the war at any cost, which made him increasingly unpopular with the working class and their parties. After issuing a note to all the Allied embassies in May 1917 stating that Russia stood shoulder to shoulder with their forces against Germany, he was forced to resign in the midst of a storm of protest. In the civil war he joined General Alexeev's volunteer army to fight against the Bolsheviks. After their defeat he moved to France to pursue an academic career, and died in Paris in 1943, aged 84.

Plekhanov, George (1857–1918)

Whilst still a teenager, in 1876 Plekhanov, as a member of an earlier party, Land and Liberty, was one of the main speakers at a rally in Kazan Square in St Petersburg. Land and Liberty split into two, with one half becoming the terrorist-based People's Will Party, with Plekhanov, opposed to violence, devoting his time to spreading the revolutionary word among the urban proletariat and the peasantry through the other faction, Black Repartition. Exiled in 1880, he soon became Russia's leading Marxist. Unlike Lenin, however, he believed that revolution by the working class could only be successful after the full development of capitalism. The idea that small, focussed groups of dedicated intellectual revolutionaries could dislodge Tsarism made no sense to Plekhanov. He did, however, work on the editorial board of *Iskra* alongside Martov and Lenin. Although there was some mutual respect between Lenin and Plekhanov, the latter did not support Lenin's proposals for seizing power. His reticence to support violent action and his support for the war in 1914–18 even cost him the loyalty of the Mensheviks. He died in 1918, aged 61.

Radek, Karl Bernhardovich (1885–1939)

(Real name Sobelsohn.) Polish-born Radek had already participated in revolutionary activity in Warsaw in 1905. When the First World War began, he was living in Switzerland and was avidly against the conflict, which, like Lenin, he saw as an imperialist war. After returning to Petrograd with Lenin, he joined the Bolshevik Party. Following the war, he went to

Germany where he helped to set up and promote the growing German communist movement. Once back in Russia, he soon fell out of favour with Stalin and was expelled from the Communist Party in 1927. Three years later he was re-admitted, and was one of the authors of the Soviet Constitution of 1936. However, he was accused of treason, tried in 1937, and died in prison the same year, aged 54.

Stalin, Josef (1879–1953)

(Real name Iosif Vissarionovich Dzugashvili.) Born in Georgia, he soon changed his name to 'man of steel' – Stalin. His parents were peasants and spoke no Russian. Until 1894 he had attended a church school and as a diligent student soon had a scholarship at the Tbilisi Theological Seminary. It was hoped that he might become a priest, but Marxism lured him away from religion. In 1902 he was imprisoned for seditious activity and later exiled to Siberia. There he met his first wife, Yekaterina Svanidze, but their marriage ended when she died in 1910. Out of eight further arrests he escaped six times, but was placed under stricter supervision when exiled in 1913. Only the revolution would free him in 1917. In support of the Bolsheviks he organized bank robberies to swell the party coffers. He edited the new Bolshevik newspaper *Pravda* and worked closely with Lenin during the year 1917, becoming Commissar for Nationalities in the first Soviet Government. He remarried, this time to a communist 22 years his junior, Nadezhda Alliluyeva. Appalled at his excesses, she shot herself in 1932.

Stalin was a skilful manipulator, a paranoid, devious plotter who, by the time of Lenin's death in 1924, was set to take over the Communist Party. For the ensuing 29 years he developed a cult built around himself and Lenin, and ruled Russia by sheer terror, responsible for the deaths of millions of people through purges, war and starvation.

He died following a stroke in the early hours of 2 March 1953. Whilst his close, sycophantic comrades stood in relief at his bedside, knowing that by kow-towing to his whims they, unlike so many others, had survived, the great mass of the Russian public, whose immense suffering Stalin had caused, plunged into a morbid period of mourning for their 'beloved father'.

Sukhanov, Nikolai (1882–1939)

Sukhanov was a member of the Socialist Revolutionary Party. At the age of 22 in 1904 he was sent to prison for a year for possessing revolutionary literature. A prolific writer and diarist, once freed he threw himself into the 1905 revolution and in 1910, after writing a series of academic works on agricultural economics found himself exiled to the Arctic Circle at Archangel. In opposition to Alexander Kerensky following the 1917 February revolution, Sukhanov became a passionate opponent of the war and helped in the formation of the Provisional Government, becoming a highly active member of the Petrograd Soviet. However, following the October coup, he turned against the Bolsheviks, especially over their brutal suppression of the free press. A colourful and highly readable author, his *Russian Revolution,* published in 1922, remains one of the great works on the event.

He became an important academic specializing in agriculture at the Communist Academy, but following his dismissal from his post in 1930, in 1931 he was convicted of counter-revolutionary activity. Eight years later, on 27 August 1939, he was shot on Stalin's orders.

Trotsky, Leon (1879–1940)

(Real name Lev Davidovich Bronstein.) Trotsky attended grammar school in Odessa and later went on to study at Odessa University where he soon developed a keen interest in Marxism. After helping to organize the Southern Russian Workers' Union he was arrested and exiled to Siberia in 1897. He escaped and fled to Europe with his new wife Alexandra Sokolovskaya. Eventually they arrived in England with their two daughters, where, after spending time with Lenin, he changed his name to Trotsky.

He managed to get back to Russia in time for the 1905 revolution, but when it failed Trotsky was arrested and once more found himself on his way to Siberia. However, he escaped and a new marital arrangement sprang up, this time with a common-law wife, Natalia Sedova. After further exile around Europe in France and Spain, he eventually arrived in New York early in 1917. After working on émigré newspapers and lecturing, with the news of the revolution he was once more bound for Russia. His trip home, however, was interrupted when the British Government imprisoned him with German POWs in Canada. He was eventually released and arrived in Petrograd in May 1917. Soon, after working closely with Lenin, he abandoned the Menshevik Party and became a Bolshevik. He played an important part in setting up the October coup and ran the peace negotiations at Brest Litovsk which brought Russia out of the war.

As Commissar for War Trotsky achieved much, building the Red Army and taking the Bolsheviks to victory in the Civil War. With Lenin's death, Stalin was able to fully exercise his loathing of Trotsky and, after expelling him from the party and the Politburo, by 1928 he was exiled to Turkestan. The following year, on trumped-up charges of being a counter-revolutionary, he was expelled from Russia and once again spent years in exile. Stalin finally had his way when Trotsky was assassinated in Mexico in 1940.

Zinoviev, Grigori (1883–1936)

Zinoviev's family in Ukraine were Jewish dairy farmers. The young Grigori grew up helping on the farm, and not attending school he received a formal education at home. He started his first job as a clerical worker at the age of 14, and in 1901 became a member of the Social Democratic Party. Following the party's split in London in 1903 Zinoviev threw in his lot with the Bolsheviks and once back in Russia he began to work for the newspaper, *Iskra*. In 1904 he moved to Switzerland where he studied chemistry at Berne University, but carried on writing for various revolutionary journals. Like many other revolutionaries, he returned home to participate in the 1905 revolution as organizer of a general strike in St Petersburg, but struggling with a heart condition he had to abandon his task and seek treatment abroad. Following his treatment and the failure of the 1905 uprising, he was back in Russia where he worked as an agitator and organizer among the St Petersburg factory workers, especially the metalworkers in such large industries as the Putilov works. After being elected to the Bolshevik Central Committee he was arrested, and although released without charge decided to carry on his work abroad, returning once again to Switzerland.

By 1912, the nearest Zinoviev could get to Russia, along with fellow exiles Lenin and Kamenev, was Cracow in Poland, but the outbreak of the First World War forced them back to the neutrality of Switzerland.

Zinoviev returned to Russia on the famous 'sealed' train in

April 1917, and soon became the editor of *Pravda*. Together with Kamenev he voted against Lenin's plans for the October coup, but did participate in the uprising. He held a number of important posts during the revolutionary period, culminating in 1919 as Chairman of the Executive Committee of the Comintern.

Both Kamenev and Zinoviev followed Trotsky's internationalist approach to spreading revolution. This was a conviction which they would temporarily have to abandon to keep on the right side of Stalin following Lenin's death. But by 1926 frustration dictated that they return to the Trotsky camp. Stalin accused them of creating disunity in the party. In fear for their lives they were forced to sign statements which promised that they would toe Stalin's line. Trotsky refused.

Both Zinoviev and Kamenev were eventually accused of various misdemeanours, such as involvement in the murder of Leningrad's communist leader, Sergei Kirov and plots to assassinate Stalin. They were shot on Stalin's orders in Moscow on 25 August 1936.

Organizations and Publications

Cheka

Bolshevik secret police force established in 1917 (see entry on Felix Dzerzhinsky). 'Cheka' is the shortened form of All-Russian Extraordinary Commission for Combating Counter-Revolution and Sabotage. The Cheka was the revolutionary successor to the Tsarist secret police, the Okhrana. The Cheka went through various transformations to eventually become the KGB in 1954.

Comintern

The shortened form of the Communist International, most commonly associated with the Third International. From March 1919 to 1935 seven Comintern World Congresses would be held. The Comintern was dissolved by Stalin in 1943. The Internationals – especially the first and second – were strongly associated with the ideas of Lenin and Trotsky. Their gatherings were devoted to promoting proletarian revolution around the globe and to providing aid for this cause. The first Comintern Chairman was Grigori Zinoviev. Because of Stalin's hand in the Third International, the exiled Leon Trotsky formed the Fourth International in 1938. Once Stalin had organized Trotsky's murder in 1940, he sought to placate Churchill and Roosevelt in 1943 by convincing them that Russia no longer supported the cause of global revolution, hence his dissolution of the Comintern.

Duma

Duma was the Russian name given to denote a 'representative body'. The first Duma came out of the failed 1905 revolution. It was a Tsarist compromise engineered to give the impression of some kind of parliamentary representation for the people. Some members were appointed by the Tsar and the gentry, with academics and industry also being represented. Nicholas II dissolved the Duma in 1906 as he found that the majority of elected delegates had come from the opposition. He also dissolved the even more radical, short-lived Second Duma of 1907. The Third Duma lasted from 1907 to 1912 and found slightly more favour with Nicholas's government as changes in electoral rules had provided him with a more docile body. However, under the Third Duma advances were made in workers' and peasants' rights. The Fourth Duma had an intermittent existence between 1912 and 1917. It was the most anti-Tsarist body of them all, and subsequently Nicholas disbanded it in February 1917, yet riding on the wave of the revolution it refused to dissolve and eventually was transformed into the Provisional Government. Today Russia has a State Duma which was established in 1993.

Iskra

Iskra (the Spark) was a newspaper founded by Lenin in 1900. It was the first illegal Marxist paper devoted to the interests of the Russian proletariat. The first issue, in December 1900, came out in Leipzig, Germany. Over subsequent years it appeared in various European locations such as London, Geneva and Munich. With the paper's 52nd edition, George Plekhanov finally took control of the publication.

Izvestia

Izvestia (News) was first issued after the February revolution of 1917. Issued daily it was the organ of the Petrograd Soviet of Workers' and Soldiers' Deputies. After the October coup it soon became established as the Soviet Government's official newspaper, and was published in Moscow, but prior to this *Izvestia*, then run by Mensheviks and the SRs' had often attacked the Bolsheviks.

Milvrekom

The shortened form for the Military Revolutionary Committee (also known as the MRC) which was set up in 1917 by Lenin and Trotsky to arm and direct the workers in preparation for the revolution.

Narodniks

An early revolutionary term which had its roots in the earlier movements of the 1860s and 1870s. 'Narodniki' means 'going to the people' which is what a dedicated band of intellectuals and revolutionaries, many of them students, did; they saw the peasantry as being unable to overthrow their masters without the aid of knowledgeable 'leaders' – the Narodniks. The conflict in the countryside, however, was not overtly at that time between the rich, land-owning gentry but between the poorer peasants and those more avaricious peasant middlemen, the Kulaks. The Narodniks underestimated the reluctance of the peasants to be 'taught revolution' by what they regarded as cocky city dwellers. They already distrusted urban intellectuals and, as 1917 would prove, were quite capable of fermenting their own uprisings. The Narodniks, however, were viciously dealt with by the Tsar's police, exiled, violently beaten and executed in their hundreds. This forced them underground as the organization known as 'People's Will', which plotted assassinations and terrorism. When the People's Will finally faded away, many of their methods became the standard in subsequent revolutionary organizations.

Novy Mir

Novy Mir (New World) was a socialist publication in the USA in the early years of the twentieth century, for which Trotsky worked during his stay in New York. It should not be confused with a present-day Russian magazine which concentrates on the arts and media from a more conservative standpoint.

Okhrana

Protecting the Tsar in the nineteenth century was the central policy of the Russian police. In 1880 the police set up a special task force to focus on this. Okhrana means 'guard'. One of this new body's first tasks was an attempt to prevent Russian workers from forming trades union. Okhrana spies infiltrated all working-class organizations and many of their secret agents had dual membership of revolutionary parties and the Okhrana. Some reached high positions, such as the metalworker Roman Malinovsky, a man in whom Lenin had the greatest faith. Even though he was reporting back to the Okhrana, Malinovksy managed to be elected to the Bolshevik Central Committee. Following the insurgencies of 1917, the Okhrana files were uncovered by the revolutionaries and what they revealed was shocking. Exposed agents were summarily killed; many fled the country. Malinovsky was imprisoned and executed by a Bolshevik firing squad. The Okhrana had huge funds at its disposal, and was able to set up branches in all the major cities in the world wherever Russian revolutionaries were exiled. They had photographic files, and a meticulous index system so that they knew the movements of every revolutionary. No one was trusted. In 1912 26,000 people in Russia were acting as paid Okhrana informers on a scale from 100 roubles per month to 2,000 roubles (100 roubles per month equalled a skilled worker's wage). Up to 30,000 people arrested by the organization were executed without trial.

Politburo

Short for the Soviet Government's Political Bureau. This was the executive arm of the Communist Party, set up in 1919. The first members of the Politburo were Stalin, Kamenev, Lenin, Trotsky and Krestinsky. It was replaced in 1952 with the

Presidium of the Central Committee, but the name returned in 1966 following Kruschev's ousting from power in 1964.

Pravda

Pravda, meaning 'truth' became the butt of a private joke among many Russians during the Soviet era. The saying was '*Izvestia nyet Pravda; Pravda nyet Izvestia*' (The news isn't the truth; truth isn't the news). The newspaper was founded in St Petersburg in April 1912 by Russian workers, and was avidly read in the big factories. It explained political and world economic events from a Marxist standpoint and often had a daily circulation of over 50,000 copies. Considered a great threat by the Okhrana, in 1912 issues were confiscated on 41 occasions. It was closed down eight times, but always reappeared under a different masthead. After being banned in the early stages of the First World War, it sprang back into life in 1917 yet was still under constant threat from the right-wing parties, with publication frequently curtailed or stopped. During Stalin's reign *Pravda* became the only Russian 'news' paper most people had access to, yet its content was so weighed down with propaganda that it became a joke. It still exists today in two different versions, both available on the Internet – and some of the content is still risible.

Soviet

Soviet is the Russian word for 'council'. The first Soviets were those organized in the 1905 revolution by the striking factory workers. After the February revolution of 1917 the Petrograd Soviet of Workers' and Soldiers' Deputies was formed, with many similar soviets being established throughout the country.

Sovnarkom

This is an abbreviation of *Soviet Narodnik Kommissarov* (Council of People's Commissars). After the Second All-Russian Congress of Soviets in October 1917 Sovnarkom had begun to issue decrees which were considered legal even if the Congress of Soviets was not in session. These 'laws' would then be approved by the Congress when it convened. Sovnarkom was, in effect, the first administrative body of the new Soviet Government following the October coup.

The name was changed by Stalin in 1946 to the Council of Ministers, also known as *Sovmin* or *Sovet Ministrov*. The term 'commissars' was changed to 'ministers' at the same time.

NOTES

Introduction

1 Marx, Karl, *Das Kapital*, Vol. I, preface to German edition, 1967.
2 Clark, Lloyd, *World War I: An Illustrated History*, Helicon, Oxford, 2001.
 See also: Keegan, John, *The First World War*, Hutchinson, London. 1998.
3 Maylunas and Mironenko (1996) (from the Memoirs of Maurice Paléologue, French Ambassador).
4 Ibid.
5 Amis, Martin, *Korba The Dread*, Jonathan Cape, London, 2002.
6 Trotsky (1986).

Chapter 1: Frozen Minds

1 Shub (1977).
2 Report filed by Robert Wilton to *The Times* on 31 December 1916. The contents of Wilton's story were deemed too sensational to print, and it was filed under 'Confidential'. It can be read at www.timesonline.co.uk/

3 Pares, B. (ed.), *Letters of the Tsarina to the Tsar 1914–16*, Krasniarkiv (Red Archive) Moscow, 1923.

4 Interview with Alice Lagnado, by kind permission of the *St. Petersburg Times*.

5 *Novaya Zhin*, published in Moscow 26 October 1917. Tables of costs and wages compiled by the Ministry of Labour and Moscow Chamber of Commerce.

6 Mikhailovitch, Alexander, Grand Duke, *Once A Grand Duke*, 1931.

7 Darby, Graham *The Russian Revolution Tsarism to Bolshevism*, Longman 2003.

8 McDonald (2001).

9 Betelheim, Charles, *Class Struggles in The USSR 1917–1924*, Harvester Press, Hassocks, Sussex, 1974. (Figures originally published in *Nardodnoye Kh. SSSR v. 1970.)*

10 Seton-Watson, Hugh, *The Russian Empire 1801–1917*, Oxford University Press, 1967.

11 Soviet Encyclopaedic Dictionary, Volume 2, 6 April 1964, Moscow. English translation of Kulak entry available at www.deanesmay.com

12 A 'Pud' is a Russian measure of weight.
   1 Pud = 16.38 kilograms
   1 Pud = 40 Funt
   A Funt is 409.4 grams.

13 Brower, Daniel R., *The Russian City: Between Tradition & Modernity*, University of California Press, 1990.

14 Shapovalov A.S., *Naputi K. Marksizmu*, 1926.

15 Breshkovskaya, Catherine, *Memoirs* 1917. See www.spartacus.schoolnet.co.uk

Chapter 2: Across The Rubicon

1 Semyanov, Demian, *To The Fallen Freedom Fighters*, poem, March 1917. See Steinberg (2001).

2 Trotsky (1930).

3 Florinsky, M. T., *The End of The Russian Empire*, Yale, 1931.

4 Interview with the author.

5 Msistlavski, S., *The Wreck of Tsarism*, Leningrad, 1927.

6 Report in the *Daily Chronicle* by Harold Williams, 13 March 1917.

7 F. Starunov, Memoir quoted in Smith (2002).

8 Moynahan (1992).

9 Buchanan (1919).

10 Shub (1977).

11 Maylunas, & Mironenko, *A Lifelong Passion: Nicholas & Alexandra, Their Own Story* Weidenfeld & Nicolson, London 1996.
12 Lieven (1994).
13 Trotsky (1986).
14 Ibid.
15 Wilcox, E. H., *Russia's Ruin*, Chapman & Hall, 1919.
16 Shliapnikov, A., *The Year 1917*, Moscow, 1925.
17 Katasheva, L., *Natasha – A Bolshevik Woman Organiser, A Short Biography,* www.marxist.com.women
18 *Pravda*, 23 February 1914.
19 Kayorov's story as told to Leon Trotsky in his *History of The Revolutiuon.*
20 Eastman, John: taped interview circa 1958 from Australian Broadcasting Corporation, supplied to the author by his daughter, Mrs Molly Williams of Birmingham.
21 Eisenstein, Sergei, *Beyond The Stars: The Memoirs of Sergei Eisenstein*, BFI Publishing, 1995.
22 Wilton, Robert, *The Times*, 16 March 1917.
23 Pipes, Richard, *The Russian Revolution 1899–1919*, Collins Harvill, London, 1990.
24 Interview with the author.
25 Maylunas (1996).

Chapter 3: The Prodigals Return

1 Interview with the author, St Petersburg, May 2004.
2 Interview with the author, St Petersburg, May 2004.
3 Acton (1990).
4 Steinberg (2001).
5 M.G. Mulhall *Dictionary of Statistics* 1884, quoted in Mc Donald, Hamish, *Russia & The USSR Empire of Revolution*, Longman, Harlow 2001.
6 Moynahan, (1992).
7 Vellacott, J., *Bertrand Russell and the Pacifists in the First World War,* 1980.
8 Saville, John, *The Labour Movement in Britain*, Faber & Faber, London, 1988.
9 Moynahan (1992).
10 *Pravda*, 28 March 1917.
11 *Novy Mir*, 3 April 1917.
12 Service (2000).
13 Ludendorff, Erich, *My War Reminiscences*, Berlin, 1919.
14 Shub (1977).

15 27 March was the date by the Russian calendar; it was 8 April in the rest of the world.
16 Wilson, Edmund, *To The Finland Station*, Fontana Edition, 1970.
17 Hill (1971).
18 Service (2000).
19 Trotsky (1986).
20 Sutton, Antony C., *Wall Street & The Bolshevik Revolution*, Veritas, Morley, Western Australia, 1981. Sutton also quotes earlier evidence of Trotsky's US passport in Wise, Jennings C., *Wilson: Disciple of Revolution*, Paisley Press, New York, 1938.
21 Trotsky (1986).
22 Taylor, A.J.P. *From Napoleon To The Fourth International: Essays on 19th Century Europe*, Hamish Hamilton, London, 1982.

Chapter 4: Red Days, White Nights

1 Pickford, E. (Comp.). Recorded by Dick Gaughan on *A Handful of Earth,* Topic CD, 12TS419 (1981).
2 Williams, Harold, Correspondent for the *Morning Post*, 8 June 1917.
3 Interview with the author, St Petersburg, May 2004.
4 Steinberg (2002).
5 Plekhanov, George, *An Open Letter to The Petrograd Workers*, 28 October 1917.
6 Buchanan, Sir George, *My Mission to Russia and Other Diplomatic Memories*, 2 volumes, Cassell, London & New York, 1923.
7 Service (2000).
8 Bonch-Bruyevich, V., *V.I. Lenin in Russia*, Moscow 1925.
9 Shub (1977).
10 Tatiana was the 20-year-old second daughter of Nicholas and Alexandra.
11 Maylunas and Mironenko (1996).
12 Ibid.
13 Farmborough (1974).
14 Sutton, Antony C., *Wall Street and the Bolshevik Revolution*, Morley, Australia, 1981. In his work, Sutton cites an article by Lt Col John Bayne MacLean, a prominent Toronto publisher and army Intelligence contact. In this a figure of $10,000 is presented to 'the Trotsky fund' by the German Imperial Bank. Among Sutton's many startling claims, based on MacLean's article, is that Trotsky was in fact a German. Sutton also reveals a $1 million donation made by W.B. Thompson, a director of the Federal State Bank, to the

Bolsheviks under the cover of the American Red Cross Mission. Trotsky deals dismissively with the German funding allegations – especially those made after the war by Kerensky – at some length in his autobiography.

15 Clark, Lloyd, *World War I: An Illustrated History*, Hutchinson, London, 2001.

16 Buchanan (1919).

17 Trotsky (1986). Trotsky actually tells the story of his rescue of Chernov with an extract from the memoirs of Lieutenant Raskolnikov, one of the leaders of the Kronstadt sailors who was present outside the Tauride Palace.

18 Trotsky (1986).

Chapter 5: From Crisis to Conquest

1 Paustovsky, Konstantin, *In This Dawn: Spring 1917–Spring 1920*, Progress Publishers, Moscow, 1967.

2 Interview with the author, May 2004.

3 Griffin, Frederick C., *History of The Trans-Siberian Railroad*, Arizona State University, 1998. The RRSC was ostensibly neutral when it arrived in Russia, but by 1919, with the advent of the Civil War, the American railroad men supported the Whites as part of the Allied intervention forces.

4 Westwood, J.N., *A History of Russian Railways*, Allen & Unwin, London, 1964.

5 Paustovsky, *In This Dawn*.

6 Beatty, Bessie, *The Red Heart of Russia*, Century, New York, 1918.

7 Schapiro, Leonard, *The Communist Party of The Soviet Union*, Methuen, London, 1983.

8 Pitcher (2001). The report that the Tauride required redecorating was filed by Arthur Ransome on 4 August.

9 Kann (1990).

10 Service (2000).

11 Shub (1977).

12 *Proletarska Revolutziya*, Moscow, 1922: David Shub points out that in this document Trotsky wrote 'I do not remember the proportion of the votes, but I know that 5 or 6 were against it. There were many more votes in favour, probably about 9, but I do not vouch for the figures.' However, the 10–2 vote does appear to have been accepted by subsequent writers, including Robert Service.

13 Darby (2003).

14 Service (2000).

15 Moynahan (1992).

16 Hill (1971).
17 Bergan (1999). Podvoysky is outlined in Bergen's work as Chief of
    Staff at the storming of the Winter Palace; Eisenstein engaged the
    ageing revolutionary as an actor, playing himself in *October*.
18 Podvoysky, N.I., *Voyennaya Organizatzia Tze-Kah Bolshevikov*,
    Leningrad, 1923. (Quoted in Shub, David, *Lenin: A Biography*).
19 Reed (1979).
20 Contrary to John Reed's attitude to the looting of the Winter Palace,
    Reed himself is rumoured to have made off with a jewelled sword
    when leaving the building.
21 Bryant, Louise, *Six Red Months In Russia*, George H. Doran, New
    York 1918.
22 Farmborough (1974).

Chapter 6: Power and Dominion

1   Interview with the author, May 2004.
2   Trotsky (1986).
3   In July 1918 Lenin spoke to the Soviets about the problem of
    workers' control, saying: 'The chief shortcoming of the masses is
    their timidity and reluctance to take affairs into their own
    hands.'
4   Paustovsky, Konstantin, *In That Dawn Spring 1917–Spring 1970*,
    Progress Publishers, Moscow, 1967.
5   Lenin, V. I. Decree *On The Press* issued Petrograd Oct. 29 1917.
6   Reed, John *Ten Days That Shook The World (Illustrated Edition)*
    Sutton Publishing, Stroud 1997.
7   Lenin, V.I. *Selected Works Vol. VI* and *Pravda*, 2 Nov 1917.
8   Appiganesi and Zarate (2000).
9   Interview with the author, May 2004.
10 Lunacharsky's *On Popular Education* was issued in November
    1917, and mentions the fact that elementary school teachers were
    earning less than 100 roubles per month.
11 Buchanan (1919).
12 Radkey, O., *The Election to the Russian Constituent Assembly of
    1917*, Harvard, 1950.
13 The White Russians derived their name from the royalist opponents
    to the French revolution. French royalists were called Whites after
    adopting the white flag of the Bourbon dynasty.

Chapter 7: Swept Away

1 Interview with the author, May 2004.
2 As a mark of how much Russia has changed, the former Cheka offices are now occupied by IBM.
3 Zubov, N., *Dzerzhinsky*, Moscow, 1933.
4 Moynahan (1992).
5 Naglovsky, A., *The Red Leaders* is quoted in Shub (1977). Shub tells us that Naglosky passed his memoirs onto him in the hope of having them published in the USA. This did not happen, but sections were printed in the journal *Sovrenmennyya Zapiski* in Paris.
6 Smith (2002).
7 The film was released in the UK as *Rasputin The Mad Monk*. When Hammer Films made a film of the same name in 1965, starring Christopher Lee, Yusupov demanded a full inspection of the script before production went ahead.
8 Bergan (1999).
9 As with Rasputin, Trotsky's demise also fascinated film-makers. Richard Burton starred as Trotsky in Joseph Losey's 1972 film, *The Assassination of Leon Trotsky,* described by critic Leslie Halliwell as 'Glum historical reconstruction with much fictitious padding'.
10 Sebag Montefoire, Simon, *Stalin: The Court of The Red Tsar*, Weidenfeld & Nicolson, London 2003.
11 Interview with the author, May 2004.
12 Sebag Montefiore, *Stalin: The Court of The Red Tsar*.
13 Reed (1977).

Chapter 8: Children of The Revolution

1 Interview with the author, St Petersburg, 2004.
2 Interview with the author, St Petersburg, 2004.
3 I was disinclined to believe this until I saw a notice written by Lenin on the wall of his secretary, Vladimir Bonch-Bruyevich's office in the Smolny Institute. Lenin's order was that no one in the government should earn more than a skilled worker. His salary as head of state circa 1917–18 was 500 roubles per month, with Bonch-Bruyevich earning 400 roubles. According to John Reed, a locksmith in August 1917 was earning 9 roubles per day. As Lenin never appeared to stop working one can assume that his salary reflected overtime rates.

SELECT BIBLIOGRAPHY

There are literally hundreds of books available in English dealing with the Bolshevik revolution. They vary enormously in scope and attitude, the latter inevitably dictated by their author's own political beliefs. Reports of what happened and when, and involving whom often vary, as do dates, statistics and spellings. The books listed here do not represent every publication consulted whilst completing this work, but they were among the most informative and consistent.

Acton, Edward, Rethinking The Russian Revolution, Edward Arnold/Hodder & Stoughton Ltd., Sevenoaks, Kent. 1990.

Appignanesi, Richard and Zarate, Oscar, Introducing Lenin & The Russian Revolution, Totem Books/Icon, New York, 2000.

Bergan, Ronald, Sergei Eisenstein: A Life in Conflict Warner Books, London, 1999.

Buchanan, Meriel, Petrograd: The City of Trouble 1914–18, Collins, London, 1919.

Darby, Graham, *The Russian Revolution Tsarism to Bolshevism 1861–1924*, Longman History in Depth, Harlow, 2003.

Farmborough, Florence, *Nurse At The Russian Front*, Constable, 1974.

Hill, Christopher, *Lenin & The Russian Revolution*, Pelican, 1971.

Figes, Orlando, *A People's Tragedy: The Russian Revolution 1891–1924*, London, 1996.

Kann, Pavel, *Leningrad: A Guide*, Planeta Publishers, Moscow, 1990.

Lieven, Dominic, *Nicholas II Emperor of All The Russias*, Pimlico, London, 1994.

Massie, Robert K., *The Romanovs: The Final Chapter*, Jonathan Cape, London, 1995.

Maylunas, Andrei and Mironenko Sergei, *A Lifelong Passion: Nicholas & Alexandra, Their Own Story*, Weidenfeld & Nicolson, London, 1996.

McDonald, Hamish, *Russia and The USSR: Empire of Revolution*, Longman, London, 2001.

Moynahan, Brian, *Comrades 1917 – Russia in Revolution*, Hutchinson, London, 1992.

Pelican, London, 1971, Longman History/Pearson Education Ltd. Harlow, 2001.

Pitcher, Harvey, *Witnesses of The Russian Revolution*, Pimlico, London, 2001.

Rabinowitch, Alexander, *The Bolsheviks Come To Power*, New York, 1976.

Reed, John, *Ten Days That Shook The World* Penguin Edition 1977.

Richardson, Dan, *The Rough Guide To Moscow*, Rough Guides/ Penguin, London, 2001.

Ross, Stewart, *Events & Sources: The Russian Revolution*, Evans Bros. Ltd., London, 2002.

Service, Robert, *Lenin: A Biography*, Macmillan, London, 2000.

Shub, David, *Lenin: A Biography*, Penguin, London, 1977.

Smith, S.A. *The Russian Revolution: A Very Short Introduction*, Oxford University Press, 2002.

Steinberg, Prof. Mark D., *Voices of Revolution 1917*, Yale University Press, 2001.

Sukhanov N.N., *The Russian Revolutions: A Personal Record*, Oxford, 1955.

Swain, Geoffrey, *Russia's Civil War*, Tempus Publishing, Stroud, Gloucestershire, 2000.

Trotsky, Leon, *History of The Russian Revolution* (1930), available at www.marxists.org/archive/trotsky

Trotsky, Leon, *My Life: An Attempt At An Autobiography*, Penguin, London, 1986

Ustinov, Sir Peter, *My Russia*, Macmillan, London, 1983.

Zinovieff, Kryil and Hughes, Jenny, *The Companion Guide To St. Petersburg*, Boydell & Brewer, Woodbridge, Suffolk, 2003.

INDEX